D0429119

2 00

MAN'S BETTER ANGELS

Man's Better Angels

Romantic Reformers and the
Coming of the Civil War

PHILIP F. GURA

THE BELKNAP PRESS OF
HARVARD UNIVERSITY PRESS

Cambridge, Massachusetts
London, England

2017

Copyright © 2017 by Philip F. Gura

All rights reserved

Printed in the United States of America

First printing

Library of Congress Cataloging-in-Publication Data

Names: Gura, Philip F., 1950– author.

Title: Man's better angels : romantic reformers and the
coming of the Civil War / Philip F. Gura.

Description: Cambridge, Massachusetts : The Belknap Press of
Harvard University Press, 2017. |
Includes bibliographical references and index.

Identifiers: LCCN 2016037370 | ISBN 9780674659544 (cloth)

Subjects: LCSH: Social reformers—United States—History. | Social problems—
United States—History. | United States—History—1815–1861.

Classification: LCC HN57 .G827 2017 | DDC 303.48/4092—dc23

LC record available at https://lccn.loc.gov/2016037370

For Maeve and Abel
Remember,
"Of all sad words of tongue or pen,
The saddest are these, 'It might have been.'"

Contents

MAN'S BETTER ANGELS

Introduction

In the spring of 1837 the silver-tongued orator and U.S. senator from Massachusetts Daniel Webster addressed an audience at a reception in his honor in Wheeling, Virginia. He painted a grim picture of the state of the nation. "So many bankruptcies among great and small dealers, so much property sacrificed, so many industrious men altogether broken up in business, so many families reduced from competence to want, so many hopes crushed." Webster had recently suffered considerable financial losses on his own investments in western lands and knew of what he spoke: "So many happy prospects forever clouded, and such a fearful looking for still greater calamities, all from such a mass of evil as I had never expected to see, except as the result of war, pestilence, or some other external calamity."[1]

The famous senator was describing the aftermath of the Panic of 1837, and his was only one of hundreds of similarly despairing testimonies as to how that great financial depression pushed the new republic into a deeper and deeper spiral of financial and social ruin. In the privacy of his journal, Transcendentalist and reformer Ralph Waldo Emerson spoke an even harsher truth: "The land stinks with suicide," he wrote. "Young men have no hope," for "society has played out its last stake; it is checkmated. The present generation is bankrupt of principles & hope, as of property."[2] Such financial crises, particularly when they occur with little advance warning, bring out the best and the worst in people. On the one hand, widespread economic upheaval provides opportunities for the wholesale structural reform of systems that, too long misunderstood or mismanaged, warp large-scale institutions as well as harm countless individual lives. Facing their own economic and political disruptions in the 1840s, for example, and frustrated by ineffectual and compromised political solutions, Europeans eventually resorted to physical force in attempts to initiate overt revolution. But Americans were a different lot and never went to the barricades. Instead, faced with immense financial losses closely linked to the cotton trade and believing in the efficacy of the emergent national two-party system to control the growing disaster, many of them offered what can only be termed highly imaginative yet often quixotic responses. Although at the time these reactions seemed relevant, they only exacerbated the nation's increasingly intolerable economic and social problems.

The issue so many American reformers sought to avoid meeting head-on, of course, was slavery, the very institution that made possible the country's inexpensive agricultural production and the attendant great profit, particularly on the export of cotton. Ironically, the circuitous road to secession was paved with good intentions on the part of many of slavery's opponents. But their inability accurately to conceive what in the nation had to be changed or redirected—in particular, how to respond to and correct an economic system seemingly run amok—provided tinder to a sectional crisis that finally burst into flame in 1861.

One American, however, finally did resort to physical force to address the nation's problems, for the violent ideas of John Brown cast a pall over these decades. What do we make of the fact that Brown, who suffered greatly and almost drowned in the financial maelstrom following 1837, was eventually invited into the parlors of prominent antebellum reformers to speak of blood and revolution? To understand why is to understand the bankruptcy of an American liberalism with which so many Americans met the nation's post-1837 crises. In thrall to a national ethic of self-reliance and ignorant of the extent to which individuals were now enmeshed in and controlled by complex political and economic institutions, Romantic activists blamed the economic disaster on their countrymen's moral shortcomings, particularly their uncontrolled greed and selfishness, not on any larger, institutional failures. As Emerson put it, State Street believed that "nobody fails who ought not to fail. There is always a reason," in other words, "in the man, for his good or bad fortune."[3]

Thus, many nineteenth-century reformers urged change through personal suasion and self-discipline and believed that eventually institutional transformation would follow such attention to personal failings. They assumed a human nature that was fundamentally good, a goodness almost always traceable back to God's intentions for man. If one were able to eliminate the social, political, and economic perversions, they believed, and assert one's indwelling goodness, individuals could not help but be mutually cooperative. Behind America's nineteenth-century liberalism stood no less an unimpeachable referee than God.

In urging individual reform, however, many nineteenth-century reformers willfully or not ignored that there was a more threatening side to this habit of reform logic. If we all have it in us to be better, and our unwillingness to do the work necessary to realize that perfection is what stands in the way of universal harmony, then a harsh judgment is certainly called for. Bracketing this possibility, many reformers frequently argued themselves into a variety of social and political cul-de-sacs of their own creation. Given their commitment to the core American principle of individualism, the social harmony they sought eluded them. Committed to an ethic of what Emerson called *self-reliance* and his friend the Unitarian clergyman William Ellery Channing termed *self-culture*, it was almost beyond the reformers' ability to imagine a different, more ameliorative, more pragmatic approach to the nation's problems, particularly through legislative enactment. Instead, they insisted that individualism was not incompatible with social utopia and offered their varied reforms toward that end.

But the possibilities and opportunities for reform differ fundamentally when one presumes, as many reformers did, that most people are inherently good rather than inherently selfish, and that what makes some individuals selfish can be purged through self-discipline of one sort or another, and that it has nothing to do with political reconstruction. For the longer an individual or society thwarts God's good intentions, the more they seem to deserve sterner, harsher reprimands. What then? What happens after a society has been punished, as the United States was in 1837 and again in the Panic of 1857, another economic meltdown? If present trials did not force enough individuals to reform, if neighbors near and far were not persuaded by example, were more extreme clarion calls licensed? These reformers naively thought not, continuing to place hope in the transformative power of individual example. Among them, however, John Brown finally lost his patience.

The majority of reform efforts from the 1830s until the outbreak of war thus remained anchored in a faith in the individual's fundamental goodness that could be called on and called forth, a God-given moral compass or sense that, once awakened, educated, and heeded, would permit (even demand) individuals to improve themselves, thereby carrying whole communities, the country, and even all humanity to the point of universal harmony.

If that faith failed, there were two stark choices. Give up on it, turn pragmatic, and embrace partial solutions attained incrementally; or, double down on that faith. This could mean an ever more inward pursuit of one's best self. Or, it could mean seeing some part of humanity so turned from God and good nature that they stubbornly, sinfully hindered a beckoning, harmonious world. Admit some part of that thinking into one's worldview and striking people with pike and bullet becomes the equivalent of doing the Lord's work.

Until the spring of 1837 most Americans uncritically believed that limitless economic expansion was assured—indeed, was the nation's divine destiny. In truth, more pedestrian and ultimately concerning reasons explained what the young Virginia lawyer Joseph G. Baldwin memorably described as "flush times." Cotton, the nation's seemingly limitless amount of arable land, and a large population of cheap—slave—labor had combined to fuel the nation's supercharged economy.[4] Since the late eighteenth century, when American inventor Eli Whitney perfected his machine for "ginning"—that is, efficiently picking the seeds from—short-staple cotton, this crop had become the country's most important agricultural product, essential to both the nation's internal and transatlantic trade.[5]

In the late 1820s and early 1830s, ever-larger textile factories began to dot the riverbanks in the Middle Atlantic and New England states, as American entrepreneurs, emulating their English counterparts, utilized increasingly sophisticated and efficient water-powered machinery to produce cheap cloth. But despite this progressive expansion of American industry, cotton from the southern United States had become an international commodity, and England remained its main market. That nation's textile works had been established almost half a century before those on the American strand. Inventions such as the spinning jenny, the power loom, and cylinder presses for printing cloth, propelled by reliable steam engines to replace ever-fickle waterpower, had made England the world's largest industrial power. By 1833 it boasted over 100,000 power looms and within two years imported through Liverpool no less than one-third of a billion pounds of American cotton; the crop's value to American investors was fifty million dollars. The ability of the United States to service this huge industry—imports from India and Egypt hitherto had dominated the market—was so significant that cotton cultivation in the American South had done nothing less than "reshape the global market."[6]

In turn, England's ever-growing demand for cotton fueled an American land boom. Through the mid-1830s savvy investors and less-savvy speculators, Webster among them, bought up as much uncultivated land as they could at the lowest prices they could negotiate, and then quickly resold it to the next wave of interested buyers, many with little farming experience but eager to begin cultivation in the belief that the market for cotton would continue to grow. The federal government reaped great rewards from such investment. Between 1835 and 1836 alone it sold off over fifty thousand square miles of its lands to those eager to begin tilling it.

Even presidential politics, divisive as it became with the emergence of the modern two-party system and escalating debates over slavery, abetted this land boom. President Andrew Jackson's deep distrust of the Eastern establishment (and particularly its chief banker, Philadelphian Nicholas Biddle) led him in 1832 to veto the charter of the Second Bank of the United States and set its expiration four years later. An unintended consequence of his action was that it allowed speculators to obtain easy credit for land purchases from the plethora of state-chartered banks that Jackson's veto had strengthened. Between 1830 and 1836, the number of such institutions more than doubled, from just over three hundred to over seven hundred.

While such state banks were required to keep on hand a certain percentage of their notes' value in specie—that is, gold and silver—to "back" or give value to the paper money they issued, Jackson's weakening of the nation's only central bank emboldened them to issue greater amounts of paper money without increasing the percentage of specie they maintained on hand. Hitherto, the Bank of the United States had implicitly kept this system of state-issued currency in check, for it accepted at its own offices at or near face value only those notes of state banks whose deposits it trusted as adequate. With the loosening of this central oversight, there was a large increase in paper money that further boosted funds available for the immense national landgrab. "The country lost its senses in its haste to be rich," one commentator observed. "The credit system was carried to an extent which those who can remember it can scarcely believe," he continued, so that "men without a thousand dollars of capital bought cotton plantations and slaves, and drew on brokers immediately, on the credit for the first crop, before the seed had been sown."[7]

As long as everyone trusted the system, investors could use the paper notes for new investment. But if for some reason too many people sought to redeem their bills in specie at the same time, there might be a "run" on the bank's reserves, leaving some note holders unable to acquire their promised specie and forcing banks to suspend such payments. The country's economic vitality, in short, rested on the uneasy assumption that public trust would hold out.

Early in 1836, increasing inflation of the price of staple goods suggested that economic matters had begun to shift and teeter. "As the manufacture of paper money proceeded," one contemporary wrote, "provisions and other necessaries of life rose in price." The result was predictable: laborers and mechanics began to demand higher wages to keep up with the increases. But this inflation alone, which hit urban areas most forcefully, did little to halt the lust for land in the West and South. "Millions of acres," this critic noted, continued to be "sold at prices utterly fictitious, and paid for in values utterly fictitious." He added, "There was no longer any *reality* in the business."[8]

Jackson only exacerbated matters when, his desire for decentralized banking unappeased after he had destroyed the Bank of the

United States, he tried to assert yet more control over the nation's banking system. In 1833, further to bolster the strength of the state banks, he issued his "Deposit Act," through which he removed significant amounts of specie from the Bank of the United States and deposited them in thirty state institutions, his "pet" banks, as they became known. This effectively further diminished the power of the nation's central bank over them and implicitly encouraged these institutions to issue yet more paper money to plow into land sales. The American banking system had become a shell game of huge proportions.

Old Hickory finally began to realize the disastrous side effects of his financial meddling. In mid-1836, alerted to the unnaturally high prices being paid in bank notes for the government's lands and worried that the federal government itself would be left holding worthless state paper because of these transactions, he issued his "Specie Circular," instructing offices auctioning federal lands to accept only specie as payment. However, this implicitly encouraged the transfer of ever more significant amounts of gold and silver from the North's and East's financial institutions to the nation's hinterlands and thus potentially jeopardized their ability to redeem notes in hard currency, should creditors so demand. Soon enough they did.

Following England's first disastrous wheat harvest in years, which prompted the purchase of large amounts of grain from Europe, London's central banks began to contract credit and raise interest rates. Alarmed by what they had heard of the Americans' unstable, decentralized banking system as well as the seemingly irrational land boom it encouraged, London's financial houses began in 1836 to squeeze the English merchants and middlemen dependent on them for financing commerce with brokers of American cotton.

By October, a ripple effect set in, and short-term loan rates in London for some of these American firms soared to 30 percent as money for any purpose, not just for new investment, tightened. English creditors began to call in more and more of their loans with American firms and demanded payment in specie, which had grown increasingly scarce in many American banks. Cotton prices began to tumble precipitously, the staple losing 30 percent of its value. "The immense [cotton] crop of 1836," one observer noted, simply "could not be sold."[9] Americans who had bet their fortunes on ever-rising prices for this commodity soon were broadsided by debt. The result was predictable: widespread failure of banks and mercantile houses, first in New Orleans, central entrepôt for cotton shipments; then in New York and other major Eastern cities; and finally throughout the United States.

The growing economic disaster leveled speculators and investors. Inevitable loss of savings and income followed, and then, of the very livelihoods of everyone, from mill owners to their factory operatives, whale ship owners to their men on the masts, plantation masters to the dockhands who loaded their staples. Hundreds of thousands of people fell into despair and with good reason. The American dream was turning into what proved an extended nightmare. By one estimate, 90 percent of the factories in the Eastern states closed by the end of 1837. Fifty thousand laborers in New York City were out of work, and two hundred thousand more were without adequate means of support.[10] One young mechanic remembered, "we had food enough in the house to last perhaps a week and my last wages lasted perhaps another week." He spent hours each day in search of some kind of employment, "but all in vain." "Starvation" looked his family "in the face," he added, and they often had to make do "with one meal a day," a privation that for his wife and children thankfully lasted only several weeks, but months or years for others.[11]

Young Horace Greeley, beginning his career as a city newspaperman, offered a chastening summary of such scenes and situations. "The times were hard," he wrote retrospectively. "Food and fuel were dear, many thousands of men and women were out of

employment, and there was general distress." "Some died of starvation," he continued. "Some were frozen to death." And "many,
through exposure and privation, contracted fatal diseases." Even
the circumstances of hitherto "respectable mechanics" were greatly
diminished, with many offering their services "as waiters in eating
houses for their food only."[12]

Greeley's grim assessment applied to communities all over the
country, whether urban or rural. In Philadelphia, for example, diarist Sidney George Fisher noted that there was "no society, no life
or movement, no topics of interest of any kind" because "everyone
has become poor & the calamities of the times have not only broken
up gay establishments & put an end to social intercourse, but seem
to have covered the place with a settled gloom."[13] In the shoemaking city of Lynn, Massachusetts, two thousand people were
out of work.[14] In nearby Nahant, one bank that failed had $215 on
hand in specie, and bank notes out to the tune of $242,965.[15] James
Kirke Paulding, novelist and former secretary of the navy, traveling
through Illinois up to the new settlement at Chicago, observed that
the people of that region "had been precipitated from the summit
of hope to the lowest abyss of debt and depression."[16]

Matters were even worse in the rural South, where many new
planters simply abandoned their lands and moved away to the vast
hinterland of Texas—then being contested between the United
States and Mexico—to escape being dunned.[17] Southerners speculated on the cause of their distress, and one firsthand witness
could not contain his sarcasm. In Alabama and Mississippi he
had seen the rise of a "new era," one of "credit without capital,
and enterprise without honesty."[18] There even was fear of outright
warfare. From everywhere, a writer for the Whig periodical the
Knickerbocker reported, comes "rumor after rumor of riot, insurrection, and tumult."[19]

New Yorker Philip Hone summed it up for the country as a
whole: "All is still as death; no business is transacted; no bargains

made; no negotiations."[20] It would be at least another seven or eight years before any genuine, stable recovery, when the Mexican War reinvigorated a nation badly in need of a new focus, and new sources of wealth. Unfortunately, the latter came with the implicit extension of slavery into new territories.

This book treats several individuals who attained considerable notice or notoriety as they struggled to understand the Panic of 1837 and its aftermath and concluded that its causes were not so much structural but were the result of personal, moral failings, to be remedied through appealing to man's "better angels."[21] Maintaining faith in the belief that, in a democratic nation based on a market economy, a person is solely responsible for his or her own failure (or success) in the economic marketplace, they offered imaginative, if frequently specious, ways for Americans to think about how, by improving certain aspects of their personal lives, they could make themselves better, more productive, and potentially successful citizens. These reformers thought that their fellow countrymen and women were sick in mind, body, and soul because of their addiction to ways of life that, while promising prosperity and success, instead brought them to what the writer and social critic Henry David Thoreau called "lives of quiet desperation."[22]

Indeed, perhaps more than any other thinker, Thoreau proved to be the system's most searching critic. He recognized that for years Americans had swallowed the pabulum that more was better, even as it became apparent (particularly in urban areas) that not all of their fellow citizens sat down to a decent meal, never mind seasoned it with choice condiments. But what could these privileged Americans do now, after full-scale economic meltdown? For two decades, until another economic catastrophe drained other reform efforts and redirected them toward the effort to abolish slavery, prophets and dreamers of all shapes and varieties scrambled to recover from the psychological shocks that had accompanied the recent panic, and they struggled to convince themselves (and as many of their fellow citizens as they could) that they might find a whole new life in the crucible of financial ruin.

Everywhere these Romantic reformers looked they saw evidence of widespread malaise—physical, moral, spiritual—and of attendant social and emotional dislocation. In the years leading up to 1837, many Americans, for example, had left farms for factories, and so they ate differently, drank more, and lived in unnaturally crowded environments. They wanted more cash and credit, and thus organized and began to patronize an economic system that further divided them into lenders and borrowers, winners and losers, and landlords and tenants, each of the latter driven to melancholy or despair, and the former, to a deceptively euphoric state of inflated self-worth. People no longer did business face-to-face but inhabited a vast, impersonal world where events across the Atlantic might impact grain prices in Buffalo, where the tightening of credit in London might bring a Louisiana cotton broker to ruin. Adamant in their self-reliance, Americans searched for religions that fit their belief in free will and flocked to new denominations or sects—Free Will Baptist, Methodist, Millerite, Mormon, even Transcendentalist, among others—that offered shortcuts to salvation, forgetting that the selfishness that underlay such desires for independence might still mark them as sinners.[23]

Many reformers viewed the nation's various transformations and proclaimed the country a moral shambles. They advocated wildly divergent panaceas—some legitimate, others quackery, pure and simple—that promised restoration of the body economic and politic through individual reformation. Remarkable idealism unified these principals. Reformers refused to accept anything as inevitable: choice and possibility, the opportunity to determine a different outcome, were writ in their very constitutions. Whether by example, education, politics, media, passion, or labor, they felt compelled to act, to influence, to effect change in the individual that then could be replicated in others. They believed that the United States had hit a dead end but also maintained a belief in the rightness of the country's ongoing democratic experiment, whose salutary end they could assure if only they identified and banished manifestations of pragmatism, expediency, and selfishness.

From their sincerity resulted, among other things, genuine efforts to provide the workingman with a living wage, proper diet, and a decent education; the mentally and physically challenged with proper empathy and care; and the institutionalized with rehabilitation. But just as often, in place of such morally sensitive work was a proliferation of pseudoscience, deficient economics, crackpot religion, or dogmatic politics. Trying to reroute the country's path, such idealists learned from painful experience that the nation's uncritical embrace of the market had instead led the nation astray. Their final inability to realize the America of their imagination provides case studies in the kinds of misjudgment and failure that can follow idealistic overreaching and that too often has marked subsequent American history in the wake of economic catastrophe.

This book weaves the stories of several influential antebellum reformers who had been indelibly affected by economic dislocation and thereupon galvanized to lives of reform. These include George Ripley, who at his Brook Farm utopian community near Boston offered a Transcendentalist's individualistic alternative to the nation's cutthroat capitalism; Horace Greeley, editor of the influential *New-York Tribune* and tireless advocate of European socialism and its attendant promise of more psychologically well-adjusted workers; William B. Greene, an erstwhile clergyman and economic theorist who, influenced by French Christian socialism, advocated a radical "mutual" or cooperative banking system that would guarantee the laborer an affordable source of credit and a

wage equivalent to the worth of what he produced; Orson Squire
Fowler, who with his brother, Lorenzo Niles Fowler, built a publishing empire around the pseudosciences of phrenology and
hydropathy (the "water cure"); Mary Gove Nichols, who with her
husband, Thomas Low Nichols, advocated women's health reform
and liberalized sexual relations; and Henry David Thoreau, arch-
individualist who sharply indicted his fellow citizens' insatiable
desire for wealth as well as the government's complicity in a transatlantic economy that thrived on slavery.

In various ways, each of these reformers queried how individuals' uncritical commitment to an unregulated and finally
impersonal marketplace, and their vulnerability to the financial
catastrophe and social disruption to which it often led, affected
what constitutes a good life, true liberty, and the morally justifiable
pursuit of happiness, goals that in one form or another remain
central to the nation's political culture. A final chapter treats John
Brown, who for two decades was the darling of many of these and
other reformers because of his seductively idealistic vision of a
fully integrated republic but whose tragic end is cautionary. Backed
against the wall because of his countrymen's unwillingness to heed
his call for immediate emancipation of the nation's slaves, Brown
finally rejected reason and compromise. His recourse to violence
starkly illuminates the inadequacy and final failure of idealisti-
cally elevating personal moral reform as a model for social action
and offering it as a substitute for whole-scale institutional change.

Before turning to the lives of these individuals, the practical and
psychological effects of financial failure on them, and the explicit
and implicit connections between them that the panic forged and
solidified, consider the broad spectrum of antebellum reform on

which they are located. In the wake of unprecedented financial disaster, they and their peers were interested in virtually any nostrum that would heal the American body, mind, or soul.

In the 1830s, health reformer Sylvester Graham questioned his contemporaries' ill-considered diet and proclivity to "wasting" bodily energy—that is, masturbation—and counseled vegetarianism and prolonged chastity.[24] Marx Edgeworth Lazarus traveled to the opposite extreme and urged uninhibited indulgence in sexual pleasure and free love. Dr. Joel Shew, R. T. Trall, and their followers championed the "water cure" for prolonged health, prescribing daily cold baths and vigorous rubbing with stiff "flesh" brushes to stimulate circulation and restore vitality.[25] "Botanical" doctors—now called herbalists—and homeopaths who believed that "like" cured "like" challenged the emergent medical profession's claims to professional knowledge and peddled countless editions of such works as *Gunn's Domestic Medicine or Poor Man's Friend* (1830) to a public willing and able to administer home cures.[26]

Other reformers queried man's relation to natural and built environments. Alarmed at the crowded and unsanitary conditions that often marked boardinghouse and apartment life, architects Andrew Jackson Downing and Frederick Law Olmsted advocated new types of interior and landscape design, including "cottages" in the country (what we would call suburbia) and octagonal homes (the famous attorney Clarence Darrow, for example, would be raised in one) in which the inhabitants' physical and mental health would be restored.[27] The plight of the laboring classes in massive, dehumanizing factories, where young children as well as their parents worked twelve-hour days, worried Frances Wright, Orestes Brownson, and other labor reformers; they rightly predicted that such institutions created an American proletariat and implicitly threatened American democratic ideals.[28]

Novel notions of the mind's complexity and its relation to bodily health fascinated other reformers. Inspired by the German physician Franz Joseph Gall, the Scot George Combe made a triumphant American tour during which he fueled widespread interest in phrenology—the assessment of character by studying the contours of the skull. By 1850 hundreds of traveling "doctors" urged deeper self-knowledge (and, implicitly, self-improvement) through feeling the bumps on one's head.[29] To anthropologists (and racists) this pseudoscience and its sister in faux-psychology, physiognomy (the study of character through indicative facial features) supported the notion that mankind was divided into separate and unequal races, frustrating the slave's claim to citizenship and even humanity.[30]

No aspect of personhood escaped the reformers' calls for renovation. The Frenchman Charles Poyen and his American disciple LaRoy Sunderland popularized "animal magnetism," or mesmerism, promising to cure diseases both mental and physical through adjustment of one's internal "electricity."[31] Their disciples often gravitated as well to Swedenborgianism, a religion that comparably stressed the literal correspondences between the material and spiritual worlds.[32] From here, it was only a small step to the séances of spiritualists and to early proponents of what became known as the "Mind Cure" and Christian Science, in which the strength of one's mental concentration defined a healthy, well-adjusted individual.[33] In different ways and to varying degrees such reformers and a myriad of others were convinced that what many so indiscriminately touted as most characteristically "American," rugged self-made success best (perhaps exclusively) measured by wealth and commercial achievement, only diminished the republic physically, psychologically, spiritually, and, as the events of 1837 made evident, economically.

This seething cauldron of equal parts discontent and ill-considered idealism was typified memorably in 1840 in Boston at the Chardon Street Convention of Friends of Universal Reform. There, attendee Ralph Waldo Emerson reported, one found

"Dunkers, Muggletonians, Come-outers, Groaners, Agrarians, Seventh-Day Baptists, Quakers, Abolitionists, Calvinists, Unitarians, and Philosophers," all of whom "came successively to the top, and seized their moment, if not their hour, wherein to chide, or pray, or preach, or protest."[34] In attendance, among others, were William Ellery Channing, the Unitarian "Pope"; Edmund Thompson ("Father") Taylor, the "sailor preacher"; Transcendentalist Bronson Alcott, planning Fruitlands, his own experiment in communal living based in radical vegetarianism and animal rights; radical abolitionists William Lloyd Garrison, Samuel May, and Maria W. Chapman; the Reverend Theodore Parker, inveighing against Boston's wealthy merchants and industrialists; free-love advocate Henry C. Wright, an early proponent of birth control; and Edward Palmer, who urged people to eschew entirely the use of money.

Alcott summed up the excitement in breathless shorthand. "Brag, & gasconade & prayer & prophecy, & blasphemy, & preaching, & contention and denunciation," he wrote. "Chardon Street & Bible, & Groton Conventions," he continued. "Abolition Mobs, & meetings of Non-resistants, & of women; Committees, the Symposeum [*sic*] Club, & the Dial; Fruitlands, Brook Farm, Parkerism, Conversations, and Emerson." These, he concluded, were "significant aspects of the time, and elements of the biography of its ruling spirits, looming forth from the canvas bold, & lurid, & serving to illustrate their ideas, endeavours, failures, and experiences."[35]

In the privacy of his diary in the same year as Chardon Street's meetings, John Quincy Adams confirmed these descriptions more acerbically, and he, like Alcott, singled out perhaps the foremost advocate of the self-made man as the ringleader in such affairs. "Ralph Waldo Emerson," he wrote, "after failing in the every-day avocations of a Unitarian preacher and schoolmaster, starts a new doctrine of transcendentalism, declares all the old revelations superannuated and worn out, and announces the approach of new revelations and prophecies." The doors simultaneously were opened, Adams continued, so that "Garrison and the non-resistant abolitionists, Brownson and the [Jean-Paul] Marat democrats, phrenology and animal magnetism all come in, furnishing each some plausible rascality as an ingredient for the bubbling cauldron of religion and politics" that marked the age.[36]

From this cacophony of voices vying to outdo each other for the public's wider attention and support, the profiles of reformers here indicate how economic upheaval and the moral obliquity that led to it made them and thousands of other Americans hope and work for a better day, though too often through extravagant and foolhardy means. Obviously, the causes of financial panic and civil war are multiple and diverse. The story about to be told is not intended to blame either event on these individuals. But collectively they do represent a significant part of America's imaginative landscape of possible solutions to what for them had become intolerable problems. Unfortunately, although their idealism was genuine, their insistence on an ethos of individualism and the transformative power of personal example did not lead to correctives that prevented further economic chaos or the bloodbath of the Civil War, nor in some cases even to significant personal reformation.

I

George Ripley,
Transcendentalist Dreamer

In the years after George Ripley's ordination in 1821 over the Purchase Street Church on Boston's waterfront, his neighborhood changed. As the city grew in size, shopkeepers and other merchants who originally built in the area to take advantage of the burgeoning coastal and transatlantic trade began to move from the wharf area to newer homes along the more fashionable western edges of the city. There, beyond the Common and out along the Charles River, work to reclaim land in the Back Bay had commenced. Those who worked the waterfront in various capacities—clerks, cart men, sailors, shopkeepers of all sorts—took their place around Purchase Street, transforming the area into a working-class enclave rather than a home to the almost exclusively "middling" sort among whom Ripley initially had settled.

In the aftermath of the Panic of 1837, the neighborhood changed even more. With work scarce, laboring families found themselves in dire economic straits, unable to pay rent or put food on the table. Ripley became increasingly concerned about the proliferation as well as the plight of this impoverished population, and also about his remaining parishioners' evident complacency toward, even callous disregard for, their less fortunate neighbors' difficulties.

In a powerful sermon, *The Temptations of the Times* (1837), Ripley proclaimed that he had identified what was troubling his city and the nation as a whole. The chief danger was nothing less than "the inordinate pursuit, the extravagant worship of wealth," which he traced back to "a constant temptation" to "an excess of selfishness."[1] The conundrum—as well as the main impediment to corrective social action—was that the source of urban misery lay in the very ethic of self-reliant individualism that distinguished the United States from other nations and in which it took inordinate pride. In the antebellum period, a faith in a God-granted and God-calibrated moral compass universal to mankind promised to channel individualism and check its selfish propensities. Believing in everyone's innate ability, spiritual in origin, to tell right from wrong, and good from bad, this ethic suggested that men and women were architects of their own fortune, or misfortune. Meaningful reform, therefore, had to center on attempts to reach an individual's conscience.

The problem, Ripley insisted, was that under the current economic system everything "tends to fix our regards upon ourselves and to withdraw them from others," while "a fixed fancied independence is counted as the highest good." Convinced that he had to reinstate a "deeper sense of our dependence on one another," he wondered whether, given his inability to spark his flock to social action, he should seek another, more independent church, as his friend Orestes Brownson had in taking up a ministry to Boston's poor.[2] Or, more radically, should he leave the pulpit altogether (as his cousin Ralph Waldo Emerson had), the better to fulfill what he regarded as his social mission?

Humble Beginnings

Born inauspiciously in 1802 in the midst of a smallpox and dysentery epidemic in Greenfield, Massachusetts, Ripley was one of six children of ambitious and hardworking parents who a decade earlier had moved from Boston to this growing town on the Connecticut River in the northwest part of the state.[3] Ripley's father, Jerome, operated a tavern and general store that eventually brought the family financial success as well as political influence. Over his career, Jerome served variously as justice of the peace, assessor, selectman, judge of the County Court, and delegate to the Massachusetts General Court. Through all these ventures, Sarah Franklin Ripley was Jerome's supportive helpmeet.

The young Ripley was raised in a home of rising economic means within a community comprised of different social classes living in relative harmony. Like most of their neighbors, his parents were Congregationalists in religion and Federalists in politics. As a family in the upper echelon of the community's civic leadership, the Ripleys expected deference and were not disappointed. Those who offered it accepted social distinctions as a matter of course, for Greenfield's citizens respected those who had obtained positions of leadership through hard work and moral rectitude. The Ripleys fit this bill.

Ripley's brothers followed in their father's footsteps in various aspects of business, but early on George was earmarked for a respected alternative, the ministry. Given his family's ambition and social stature, this meant an education at Harvard or Yale College, not yet at upstarts like Williams or Amherst College, even though they were closer to Greenfield. As a teenager Ripley prepared at an academy down the Connecticut River in Hadley, Massachusetts, and eventually decided on Harvard, in large part because his father's embrace of what then was termed "liberal Christianity," which many of Harvard's divinity faculty professed. They believed that Christ was not God the Father's equal but a separately created, subordinate being through whom He had revealed his wishes for mankind. This belief formed the bedrock of "liberal Christianity" and, soon enough, of what was termed Unitarianism.

Given the rigor of Harvard's admission requirements, early in 1819 Ripley furthered his studies with family relatives in the eastern part of the state. These included the venerable Dr. Ezra Ripley, who had prepared countless other youths for Harvard. Ripley could also discuss his emergent religious beliefs with another nearby relative, Ralph Waldo Emerson, then a sophomore at Harvard.

Ripley applied himself diligently and was admitted in the fall of the year; he graduated at the head of his class four years later. Not yet as committed to liberal Christianity as his father, as a next step he considered attending the Andover Theological Seminary, founded in 1807 by conservative stalwarts who feared Harvard's increasing commitment to the theological liberalism that was soon to flower in the Unitarian movement.[4] Ripley appreciated the fact that, while avowedly Trinitarian, Andover's faculty was open to liberalizing influences from European scholars, particularly in scriptural study, that were finding their way across the Atlantic. But once again, Jerome Ripley exerted his influence. His son remained in Cambridge, where a cohort of professors led by Henry Ware Jr., two years earlier appointed to the prestigious Hollis Professorship of Divinity, and Andrews Norton, the Dexter Professor of Sacred Literature, similarly were adopting the "Higher Criticism" of scripture, but in defense of Unitarianism.[5]

Within a year, his teachers' arguments swayed Ripley. He became convinced of the unity of the Godhead, the prime Unitarian tenet, and rejected Calvinism's dark vision of predestination, original sin, and stark damnation. He also came to regard dry theological wrangling of the sort in which theologians too frequently engaged as a pointless diversion from a true life of the spirit. The young divinity student wanted to work in the world. Religious experience and its attendant effect on ethics, he concluded, mattered most. By his last term, however, Ripley was regarded as so promising a scholar that he was invited to publish articles in a Unitarian periodical, the *Christian Register*. Friendship with the eminent

William Ellery Channing, pastor of the large Federal Street Church in Boston and nicknamed the Unitarian "Pope," further bolstered Ripley's Unitarian résumé.

Soon after his graduation in 1826, Ripley was settled over a liberal church in a new meetinghouse on Boston's waterfront, at the corner of Griffin and Purchase Streets, near Griffin Wharf. Its cornerstone had been laid in 1825; and many of Ripley's Harvard professors, including Ware and Norton, attended his ordination. Ripley's fiancée, Sophia Dana, whom he married a year later and who would prove an equal partner in his future endeavors, also was present. By the 1820s Ripley was a graduate of Harvard, a published scholar, a leader in the city's liberal theological and philosophical discussions, and had married into one of Boston's best families; his prospects seemed assured.

Continuing Education

The young clergyman quickly learned that ministering to a congregation in the city's swelling wharf district, filled with dockworkers and cart men as well as the "middling-class" merchants who owned the nearby warehouses and shops, and who comprised the bulk of his parishioners, was a far cry from writing essays for Unitarian periodicals or debating religious beliefs with his erudite classmates.

Hitherto, he had traveled among the region's elite, for whom economic matters were not paramount: many early American Unitarians were wealthy lawyers, doctors, and merchants. But as the Purchase Street neighborhood grew, its population changed; and, after 1837, as economic dislocation spread, Ripley saw more vividly the harsh circumstances in which most of the city's population lived. Poverty and vice proliferated. Among the once-comfortable homes of middle-class merchants and tradesmen he saw numerous taverns, gambling houses, and even houses of prostitution, the

kinds of businesses that flourish even in severe economic down-
turns, because they help people forget their disappointments and
anxieties.

Ripley also realized that the traditional steps the clergy took to
address such ills—urging citizens to join an Evangelical Missionary
Society or a Sunday School Union—did little to alleviate economic
hardship or growing social tensions. To his protégé, John Sullivan
Dwight, whose ordination sermon Ripley recently had preached
in Northampton, Massachusetts, he complained that his parishioners "wish for a priest & a spiritual guide, not to say a dictator,
rather than for a fraternal helper. . . . They would rather be exhorted
than enlightened."[6] But dictating conduct was not just perilous for
parishioner and priest but, far worse, a perversion of each individual's ability to be guided by a far greater and unerring power. Ripley's profound belief in the guidance of a transcendent spirit with
whom each being could be in touch only furthered his belief that
the best way to solve society's myriad problems was to persuade by
example, not to reengineer society as a whole. Eventually, he began
to wonder whether the ministry offered the most effective way to
address the manifold challenges Boston's citizens faced.

Ripley did not immediately sour on pastoral work, though, for
his congregation genuinely welcomed his preaching and service.
Moreover, he found time to continue his already prodigious intellectual growth; a rigorous program of reading and study helped
push aside any creeping doubts of his effectiveness as a clergyman
or scholar. As an alumnus, he frequently visited the Harvard College library, and he joined the Boston Athenaeum for reading privileges there.

He also borrowed books from fellow clergymen and eagerly
bought other volumes, beginning to assemble what eventually became one of the city's best private libraries of religious and philosophical works, in several languages. From his study he navigated
Europe's theological and philosophical currents, particularly the

brave new course of the Higher Criticism of the Bible, and that of the philosophical Idealism spawned by Immanuel Kant and promulgated and extended by a subsequent generation of philosophers: Friedrich Schleiermacher, Johann Gottlieb Fichte, and Friedrich Wilhelm Joseph Schelling, among others. Soon even Unitarianism began to seem stuffy and conservative, unable to satisfy Ripley's growing faith in what Emerson termed the "the infinitude of the common man."[7]

These thinkers had convinced Ripley of an order of truths that, as he put it, "transcends the sphere of external senses," and that thus indicated the supremacy of mind over matter. There is a faculty in all, he believed, even in the most degraded, ignorant, or obscure, to perceive spiritual truth directly, so that the ultimate arbiter of moral questions was not "a jury of scholars, a hierarchy of divines, of the prescriptions of a creed," but the instinctual common sense of the individual.[8] Innately present in each individual, in other words, is a spiritual principle that, of itself, without any external stimuli, allows one to distinguish between right and wrong, good and bad, God and Satan, and supersedes any outward laws and injunctions. The highest law comes from the promptings of the spirit, a potentially anarchic belief held in check, he believed, by the universality of the religious sentiment.

Conversations with friends among the younger clergy also fertilized Ripley's intellectual growth and as well awakened his social conscience. None of these was more influential than Orestes Brownson, a self-educated Vermont farmer's son who in the course of a circuitous religious pilgrimage already had moved away from conservative Presbyterianism and Universalism, another liberal faith whose followers believed in the eventual salvation of all men and women. By the time Ripley moved to Purchase Street, Brownson was under the sway of Frances (Fanny) Wright and Robert Dale Owen, freethinkers and leaders of the radical Working Men's Party.[9]

Brownson next discovered William Ellery Channing as well as French Christian socialist Claude-Henri de Saint-Simon. Swayed by Channing's emphasis on the inherent goodness of all mankind and Saint-Simon's belief that true Christians should work for social justice and harmony among all classes, Brownson embraced Unitarianism. By 1832 he was leading a small congregation in Canton, Massachusetts, near Boston, and began to circulate among the area's liberal clergy. He soon became an important ally in attempts to extend Unitarianism to the urban masses. Foremost among his new friends in this endeavor was Ripley, who, alerted to the plight of the city's poor by growing numbers of the working class in his own neighborhood, welcomed another voice for the city's disadvantaged.

Brownson soon had the opportunity to work toward just that end, for he replaced Joseph Tuckerman as "minister-at-large" to Boston's indigent.[10] He moved to Chelsea, on the city's harbor and near the center of the Unitarian universe. He walked shoulder to shoulder with other liberal Christians, Ripley among them, who testified to their faith by urging more attention to those at the lowest rungs of the economic and social order.

The Lure of Transcendentalism

The key moment in Ripley's intellectual development in these years came in September 1836, after the bicentennial celebration of Harvard College, when he met at the Willard Hotel in Boston with fellow alumni Emerson, Frederic Henry Hedge, recently named minister to a Unitarian church in Bangor, Maine, and George Putnam, who oversaw a liberal congregation in nearby Roxbury. They would "confer together on the state of current opinion in theology and philosophy."[11] The initial discussion went well, and a week later at Ripley's invitation a much larger group met at his home in Boston.

Over the next four years this group, with an ever-shifting membership, but with Emerson, Hedge, and Ripley its anchors, met nearly thirty times, maintaining a focus on significant religious and philosophical issues while occasionally broaching topics of wider concern, including questions of social reform. An interest in the philosophy coming to be known as "Transcendentalism" linked these disparate individuals, known eventually (but always informally) as members of the "Transcendental Club." At these meetings, Ripley assumed a leadership role.

What precisely did it mean to be one of these "Transcendentalists," and what was the group's allure? Almost all of these individuals self-identified as "liberal Christians." In particular, they rejected Calvinism's harsh tenets, particularly the belief in man's inherent sinfulness. They also embraced the revolution in philosophy wrought principally by Kant, who championed the inherent power of the human mind, against the empirical philosophy of John Locke and his followers, who believed that external circumstances primarily formed man's consciousness.

Transcendentalism thus is best understood as a way of perceiving the world centered on the individual himself rather than on anything external. This emphasis on the primacy of self-consciousness and, by implication, the sanctity of each individual aligned the movement with the political principles of the new nation. The Founding Fathers had declared that all men were created equal and had certain inalienable rights; here was a faith in the equality and infinitude of our spiritual lives congruent to that political formulation. Moreover, Transcendentalism, with its attendant emphasis on individual self-reliance, fit perfectly well with the emergent capitalist market that drove the nation's ever-growing economy.

What did this position mean for Emerson, Ripley, and others' understanding of and commitment to social reform? When it came to the practical consequences of such Idealism, the key players disagreed. Emerson, in one of his popular "Lectures on the Times" delivered in the early 1840s, criticized those who, purporting to follow the spirit within, became too absorbed in social issues rather than attending properly to their own spiritual regeneration. It was too easy, he thought, to be swept up in larger causes and to believe that such participation validated one's moral rectitude. In fact, such outward activity just as easily could mask a deeper moral obliquity. The better—and, he believed, correct—route was to purify one's own soul and live with full integrity, to become a model for, rather than a nagging goad to, others.

"The great majority of men," he asserted, "unable to judge of any principle until its light falls on a fact, are not aware of the evil that is around them, until they see it in some gross form, as in a class of intemperate men, or slaveholders, or fraudulent persons." Only then are they greatly moved, he continued, "and magnifying the importance of that wrong, they fancy that if that abuse alone were redressed, all would go well, and they fill the land with clamor to correct it."[12] It was too easy, in other words, to work to eradicate a single outward manifestation of human corruption rather than attempting to attack the disease at its source, within the individual's constitution proper.

Others, however, argued that this dodged the central question. What relief did Emerson's way offer those who actually suffered from social evil? He might preserve the sanctity of individual conscience, but he offered little to ameliorate what, after 1837, proved ever more divisive social inequalities and the very real pain that accompanied them.

In the late 1830s Emerson's views, though increasingly influential, had not yet carried the day. In this phase of the movement, Ripley and Brownson wielded significant influence, particularly among younger Unitarians who insisted on vigorous, immediate attention to social problems. These crusaders focused on the social implications of "spontaneous reason" and perceived themselves as prophets of a wholly new secular as well as spiritual order.[13] They believed that political freedom had not been accompanied by a requisite liberality of mind. "These brave souls," Transcendentalist and pioneering feminist Margaret Fuller wrote in 1840, "tried to quicken the soul, that they may work from within outwards." "Disgusted with the vulgarity of a commercial aristocracy," she continued, many disaffected men and women whom she knew "bec[a]me radicals" in order to help their fellow men and women, pushed and pulled by the crosscurrents of the nation's economic riptides.[14]

Fuller and her peers had discovered that the heady premise of having God within bore direct relation to the democratic sentiment that all men (and women) are created equal. They also realized, however, that unchecked capitalism, and particularly the self-interest it encouraged, stunted the practical realization of this principle. Reformers like Ripley, Brownson, and others called for concerted action to make America's democratic promise a reality.

But although a real and meaningful gulf widened between Emerson and Ripley, they and their respective cohorts shared a chief premise: meaningful and lasting reform derived from personal example. Yes, Emerson looked inward and Ripley looked outward; the former came close to conceding that the best he could aspire to was to help himself while the latter wished to set an example that in theory the entire world could follow. But both were united in their wish to persuade the world how different life could be when men and women effected true reformation in themselves.

So within Transcendentalism, debate raged over which sort of example should be set. Transcendentalist Elizabeth Peabody had a word for Emerson's way of thinking: "ego-theism," a term she used to register her harsh disapproval. The problem with viewing the world as an Emerson rather than a Ripley, she maintained, was that people "deified their own conceptions" of things even as they dismissed others'.[15] This too often led to an insufferable self-righteousness and a concomitant inability to admit one's errors. One auditor of Emerson's "Lecture on the Times" was more severe: "So

we would ask Mr. Emerson," he wrote, "whether the Poverty, Ignorance and Misery of the human race and the devastated and neglected conditions of the Globe are not objects great enough to
arouse the philosopher of the Transcendentalist School to action."[16]

Emerson's close friend, the theologian Henry James Sr., baldly
leveled the same criticism. "The curse of our present times," he
observed, is the "selfhood imposed on us by the evil world," a
situation to which too many Transcendentalists acquiesced.[17] To
accomplish meaningful social reform, one had to overcome the
dangerous self-centeredness that the movement encouraged. The
problem for Brownson, Ripley, and others was whether, having
had their thought tempered in Transcendentalism, they now
could escape the bogey of individualism that had settled on Emerson and his particular acolytes, for Ripley and Emerson both still
identified the chief obstacle to reform as recalcitrant individuals
who had to be enlightened through example.

Brook Farm's Incubation

In the early 1840s Ripley finally freed himself from Emerson's grav-
itational pull. He would attempt to harmonize individualism with
social cohesion and reduce or eliminate complicity with the more
destructive aspects of the marketplace. He would eventually plan
Brook Farm, which he envisioned as nothing less than a new kind
of community that would serve as a city on a hill, as once the Puritans' Boston had been. His was indeed a noble, if grandiose, ambition, for its beacon, Ripley believed, might eventually shine not
only on Massachusetts and America but on the entire world.

He began to move in this direction as early as 1836, shortly after
Brownson offered the public *New Views of Christianity, Society, and
the Church*. Therein Brownson preached a gospel of union and progress, and exposed what he believed was the destructive worm at
the nation's core: an economic system that disregarded the inherent

dignity of each human being—mill owner or working woman, plantation overseer or slave—and rewarded cutthroat capitalism.[18] The market, in other words, tore at the New Testament (and Transcendentalist) vision that found divinity flowing through every being, regardless of social position.

If his friend Brownson provided a particularly local source for the contours of Ripley's ministry, his chief philosophical muse was the German theologian Friedrich Schleiermacher, whom Ripley had approvingly introduced to American readers in 1834 in the *Christian Examiner,* the premier Unitarian periodical.[19] Schleiermacher insisted that what best defines spirituality is *feeling,* not some abstract intellectual proposition. Through feeling, one perceived the divinity of the quotidian, an insight that transformed one's entire life into an experience of the holy, and this led to sympathy with all humanity and so to commiseration with the plight of the underprivileged. For a social reformer such as Ripley, there was a domino-like quality to this worldview. As awareness of that divinity in each person spread, so too would sympathy and commiseration, and consequently lives, communities, and even nations would be transformed, leading to a new social harmony.

For Ripley, the Panic of 1837 and the subsequent destruction and disillusion it wrought underscored how dulled Americans' perception of their inherent spirituality had become and, as a consequence, how urgent the need to lead them back to such awareness. There is no denying the impact of the contemporary financial upheaval on sensitive young reformers like Ripley. Fellow Unitarian Samuel K. Lothrop succinctly captured its shock: "We were in the midst of peace, apparent prosperity, and progress," Lothrop observed, "when, after extensive individual failures, the astounding truth burst upon us like a thunderbolt." Quite simply, "we were a nation of bankrupts, and a bankrupt nation."[20] To Ripley, Brownson, and others in their cohort, whoever ignored the immediate effects of this catastrophe did nothing less than abdicate his Christian duty.

Observing the growing inequality among classes on and around the Boston waterfront, Ripley understood the justice of what Brownson had written in 1840 in his lengthy essay, "The Laboring Classes," and a later, even longer, defense of the essay. There he identified the canker at the heart of American democracy as the system of wage labor that capitalism enabled and encouraged. He also prophesied an escalating confrontation between labor and capital that might end in outright warfare, a prediction that alienated him from many of his fellow Democrats, especially his friends among the political elite, who feared that Brownson's incendiary rhetoric would cost them votes in state and national elections. The factory owner who employs the workmen, Brownson wrote, is nothing but "one of our city nabobs, reveling in luxury; or he is a member of our legislature, enacting laws to put money in his own pocket; or he is a member of Congress, contending for a high tariff to tax the poor for the benefit of the rich; or in these times he is shedding crocodile tears over the deplorable conditions of the poor laborer, while he docks his wages twenty-five per cent."[21] The logic of Brownson's lengthy analysis was clear. To avoid an even bigger catastrophe than the Panic of 1837 and escape an upheaval that might include literal warfare, Americans had to recognize that the great cause of the age was the elevation of the laborer.

But Democrats had more immediate worries. In 1840, the modern two-party political system had come into its own, and Democrats had good reason to fear the loss of the presidency. The Whigs had stumbled on the memorable slogan, "Log Cabin and Hard Cider," as they attempted to wrest lower-class votes from the incumbent Democrat Martin Van Buren for their candidate, William Henry Harrison. Van Buren labored under the weight of the depression that arrived virtually simultaneously with his inauguration, and so the Whigs pushed Harrison, a hero of Indian wars in the Ohio River Valley, as a man of the people who would end the nation's economic suffering. Appealing through him to farmers, mechanics, and shopkeepers—men of little or middling means—the Whigs handily won the election. Neither candidate, however, shared Brownson's view of the nation's economic situation. So, despite Harrison's folksy credentials and the subsequent goodwill of his successor, John Tyler (Harrison died a month after taking the oath of office), in the early 1840s the nation's underlying structural problems remained unaddressed.

Brownson's radicalism was clear, if frightening, to many. He sought genuine change, to realize in "social arrangements" and in "the actual conditions of all men" that "equality of man and man" that God had established but that the nation's runaway economic system had progressively destroyed.[22] He rejected outright Emerson's elevation of self-culture over social activism. Self-improvement would not abolish inequality nor restore workers' rights, and bore no relation to the wholesale changes to the system of wage labor that the times demanded. One had to change the economic system, not worry about the drinking habits or reading lists of its managers. He did not say how precisely this was to be accomplished but left the question to others, like his friend Ripley.

But Brownson also knew that few contemporary clergy were brave enough to undertake the radical step of remolding society to God's will. They dared not question established social relations, he noted, lest they "incur the wrath of infidelity, and lose their standing, and their salaries."[23] Ripley knew firsthand to what Brownson alluded here; for the last several years, he had met increasing recalcitrance to his ever more frequent appeals to his congregation for stronger commitment to social action. Even though they had seen the devastating effects of the financial panic themselves, they did not react as Ripley did and did not share his fervent desire for change. Even as Brownson's "Laboring Classes" ignited a firestorm of criticism, Ripley's frustration reached the tipping point.

Ripley at the Rubicon

Ripley's personal crisis came to a head in May 1840. He wrote to his church, indicating his wish to resign if they consented. The church asked him to stay, but he had embarked on a path on which he felt compelled to continue. His friends recognized this. Fuller commented that Ripley seemed "most happy in the step he has taken" and seemed almost "newborn."[24] Emerson, too, who himself had taken such courageous action to better move in the direction of self-culture, approved. He commented that Ripley had done a "brave" thing and "stands now at the head of the church militant."[25] Over the next few months, Ripley gathered his thoughts more completely and in October offered his church a more substantial document in the form of a letter of resignation.

Ripley's missive was poignant. Even if some of his preaching had been effective, he observed, too often topics of concern to him simply failed to attract his congregation's attention or raised their ire. He believed, however, that unless a minister could speak out "on all subjects [that] are uppermost in his mind, with no fear of incurring the charge of heresy, or compromising the interests of the congregation," he could never do justice to his profession or himself.[26]

Ripley's disappointment with the ministry went beyond his difficulties with a complacent congregation. He also was frustrated with those Transcendentalists who continued to argue that the city's social problems were best addressed through calls for personal regeneration. "The attention of some good men," Ripley wrote (no doubt with his cousin Waldo in mind), "is directed chiefly to individual evils." These reformers wished to "improve private character" but neglected to attack those "social principles which obstruct all improvement." Others, however, himself included, wanted to focus on "the evils of society," because they believed that "private character suffers from public sins." Still enough of a Transcendentalist to value self-culture highly, he believed that it was imperative to find ways for people to realize their spiritual selves. Ripley sought to establish what he termed a "social worship," so that religion would "redeem society as well as the individual from sin." After the Panic of 1837 he witnessed everywhere "glaring inequalities of condition, the hollow pretension of pride, the scornful apathy with which many urge the prostration of man, the burning zeal with which they run the race of selfish competition, with no thought for the elevation of their brethren, without the sad conviction that the spirit of Christ has well-nigh disappeared from our churches, and that fearful doom awaits us." Such views, he insisted, seemed "the very essence" of the religion that he had been taught.[27] To recapture this spirit would allow individuals to establish the much-sought social harmony that the nation's political principles promised.

Ripley moved forward. At the first of the year he requested formal dismissal. The parish consented, and on March 28, 1841, he delivered a moving farewell sermon, notable for its lack of rancor. It simply boiled down to this, he said: he could dissimulate no longer. He confessed that he was "a peace man, a temperance man, an abolitionist, a transcendentalist, [and] a friend of radical reform in social institutions." And although he lamented his flock's unwillingness to join him in these causes, he did not condemn their recalcitrance. He and they parted in peace.[28]

Brook Farm: Theory

Unencumbered by pastoral obligations, Ripley did not lack for ideas about how next to proceed. Most appealing was the notion of an entire community devoted to the kind of self-improvement that he envisioned and that could serve as a model for the society of the future. Its success at all levels—economic, social, and intellectual—should be worthy of emulation by the nation and, eventually, the world at large.

Ripley broached his ambitious ideas at one of the Transcendental Club's meetings. In a letter to his protégé Dwight, Elizabeth Peabody, who owned a foreign-language bookshop in Boston where Club members frequently browsed, noted approvingly Ripley's claim that "the ministers & church are upheld in order to uphold [a] church society vicious in its foundations—but which the multitude desire should continue in its present conditions," a position opposed by Transcendentalist fellow-traveller, Hedge, who from his pulpit in Maine continued to defend the traditional church.[29] Ripley revisited the question at the next and final meeting of the Club, but both times it met with only a lukewarm reception.

Aware of similar efforts being undertaken by others, Ripley was on fire to act. He soon decided to go forward with a model community where labor and capital would enter into a new relationship, freeing individuals for self-culture. Fuller, though, worried about whether Ripley had the right temperament for such an undertaking. Was he was up to the challenge of defining his community in terms radical enough to attain its stated goals of reconfiguring social relations? Ripley was adamant and made plans to move his family to a dairy farm in West Roxbury, Massachusetts, where he recently had boarded. There he envisioned the establishment of a new, harmonious social order that had the individual's spiritual welfare at its center.

Ripley spent the late fall and winter months of 1840–1841 trying to drum up financial support for what admittedly was still a rather vaguely outlined plan. In particular, he sought the commitment of prominent Transcendentalists—Emerson, Fuller, and educational reformer Bronson Alcott, among them—in hopes that their endorsements would generate further interest and support, but none jumped aboard. Alcott, for example, had his own ideas for a utopian venture, a "simpler New Eden," he termed it, where, after its members had surrendered their desires for all selfish gratification, they would live in harmony with the universal spirit. His plan eventuated in the short-lived Fruitlands experiment, where the few members toyed with vegetarianism, animal rights, and celibacy.[30] Fuller, too, resisted Ripley's plea. She supported his ideas in principle but wondered not only if he was the right person to organize such a venture but also whether it would fulfill its mission. "I doubt," she concluded presciently, that the reformers "will get free from all they deprecate in society."[31]

Not surprisingly, Emerson, too, balked at Ripley's plan. After a lengthy discussion at his Concord home at which Ripley outlined some of his goals to Emerson and other friends, Fuller reported that, overall, the talk proved "useless." It only brought out "in strong relief" Ripley's and Emerson's "different ways of thinking."[32] But Ripley did not give up. In early November he sent his cousin a long letter in which for the first time he tried to spell out his goals for the social experiment. Brook Farm, he explained, would "insure a more natural union between intellectual and manual labor than now exists." Toward that end, the new community would

> combine the thinker and the worker, as far as possible, in the same individual; to guarantee the highest mental freedom, by providing all with labor, adapted to their tastes and talents, and securing them the fruits of their industry; to do away with the necessity of menial services, by opening the benefits of education and the profits of labor to all; and thus to prepare a society of liberal, intelligent, and cultivated persons, whose relations with each other would permit a more simple and wholesome life, than can be led amidst the pressure of our completive institutions.[33]

He had a site in mind, he told Emerson, in West Roxbury, where a large dairy farm would form the basis of their labor and where they also would operate a progressive school for the children of members and for others by tuition.

For over a month Emerson balked at his cousin's calls for his support. After much soul-searching, Emerson finally wrote that he could not join the admittedly "noble & humane" enterprise that Ripley proposed. His reasoning typifies the position of Transcendentalists most seduced by his appeal to individual self-culture. Trying to soften the rejection, Emerson explained to his cousin that the ground of his decision was "almost purely personal." He was content with his home, the neighborhood, and the institutions in Concord around which he had built his new career as a writer and lecturer. More tellingly, he explained that to join Ripley's community seemed "a circuitous & operose [arduous] way" of relieving himself of "any irksome circumstances," and putting on Ripley's community the task of his "emancipation" that he ought to take on himself. Emerson supported the kind of reform that was best accomplished in the privacy of one's closet.[34]

Ripley was determined to find other supporters. He thought that his community would require about a $30,000 investment, raised primarily by selling shares in a joint-stock enterprise.[35] Surely he was aware of the irony of having to depend on precisely the sort of financial arrangements in part responsible for overheating the nation's economic engine just prior to the 1837 panic. His intended earthly paradise, purportedly removed from competitive institutions, was in fact a joint-stock company that would survive by taking in income from school tuition and selling produce to the Boston market, so that investors might reap a percentage of any profit. Ripley evidently was willing to rationalize this incongruity. Ultimately he and his investors and loyal supporters promised to remake what it meant to live in a commercial world.

One model for this reformation of daily life lay in the various religious communities that dotted the landscape, particularly those of the Shakers, whose village at Harvard, Massachusetts, was only twenty-five miles from Boston. It was long established and solidly self-sufficient. But with its complex theology, segregation of the sexes, and enforced celibacy, the United Society of Believers in Christ's Second Appearing did not offer much inspiration to a lapsed Unitarian, save for a glimpse of the harmony possible in a community removed from entanglement in a corrupt world. More immediately influential may have been the German community of Separatists at Zoar that the Ripleys had visited in 1838 when George was preaching in the Ohio River Valley. The group's social harmony and their enjoyment of various kinds of labor, which never seemed tedious, much impressed Sophia, who described her experience in the *Dial.*[36] Ripley also consulted with Adin Ballou, a Universalist minister who was starting a utopian community in nearby Mendon, Massachusetts. The two even considered uniting their efforts, but negotiations between them fell apart because Ballou insisted that members assent to an explicitly Christian creed. Ripley wanted to welcome all faiths and denominations at his community.[37]

Unsurprisingly, though, most of Ripley's guiding principles came from his own Transcendentalist beliefs and a desire to apply them to the growing economic and social chaos around him. For example, he appeared most troubled by the exponential growth of a working class whose harsh and unprofitable labor prevented them from fully developing their intellectual and spiritual capacities. Ripley's shock at the widespread unemployment after the Panic of 1837 lay behind this. Despite the fact that laborers wished to return to work, for example, they remained unemployed. This seemed illogical, for society had the same material needs after the economic disaster as before. But those who controlled capital and, by implication, production had been so financially crippled that they were slow to reinstate workers and, as a result, further mired them in poverty and vice. Somehow, this had to be remedied.

That remedy, however, was but the starting point, not the finish line, for Ripley also believed in meaningful work. An individual should embrace labor as a joy and not a duty, and any task one is asked to do should be congruent with one's interests and talents. Conversely, to make someone perform unsuitable or unattractive labor only resulted in disgruntlement or poor performance. Adequate wages, for no matter what the work, also were important, but they were not all. At Brook Farm, the necessities of life—food, clothing, shelter, health care, and schooling for the children— also would be guaranteed. But the sort of social safety net of which twenty-first century liberals dream was never the goal. Rather, Ripley sought something more. Yes, he wished to replace a bitter, class-ridden society with contented, well-educated individuals; but the higher end was each member's self-culture and spiritual redemption.

Precisely how was all this to be accomplished? Who should he recruit, and how many members should there be? What agricultural products would the farmland best support? What would be the relation of the school and its charges to the laboring force? Could people who sought to improve their spiritual and intellectual lives but did not wish to become members stay at the farm and simply pay for room and board?

An article in the Unitarian *Monthly Miscellany of Religion and Letters* pointed out Ripley's seeming confusion in these matters. The writer observed that Ripley's plans were chiefly "connected with the education of the young of both sexes" in a "cooperative association for practical education." But then he cited another notice, from the *New England Farmer*, a well-regarded agricultural journal. It suggested that the community's main means of support instead would be through farming. Ripley, this journal reported, intended to focus on scientific methods of crop and dairy production, and through them to make farming a profession worthy of respect, even among intellectuals. The journal also seconded the other report, mentioning Ripley's educational goals and linking them to progressive farming. The ex-clergyman, the writer explained, planned a "Practical Institute of Agriculture and Education" where he would "furnish the means of a liberal education to those who are not intended for the learned professions." There he would "increase the attachment of the farmer to the cultivation of the soil, by showing the divinity of the pursuit," and as well provide the "knowledge and ability" that the work demanded so that young farmers could "intelligent[ly] discharge the duties of their calling."[38] As these reports suggest, Ripley himself seemed unsure of just which way to proceed—toward education or agriculture, or both. Thus, Emerson's hesitation in answering Ripley's request for him to join the enterprise is understandable.

Brook Farm: Practice

Even though no prominent Transcendentalist joined or even invested in the community, by the spring of 1841 Brook Farm became a reality. Ripley had settled on the Ellis farm in West Roxbury, a property familiar to him that was currently for sale. Eight miles west of Boston, the farm consisted of 170 acres of pasture and meadowland, some hardwood lots, and a pine forest. The land had been used primarily for dairy farming, its surplus hay sold locally and to the Boston market. The main dwelling was a two-and-a-half-story white clapboard building with a long ell, a sizable structure called "the Hive." The property also included a large barn with stalls for forty cattle and horses. By all accounts, the farm was a place of great natural beauty that combined proximity to the city with the repose of the countryside. Unfortunately, the land was not well suited to large-scale production of profitable crops.[39]

Ripley and a handful of others soon began to live and work at the rented farm. In addition to Sophia and George, the earliest inhabitants were William Allen, a young, experienced farmer; Frank Farley, a "mechanic" whom Ripley knew; and Elise Barker, a young "domestic" from Boston, a living, breathing reflection of Ripley's desire to form a society where social class no longer mattered. Soon

Warren Burton, Ripley's classmate at the Divinity School, arrived; and then the aspiring fiction writer Nathaniel Hawthorne, who, in addition to wanting a bucolic place at which to write, sought to profit from his investment. Affianced to Sophia Peabody (Elizabeth's younger sister), he bought two shares of stock in the venture at a cost of one thousand dollars, and hoped that interest on his investment would provide a nest egg.

The social experiment, though embryonic and not yet even formally announced, began to draw attention. Visitors from Boston either came for the day or, as space permitted, began to board outright, for which they paid a nominal fee. Such prominent Transcendentalists as Theodore Parker and Elizabeth Peabody were among the first guests; Emerson, Alcott, Fuller, and Henry Thoreau visited soon thereafter.

Preoccupied with overseeing Brook Farm itself, Ripley left it to his friend Peabody to spread word of the community, which she did in a number of publications in 1841 and 1842. She based her pieces primarily on the "Articles of Agreement" that Ripley had proposed and the first members had approved.[40] "In order more efficiently to promote the great purposes of human culture," Ripley had written in the document's preamble,

> To establish the external relations of life on a basis of wisdom and purity; to apply the principles of justice & love to our social organization in accordance with the laws of Divine Providence; to substitute a system of brotherly cooperation for one of selfish competition; to secure to our children & those who may be entrusted to our care the benefit of the highest physical, intellectual, & moral education which in the present state of human knowledge and resources at our command will permit; to institute an attractive, efficient & productive system of industry; to prevent the exercise of worldly anxiety by the competent supply of our necessary wants; to

diminish the desire of excessive accumulation, by making the acquisition of individual property subservient to upright & disinterested uses; to guarantee to each other forever the means of physical support & spiritual progress; & thus to impart a greater freedom, simplicity, truthfulness, refinement & moral dignity to our mode of life,—we the undersigned do unite in a voluntary Association.[41]

A renovation of the economy's moral basis would follow a renovation of its financial grounds. Once cooperation replaced competition, enlightened disinterest superseded thoughtless accumulation, and when one's physical well-being was ensured, spiritual harmony would follow.

Outlining the "Plan of the West Roxbury Community" in the January 1842 issue of the *Dial,* Peabody detailed the new community's organization, which resembled a combination of free-market capitalism and watered-down socialism. Brook Farm's "subscribers"—shareholders—were guaranteed 5 percent annual interest on their investment and shares set at five hundred dollars each—no small amount but necessary to enable the down payment on the land, which Ripley wished to purchase. All members paid for room, board, fuel, lighting, and washing through directly proportionate labor, "one year's board for one year's labor; one-half year's board for one-half year's labor, and if no labor is done the whole board shall be charged," four dollars per week. Men and women were compensated at the same rate, and members chose what work most appealed. No particular job, no matter how menial, was coerced, because all labor was "sacred, when done for a common interest." No one worked more than a ten-hour day, an enlightened idea for the time, or a six-day week.[42] Peabody remarked on their sincerity in these matters. The first farmers, she wrote, "cleaned the stable[,] arranged the house[,] ploughed & planted—going through the harvest & most disagreeable work they will ever have to do."[43]

In addition to room and board, members were guaranteed "medical attendance, nursing, education in all departments, [and] amusements," and everyone between the ages of seven and ten, and anyone who was sick, had free board, unless they were shareholders whose 5 percent interest could support them. Students of nonmembers who attended the farm's school paid four and, later, five dollars a week for board and tuition, three-and-a-half dollars per week for those under three.[44]

Ripley, though, was most concerned with the individual's intellectual and psychological development. Brook Farm, Peabody explained, "aims to be rich, not in the metallic representative of wealth, but in the wealth itself, which money should represent," that is, "LEISURE TO LIVE IN ALL THE FACULTIES OF THE SOUL." Thus, in addition to supplying members with room and board, Brook Farm provided them with "the elegances desirable for bodily and spiritual health—books, apparatus, collections for science, works of art, means of beautiful amusement"—for these should not be luxuries but common to all. Because such things alone "refine the passion for individual accumulation," where all shared in the cultural resources the "sordid passion" of selfishness soon would begin to disappear.

What would pay for all this? Brook Farm could provide such amenities because—as its organization as a joint-stock company already indicated—it would profitably "traffic with the world at large" by marketing its surplus agricultural goods, including milk from the herd of cows. This seemed reasonable, for such commerce increased as farms in towns surrounding Boston became essential to the metropolitan area's food supply.[45] Ripley also would take in nonresident students at Brook Farm's school, which soon enough proved the most profitable part of the venture.

In his fictional account of life at the community, however, Brook Farm member Hawthorne saw the inherent incongruity in having to compete against other farmers for market share. "It struck me as rather odd," says Miles Coverdale, the narrator of *The Blithedale Romance*, "that one of the first questions raised, after our separation from the greedy, struggling, self-seeking world, should relate to the possibility of getting the advantage over the outside barbarians in their own field of labor."[46] For all its high-minded idealism, from economic necessity Ripley enmeshed Brook Farm in the system it sought to replace. He sought to have Brook Farm influence the world, and yet from the outset, the world was having its say about the farm's very organization, if not its goals.

By the fall of 1841 ten subscribers had pledged to purchase twenty-four shares of stock in the Brook Farm Institute of Agriculture and Education. Even though all the money was not in hand, Ripley felt confident and precipitately contracted to purchase the Ellis farm as well as an additional parcel, including another house, barn, and outbuildings, for $10,500. He also began new construction, and by March the group had completed another domicile, the Eyrey [*sic*]. Several hundred yards behind the Hive, it housed Ripley's library, a music room, and living quarters on the first and second floors. Hawthorne's room was there, aside Ripley's impressive collection of books in French and German as well as English.

Over its first two years Brook Farm's population grew from about twenty to seventy; but, disappointingly, many of these were boarders or students who, while providing important income, never became members. Thus, while Ripley and other of the community's prime movers were compelled to construct new buildings to house these individuals, the population as a whole did not necessarily contribute to the agricultural labor or to the larger purpose of shared community. Many were there on quests for self-development. Others were just curious and wished to experience Brook Farm's novelty.

To accommodate such interest, Brook Farm began to charge overnight guests thirty-seven cents each, which included dinner, supper, and a night's lodging; "day-trippers" were welcomed as

well, gratis. A conservative estimate suggests a remarkable eleven
hundred visitors a year—"of all religions; bond and free; transcendental and occidental; antislavery and proslavery; come-outers;
communists, fruitists [those who subsisted on fruit alone] and
flutists; dreamers and schemers of all sorts"—who brought in
income but did not contribute a day's labor.[47]

Those who participated in Brook Farm's educational and cultural programs in its first two years, whether as members or students, virtually unanimously praised Ripley's ideals and the ways
in which he sought to realize them. Membership now included
George P. Bradford, another of Ripley's Divinity School classmates;
Providence, Rhode Island, native Charles King Newcomb, swaying
in Emerson's orbit; and Ora Gannett, the teenage niece of Unitarian clergyman Ezra Stiles Gannett. Soon enough, Dwight left
his pulpit in Northampton and took up residence. Other important additions in this period included Charles Anderson Dana, Sophia's distant cousin who had dropped out of Harvard after two
years for health reasons; experienced farmer Minot Pratt and his
family, who purchased three shares of stock and on whom Ripley
soon began to depend for all sorts of practical matters; and En-
glishwoman Georgiana Bruce, who worked in the nursery with the
youngest children.

These individuals shared the domestic, agricultural, and educational labors, which varied according to one's wishes. One student
at the school later recalled (accurately) that in this early grouping,
there was a preponderance of Unitarians, a sameness in outlook that
could be summed up as a commitment to the "philosophy of the
Here and Now": "Here and now; on the spot, with the goods, at
the moment. Not yesterday; not tomorrow, but to-day, this hour,
this instant is the appointed time to live for all you are worth. Put
your heart in your work right Here. Give your mind, your skill,
your energy to whatever you have just Now. . . . Hope for the future
is all right, but let not dreams of the good time coming becloud

clear comprehension of the realities at hand. Here and Now."[48] Such an ethic, Ripley soon discovered, could create its own problems. Entertainment and enlightenment were available to all and comprised an important component of daily activity. There were frequent picnics, concerts, dances, *tableaux vivants,* and endless delight in punning and wordplay. Lectures and discussions on topics of compelling interest, too, were frequent, not only by fellow-traveling Transcendentalists like Emerson, Fuller, and Parker, but also by abolitionists and reformers like Maria Weston Chapman, Lydia Maria Child, and others. Dwight frequently discussed the latest European music, particularly Beethoven, who was becoming all the rage in the Boston area. Such activities were not mere diversions but went hand in hand with Ripley's effort to make Brook Farm an environment where the whole being—physical, mental, and spiritual—was cultivated.[49]

But while social and cultural life, organized and informal, blossomed in myriad ways at Brook Farm, financially it struggled. By the end of 1842, Ripley and other investors had to rethink its economic basis. Eager to welcome those who seemed genuinely interested in the community, Ripley had continued to construct new buildings, for which the institute took out mortgages totaling over six thousand dollars. Debt management and expenses soon began to outpace revenues. Some original members, including Burton and Hawthorne, left, the latter also seeking to recoup his investment as well as the yearly interest still owed him. Ripley's experiment was at a critical juncture.

Brook Farm in Crisis

As Ripley brainstormed about how to raise the funds to keep Brook Farm solvent, the most pressing issue was precisely that which split the Transcendentalist movement as a whole: how to balance individual and communal interests so that the primacy of conscience was preserved, even as the communal enterprise was forwarded. This conflict had bubbled beneath the surface from the beginning but came to a head as Ripley began to realize that the community needed a significant infusion of capital.

Again, Hawthorne identified the root of the problem. His character Miles Coverdale noted the difficulty with persons of such "marked individuality—crooked sticks, as some . . . might be called"—is that they are "not exactly the easiest to bind up into a faggot." Too many who comprised the unusual population at Brook Farm were fertilized by Transcendentalism and predisposed to ride their hobbyhorses rather than clean the cattle stalls. The experiment, Hawthorne continued, could not "reasonably be expected to hold together long."[50] He himself was one of these "crooked sticks" and in the fall of 1841 decided to leave. Before he told Ripley of his intention, he dropped from the labor rolls and began to pay his way as a boarder, so that he would have more leisure and inclination to write. Brook Farm resident Georgiana Bruce put it best. "No one could have been more out of place than he [Hawthorne] in a mixed company," she recalled years later, for he was "morbidly shy and reserved, needing to be shielded from his fellows." "He was therefore," she concluded, "not amenable to the democratic influences at the community."[51] Relations between Ripley and Hawthorne subsequently deteriorated, particularly after the latter had to sue him for the return of his initial investment.

Horace Greeley, editor of the *New-York Tribune*, strong advocate of such experiments, and a visitor to Brook Farm, viewed its problems similarly to Hawthorne. In addition to drawing many individuals whose impulses were noble and purely philanthropic, he wrote, a community like Brook Farm too often could easily serve as a magnet for "the conceited, the crotchety, the selfish, the headstrong, the pugnacious, the unappreciated, the played-out, the idle, and the good-for-nothing generally."[52] Greeley saw that Ripley's experiment had become turned on its head. Rather than elevating selfish individuals to a new communal moral clarity, the conceited might swamp such fine hopes and drag down the whole effort. Ripley's good friend Theodore Parker made a similar observation more pithily. Asked how Ripley was getting along with his "Community," he replied humorously, "Oh, Mr. Ripley reminds me, in that connection, of a new and splendid locomotive dragging along a train of mud-carts."[53]

Admittedly, the necessity to recruit new members meant that Ripley did not always have the luxury to sort out whether someone might be ill suited for the work. The result was predictable. He had brought in too many such "crooked sticks" and was having difficulty binding them into the neat bundle he had imagined. The Englishman Charles Lane, who was to join Bronson Alcott in his version of utopia, was acerbic. A residence at Brook Farm, he observed, "does not involve a community of money, of opinions, or of sympathy," for the motives that brought individuals there were "as various as their members." He found their level of commitment pitifully low, for at its height Brook Farm comprised "eighty or ninety persons playing away their youth and daytime in a miserable, joyous, frivolous manner," leaving only "four or five who could be selected as really and truly progressive beings." The presence of so many persons "who congregate merely for the attainment of some individual end" weighed "heavily and unfairly" upon those whose hearts really were "expanded to universal results."[54]

Another early member, George William Curtis, who went on to a distinguished career as a writer and editor of *Harper's Magazine,* echoed such criticism. To Dwight, who had left the ministry to join the experiment in West Roxbury and soon became the country's most respected music critic, he observed that, "in the midst of busy trades and bustling commerce," Brook Farm was "a congregation of calm scholars and poets, cherishing the ideal and the true in each other's hearts" but never enough focused on the hard work at hand. "It needed," Curtis continued, "a stricter system to insure success."[55] John Thomas Codman, an early member of Brook Farm and author of one of the most detailed accounts of life there, agreed. "There were philosophers enough in it," he explained. And there were "plenty of sweet, charming characters and amateur workmen in it, but the hard-fisted toilers and brave financiers were absent."[56]

Curtis also alluded to a practical problem. Ripley mistakenly believed that Brook Farm could succeed solely as an institute of "Agriculture and Education." But given the number of members, boarders, and visitors to be fed, few farm or dairy products remained for outside sale, as Ripley originally had hoped. He would have done better to find a different and firmer financial footing for the community, but his population lacked the requisite skills and the property the infrastructure to turn the project in other directions.

The problems Ripley's critics identified, however, had a deeper source. Ripley's goal, after all, was not only an economically sound enterprise (though that was crucial to its success) or a tight-knit community of idealists with shared passions. The moral and spiritual benefits that would arise from life at Brook Farm, he posited, would arise precisely because economic considerations remained secondary to self-culture. At the farm, domestics, farmers, carpenters, and mechanics would learn to appreciate European classical music, take part in charades and plays, and, most remarkably, reside alongside philosophers.

How different it was at another contemporary utopian community. Ripley's one-time associate David Mack initially had signed Brook Farm's Articles of Agreement, but he never actually lived there. Rather, he helped start the Northampton Association of Education and Industry in the western part of the state.[57] This community, which opened its doors a year after Brook Farm, was dedicated to the support of William Lloyd Garrison's "nonresistance" arm of the abolitionist movement. Only those committed to an ideal of racial equality and willing to resist any coercive authority, including a federal government that tolerated slavery, were admitted.

Mack thus built into the Northampton community a single-mindedness that Brook Farm lacked, and this in turn led to a different process of self-selection in its membership. He and the other organizers of Northampton also established it on a different, sounder economic basis than Ripley had done in West Roxbury: they purchased an extant silk manufactory and defined labor around it. They raised mulberry trees to feed silkworms, cultivated the insects, processed their silk, and turned it into thread in a large, complex factory. In contrast, economically, Brook Farm always was a catchall enterprise, with Ripley at its intellectual center but with its "industries" dependent on what skills individual members brought: variously, farming, cultivating greenhouse flowers for market, and making shoes and window sashes by hand.

Further, whereas Northampton's members coalesced around a cause and against an institution, Brook Farm members paraded their much-lampooned individualism and idiosyncrasies. Interest in vegetarianism, women's rights, educational reform, hydropathy, religious freedom, and, inevitably, abolition, were predictable. In his late teens when he joined the enterprise, Codman admitted that he had more profitably spent his time walking out in nature than in listening to "the arguers and the disputants who talked anti-this and anti-that, the new sciences of medicine—the water-cure and homeopathy; who disputed doctrines of community of property, western lands, politics, [and] approaching war with Mexico."[58]

Against a backdrop of economic dislocation in the wake of the 1837 panic, divisive national politics, and a threatening war in the Southwest with Mexico that promised to roil the economy and secessionist fears, what to make of the Brook Farm member who purported to have given up sleep; or another, the use of all money; or he who eschewed shaving his beard; or another, the wearing of clothing? Such individuals were the butt of good-natured humor within Brook Farm and outright derision outside it, but also could not help but distract attention—again, internally and externally—from Ripley's lofty goal of a harmonious community based in self-culture.

Caught in a vise that his creditors tightened, Ripley tried to stabilize his community by seeking new and different blood. Tellingly, he sought it after adopting explicitly European socialist ideas, specifically those of Charles Fourier, of which Ripley had known earlier but had passed over. As early as 1840, for example, Unitarian clergyman Samuel Osgood reported that he had been reading "[Albert] Brisbane's book on the reorganization of Society," but had heard that the "new light socialists [at Brook Farm] eschewed [his] dictum."[59]

In August 1843, having heard much about the "Associationist" movement spawned by this French social theorist's growing number of American proselytizers, Ripley attended a meeting in Albany, New York. Here he heard advocates tout the planned North American Phalanx in Red Bank, New Jersey. In Albany Ripley also crossed paths with Albert Brisbane, Fourier's premier American advocate, whose book on the subject Osgood knew; and Greeley, who strongly supported the French thinker's ideas. Amidst the manifold problems overwhelming Ripley's new Eden, the growing influence of these and other socialists over Ripley and others who managed Brook Farm's finances soon transformed the idealistic Transcendentalist experiment into something very different.

Hard Truths

Late in his life, the Reverend William Henry Channing, the Unitarian leader William Ellery Channing's nephew, and Ripley's close friend and at one time a strong supporter of the West Roxbury community, offered a searching assessment of Brook Farm's failure. He mentioned Ripley's poor planning and lack of common sense. "The attempt was ill conceived, worse executed," he wrote to a friend. "The land was only moderate," he continued. "The water-power [was] wanting, markets not accessible, the capital insufficient, the debt oppressive, the houses ill-built, badly placed, insufficient, water scantily supplied, industry unorganized, business entangled, etc. etc."

More important, Channing, who was a committed convert to Fourierism, questioned the members' overall motives and commitment. Members of Brook Farm were unwilling to dismount their hobbyhorses—their various, often self-indulgent, attempts at self-culture—for the good of the whole. The "great evil," he continued, "the radical, practical danger," was "a willingness to do work [only] half through, to rest in poor results, to be content amidst comparatively squalid conditions, to form habits of indolence." "There was too much haste," Channing wrote, "too much spasm." And perhaps most troubling, Brook Farm's futile attempt at community seemed "at once an impossibility and absurdity" because "its ownership of land, its mode of acquiring and holding property,—its relation of barter on all sides,—and its necessarily exclusive position [that is, its separation from the world]" violated the very principles so necessary to true reform of the present economic order and its attendant class stratification.[60]

Ironically, what ruled at Brook Farm was precisely the kind of self-culture that Ripley's cousin Emerson had counseled as the bedrock of meaningful reform. Emerson sought it in his closet; Ripley hoped to provide it within his community. The grander ambition of Ripley's carried with it the possibility of a more public failure: what if the presumed harmony of enlightened self-interest failed to materialize? What if it were found that self, not social harmony, still ruled at Brook Farm? Emerson himself noted this. "At Brook Farm is this peculiarity," he wrote, "that there is no head." There is "no authority, but each master and mistress of their own actions,—happy, hapless, *sansculottes* [*sic*]." "Mr. and Mrs. Ripley," he added, "are the only ones who have identified themselves

with the Community. They have married it, and they are it." The
others were but "experimenters" who would remain with it only
if it thrived.[61] As a result, Brook Farm was "a perpetual picnic, a
French Revolution in small, an Age of Reason in a pattypan."[62]

Ironically, in a final attempt to save what he believed to be a bold
experiment in social renovation, Ripley adopted Fourier's doctrine
of "Association" that, while itself promising a brave, and better, new
world, would only further reinforce the imperial selfhood that
marked so many of Ripley's fellow Americans. One thing was clear,
however. Fourier had no use for Emerson's insistence that moral
and spiritual regeneration was best achieved in isolation, and was
not instead enabled by where, among whom, and in what way an
individual lived. In Brook Farm's first years Ripley went tentatively
down this path, for he thought that such spiritual enlightenment
and harmony might indeed be achieved communally, even as one
respected the rights of each individual. He learned, however, that
he would have to restructure Brook Farm more radically if he was
to realize his dream of a new kind of community that might then
serve as example and catalyst for the world to achieve the same.

But we should not let doubting voices like Emerson's have the
last word, for at Ripley's Brook Farm there was a sincerity and singular dedication to a host of worthwhile ideals, among them, the
dignity of labor, the need for intellectual and spiritual growth, and
the hope for a classless, harmonious society. In his way, Ripley was
trying to realize the nation's democratic promise; but, like his friend
Henry James Sr., he believed that this did not so much have to do
with "national aggrandizement" as self-realization. As James put it,
"Our glory is to be an inward rather than an outward one."[63]

It is too easy to ridicule or condemn Ripley's efforts while forgetting their nobility. There was some reason why a thousand visitors a year came to view its progress, and many of the age's chief
intellectuals sought to speak to its members. Or why someone like
Nathaniel Hawthorne thought that, in addition to being a good

investment, it offered him the opportunity to become part of something potentially world changing. Far from an outlier, Ripley and Brook Farm stood squarely in a vanguard of hopeful effort and expectation that its singular difficulties scarcely dented. As Hawthorne's character Miles Coverdale puts it, "whatever else I might repent of, therefore, let it be reckoned neither among my sins nor follies that I once had faith and force enough to form generous hopes of the world's destiny . . . and to do what in me lay for their accomplishment."[64]

George P. Bradford, one of Ripley's associates, agreed. Late in his life Ripley was asked to contribute a chapter, which he titled "Philosophic Thought in Boston," to Justin Winsor's *Memorial History of Boston*. His health failing, he completed only a few pages of it, and his classmate Bradford worthily finished the assignment. Assessing the Brook Farm years, Bradford cautioned the reader not to dismiss the episode too readily. Yes, he admitted, "it was natural enough that an institution so novel in its arrangements and its claims, so opposed to conservative notions and feelings, should encounter prejudice, misapprehension, and ridicule." And yes, "embracing in its members such heterogeneous materials, and naturally attracting persons of fantastic notions, with various peculiarities and singularities of character," it was to be expected that some of them "would have vagaries, and some affect singular ways." Because of these things, Bradford admitted, "the public very legitimately had its laugh."

But, Bradford continued, it is hardly fair "to fix on these oddities and absurdities as the salient and chief characteristics of the enterprise in which many sensible, thoughtful, worthy, and benevolent persons set themselves seriously to work to carry out an experiment" that "they fondly and generously . . . hoped would lead to important benefit for mankind." To overlook "their humane and generous aims and objects," Bradford urged, to ignore what Ripley and his cohort accomplished, and to "fix attention instead on the mistakes and ludicrous aspects" of the enterprise, is simply "not quite just."[65] Indeed, to mock Ripley's and his followers' hopes is to mock a majority of his contemporaries who held similar faith and expectations. For all its foibles, Brook Farm was testament to Ripley's belief that the fulfillment of the nation's democratic promise was not an ever-receding pipe dream but instead within close reach, if only people realized that living in the spirit trumped a good rate of interest on their investment. And he was hardly alone, then or since, in holding that belief.

2

Horace Greeley and the
French Connection

In the antebellum period, the most revolutionary solutions to America's ills were imported from Europe, and one crucial vector for their introduction was the tireless, charismatic Albert Brisbane. A sense of his peripatetic path and the tightly interlocking circles of American reform are caught in George Ripley's friend James Freeman Clarke's mother encountering Brisbane far out in the Ohio Valley in 1839 and bringing his news back to New England for the Transcendentalists to ponder. With the 1840 publication of *Social Destiny of Man; or, Association and Reorganization of Industry*, this tall, slender young man (recalled by one less-than-sympathetic wit as looking as "if he were attempting to think out some problem a little too hard for him") would be famous, at least among American reformers.[1]

Comprising translations of and commentary on the French social theorist Charles Fourier's elaborate scheme for universal reform, *Social Destiny of Man* grabbed the attention of an ambitious young New York newspaper editor, Horace Greeley. The admiration was mutual: Greeley's editorials on the subject of labor had caught Brisbane's eye as well. And Greeley soon became an enthusiastic convert to the cause of "Association," as Brisbane, Parke Godwin, and other Fourier acolytes termed the system, touting the book and its solutions in his popular and influential newspaper, the *New-York Tribune*. For over a year in 1842 and 1843 he leased Brisbane space on the paper's front page to promote the Frenchman's views, for he believed that they provided a way to address the unconscionable exploitation of the American working class that unbridled capitalism had unleashed. Brisbane later testified that Greeley did for the "Fourierists" what they could never have done themselves: "He has created the cause on this continent."[2]

Because of Greeley's contagious enthusiasm, fellow reformer Thomas Wentworth Higginson quipped, by the 1840s the *Tribune* had become nothing less than "the working centre of much of the practical radicalism of the country."[3] A popular lecturer and writer in his own right, Greeley filled his newspaper's pages with assessments of all manner of reforms in which he was interested—temperance, vegetarianism, hydropathy, phrenology, women's rights, prison reform, to name but a few—that proliferated in the years after the Panic of 1837, and, because of the popularity of the *Tribune*, he was able to disseminate his views on these issues throughout the nation. Greeley's embrace of Brisbane and Fourierism generally nevertheless remained firmly constrained by his commitment to the nation's reigning middle-class liberal ethos, the bedrock of the Whig Party. In the hands of Greeley and Fourier's other American disciples—including Brisbane and the prominent Democratic Party member Godwin—the Frenchman's promise of "Association" defined the true equality of mankind as a kind of middle-class socialism.

Thus, it is unsurprising that when George Ripley cast about for a way to stabilize and redirect his novel experiment in social theory at Brook Farm, proponents of Association (including his new friends Greeley and Brisbane) urged him to adopt Fourier's system. Long after Brook Farm was a memory and hope for social reform had faded with the escalation of the sectional crisis, this middle-class ideal dressed as a universal brother- and sisterhood continued to energize Greeley's activism as well as cement his close relationship to Ripley.[4]

Youth and Apprenticeship

For someone who became one of the nation's best-known intellectuals—indeed, one of its most widely recognized public figures—Greeley came from humble origins. He was born 3 February 1811, on the outskirts of Amherst, New Hampshire, near Bedford in the southern part of the state. He was the third of Zaccheus and Mary Woodburn Greeley's seven children, two of whom died before Greeley's birth. He was named after one of the deceased. Greeley's own survival had been in question: it was said he did not draw a breath for the first twenty minutes of his life.[5]

The Greeleys had moved to Amherst two years earlier, and, on what had proved poor land, Zaccheus was struggling to provide for his family. Mary spun wool and flax for the budding textile factories of the region in whatever spare time she could find. Young Horace later described himself as having been "a feeble, sickly child, often under medical treatment."[6] This did not exempt him from necessary work for the family's welfare, however. Greeley remembered the kinds of hard work he was expected to contribute: plowing all day long, staying up night after night to burn wood into charcoal in deep pits covered with sod, picking stones that the frost had heaved into fields, harvesting and drying hops.[7]

Probably because she had lost another son by Horace's name—so he later speculated—Mary Greeley doted on him. He was "her companion and confidant" as soon as he could talk and learned to read "at her knee." By the age of four he could make his way through virtually any book, the Bible included. She taught him well, and he proved an autodidact: by Greeley's account, each year he attended school only for relatively brief periods before seasonal farm work took him away. Despite the erratic nature of his education, through his independent reading he eventually commanded the sweep of Western history and culture as well as a rich colloquial language— his mother filled him with an "abundant store of ballads, stories, anecdotes, and traditions"—that later served him well on the lecture platform.[8]

In 1817 Zaccheus moved the family to a larger farm closer to Bedford. But soon enough he was caught in the economic downturn called the Panic of 1819. In that year, the Second Bank of the United States, to curb excessive purchase of public lands with paper currency issued by state banks, called on these institutions to repay their loans in specie. To meet their obligations, the state banks began to foreclose on heavily mortgaged businesses and farms. Unfortunately, the Greeley family, over one thousand dollars in debt, was one of these. One morning the sheriff and other town officials arrived with a few of the family's major creditors and "proceeded to levy on farm, stock, implements, household stuff, nearly all of our worldly possessions but the clothes" on their backs. The family essentially was reduced to tenant farming, a humiliating experience that Greeley never forgot.

Matters grew worse. Zaccheus soon had to move out of state to avoid imprisonment, the full amount of his liability not satisfied. After some wandering, he retrieved his family and loaded them on a borrowed two-horse sleigh. They resettled in West Haven, Vermont, near Lake Champlain, where Zaccheus chopped wood for the landlord from whom he rented a small outbuilding.[9] Now, Greeley recalled, the family "made the acquaintance of genuine poverty, not beggary, nor dependence, but the manly American sort," and the ten-year-old Horace was put to heavy, monotonous work.[10]

Given his interest in books and reading, in his early teens Greeley decided to leave the family to find work as a printer.[11] When he was fifteen he was apprenticed to the publishers of the *Northern Spectator*, a weekly newspaper in Poultney, Vermont. He learned to set and redistribute type, ink the forms, and pull the platen of the small press on which the printer produced the local paper. His skill in reading quickly earned him a reputation as an invaluable proofreader.

He joined the local debating society and Poultney's social lending library, and as well began to develop what became a life-long, consuming interest in politics. The majority of his neighbors were independent Vermont farmers who sought strong tariffs to protect their grain production and the wool industry—many raised sheep for the proliferating New England factories. Like these farmers, Greeley aligned himself with National Republicans who despised Democratic president Andrew Jackson and his aggressive free-trade policy. Then, in 1826 after a furor broke over the purported abduction and murder of disgruntled ex-Freemason William Morgan, who had threatened to publish the secret order's ritual, Greeley joined and remained a longtime supporter of the Anti-Masonic Party. In particular, he was sympathetic with its avowed purpose of eliminating the social privilege that accompanied membership in such societies.

Greeley also recalled his first encounter with slavery. In Poultney he witnessed an unsuccessful attempt to recapture a runaway. Although New York had abolished the institution several years earlier, those born slaves in the state had to remain such until they were twenty-eight years old, when they were manumitted. A young slave, Greeley recollected sarcastically, "uninstructed in the sacredness of constitutional guaranties [and] the rights of property," had the temerity to take his life into his own hands and move across the border to Vermont where all slavery was abolished. His master came calling, but met with an unanticipated reception. Greeley had never seen "so large a muster of men and boys" arise so suddenly. "Nobody suggested that envy or hate of 'the South' or of New York," had impelled the runaway's rescue, but Vermont's citizens sent the master away "disconsolate and niggerless." They "hated injustice and oppression" he wrote, and had "acted as if they couldn't help it."[12]

When the *Northern Spectator* closed its doors in 1830, Greeley rejoined his parents in southwestern New York. In nearby Erie, Pennsylvania, he again found work as a printer, on the *Erie Gazette*, whose editor shared Greeley's anti-Masonic views. In part because of his father's too frequent drunkenness, Greeley also began to support the temperance movement, eschewing all alcohol. He also began to worship with Universalists who believed in Christ's salvation for all men and in man's free will. The need to work for moral reform, to better one's fellow men's existence, continued to flow naturally from this faith.[13]

New York City

In the summer of 1831 Greeley made the momentous decision to move to New York City, the center of the nation's economy and as well as of its burgeoning print culture. In a passage in his memoirs reminiscent of Benjamin Franklin's in his popular *Autobiography* (about entering Philadelphia as an impoverished young man eager to establish himself as a printer), Greeley similarly described himself coming to the new metropolis: a "tall, slender, pale, and thin" twenty-year-old, with ten dollars in his pocket, "summer clothing worth perhaps as much more," nearly all of it in a sack over his shoulder. He knew no one within "two-hundred miles" and only had the skills (as well as the characteristic wide-eyed demeanor) of a greenhorn who had learned the printer's trade in a small office.[14] Fortunately, some friendly Irish immigrants whom he met at a boardinghouse (as much "grog-shop" as hostelry, Greeley noted) steered him to the printing shop of John T. West, in the same building as the publishing house of McElrath and Bangs at 85 Chatham Street. West hired him, and his metropolitan career was launched. Later, McElrath would become his business partner.

West had not taken him on permanently, but specifically to work two particular "jobs," setting a polyglot New Testament in minuscule type and a commentary on the book of Genesis by orthodox theologian (and later Swedenborgian) George Bush, from his (evidently abysmal) handwriting. After accomplishing these tasks in December, in the midst of a great cold snap, Greeley found himself out of work. The price of coal soared to sixteen dollars a ton; that of necessities rose accordingly. Mechanics and laborers tried to live off their earnings from the previous summer and fall, and then, if lucky, from credit offered by grocers and landlords. Fortunately, by the first of the year Greeley again found work, on William T. Porter's "sporting" journal, *The Spirit of the Times.*[15]

Like thousands of other young, unmarried men who moved to the city to work as apprentice tradesmen, clerks, and other functionaries, Greeley lived in a boardinghouse, in his case, in one where the clientele shared a commitment to temperance, vegetarian diet, and a decided moral purity.[16] Greeley's domicile was particularly strict, devoted to the principles of well-known health reformer Sylvester Graham. In addition to condemning the use of all alcohol and other stimulants such as tea, coffee, tobacco, and opium, Graham also rejected all spices and condiments, and of course meat and fish, though he later admitted indulging in black tea and coffee. From such ideas, further health reform flowed naturally. When Greeley arrived in New York, he was already interested in the growing fad of "physical culture." Always concerned with his health because of his frequent childhood illnesses, he tried to take frequent long walks and to lift weights, which one could do in one of the early "health" clubs that proliferated in the city.[17] Such healthy habits also helped fuel his astonishing work ethic.

As Greeley began his editorial career, even in this teeming city he cut quite a figure. Over six feet tall, thin and wan, with long, light, wispy hair and beard and wire-rimmed glasses, he looked the part of a preoccupied scholar. He never cared much for his appearance, and his dress was usually disheveled——pantaloons that seemed too large, a trademark white linen coat that he seemed to have had forever, hastily tied cravat, and tall boots of the sort that a farmer's son would wear. But his intelligence and enthusiasm, and his company, made him attractive. Mary Cheney, a schoolteacher whom he had met at the boardinghouse and who shared his interests in vegetarianism and other health reforms, was one of his admirers. They began courting in 1834 and married two years later.[18]

Greeley and the Whig Party

Through the 1830s Greeley entered into a series of publishing ventures, either as editor or, securing financial backers, owner. None brought him financial success, but they did circulate his name in the industry. In 1834 he caught a break when he aligned himself with the national Whig Party, which emerged to challenge the Jacksonian Democrats. The Whigs comprised a union of the old National Republican Party descended from Thomas Jefferson, the Anti-Masonic Party, and Southerners who despised Jackson's refusal to lower tariffs (which had resulted in the Nullification Crisis of 1832 when the state of South Carolina refused to recognize the legislated tariff). Led by Henry Clay, the new party quickly gained traction, particularly among small businessmen who wanted protective legislation and speculators who favored government-sponsored internal improvements to strengthen the nation's economy. In these years, Whigs sought a stable medium of exchange, well-regulated markets, and a national government that looked out for their interests, including their drive for profit. Given Greeley's background, this new national party provided a comfortable home.

In 1834, when he was still only twenty-five, Greeley was tapped to print the Whig's campaign newspaper, *The Constitution*. At the same time, he began to edit the *New Yorker*, a sixteen-page weekly magazine that included a potpourri of articles—on literary, political, and reform topics—and that within a few years reached a circulation of over nine thousand. Greeley's new ventures reflected his already long-standing interests: temperance, the plight of the workingman, Henry Clay's so-called American System of internal improvements, and free public education, among others. To these, Greeley added antislavery, a cause that he presented gingerly, for he feared what outright abolition would do to the country's economy as well as how it might divide the new party.

As Greeley sought to establish himself in the city in these first years, more than anything else he feared getting mired in debt. "I would rather be a convict in a State prison," Greeley later wrote, or "a slave in a rice swamp, than to pass through life under the harrow of debt." "Hunger, cold rags, hard work, contempt, suspicion, unjust reproach" all were disagreeable, he continued. Recalling his difficult childhood, brought on by his parent's frequent insolvency, he knew that debt was "infinitely worse" than any of these.[19]

The Panic of 1837 and its aftermath greatly challenged Greeley's values, as well as his livelihood. He later carefully dissected the panic's causes, consequent to President Jackson's disastrous issuance of the "Specie Circular" that prescribed that public lands henceforth could only be bought with specie. Greeley noted that there had been a poor harvest in 1836, necessitating the importation of foreign grain and compounding the country's already large debt to Europe for other goods. Banks thus were drained of hard currency in two directions: from those who had to pay creditors across the Atlantic and others who sought to purchase new lands in the West and South. Access to specie tightened, and, after the failure of a major New Orleans brokerage, finally, on 10 May 1837, New York banks suspended payments in specie, and financial panic began in earnest, soon spreading throughout the nation.

Many manufacturers closed their factories and peremptorily dismissed their mill hands. Those who still could find work saw wages plummet, sometimes in half. Prices of staple goods and housing increased, often to prohibitive levels, creating a population of literally hundreds of thousands of homeless in the nation's cities. Disease and abject poverty abounded. Trade was stagnant. Bankruptcies were everywhere, with property sacrificed at auction at a fraction of its cost. The American dream of ever-increasing prosperity had gone up in smoke. "Thousands," Greeley remembered, "who had fondly dreamed themselves millionaires, or on the point of becoming such, awoke to find that they were bankrupt."[20]

The ways in which the social as well as economic crisis affected the nation's largest city provided Greeley with plenty of journalistic fodder, and he managed to keep his paper afloat. A Universalist who believed that everyone is equal under the Fatherhood of God, and that all humanity ultimately would be redeemed, Greeley's commitment to reform only strengthened and broadened through the late 1830s.

In these dire circumstances he famously first urged young men to "Go West!" Although it is unclear whether he ever used precisely these words at the end of the decade, he did begin to counsel those whom the economic upheaval had displaced to consider the trans-Mississippi lands as a place of not just refuge but also of moral and spiritual renovation.[21] This admonishment to migrate, however, was well in keeping with the reform solutions he embraced closer to the eastern seaboard. Committed as he was to social change through extant political channels, he ceaselessly cast about for ways to improve the workingman's lot without threatening individual property rights or otherwise challenging, or exacerbating, already-high tensions among classes.

Although the *New Yorker* never became lucrative, its eclectic mix of politics, literature, and social commentary brought Greeley much attention. In 1838, well aware of its success in its particular niche, prominent Whig politician Thurlow Weed asked him to edit the *Jeffersonian*, the party's campaign newspaper, for the upcoming New

York gubernatorial race. Greeley consented and began to split his time between New York City and Albany, gathering news from the state capital even as he continued to edit the *New Yorker.* Weed's candidate, William Henry Seward, won handily. When, two years later, the Whigs again knocked at Greeley's door, asking him to work for the election of their presidential candidate, William Henry Harrison, he consented. He was hooked on national politics.

Greeley subsequently played a major role in what has been termed the first modern political campaign, helping to forge a national coalition that elected the putative dark horse, Harrison, over the Democratic incumbent, Martin Van Buren, in a landslide. Greeley contributed to this victory through his own brainchild, a campaign newspaper called the *Log Cabin,* whose title played on Harrison's humble origins. He filled it with witty cartoons, catchy songs, and political slogans, as well as Greeley's pithy, colloquial pro-Harrison editorials that appealed to Greeley's beloved working-class and artisan readership, and made the paper an overnight sensation. Soon he was so swept up in the election that he took to the campaign trail throughout New York, sometimes even firing up crowds by leading them in catchy lyrics that he had penned.

After Harrison's victory, Greeley not only refused all political spoils, he surprised everyone by relinquishing the *New Yorker* and starting a daily paper, the *New-York Tribune,* to compete with Scottish immigrant James Gordon Bennett's popular *New York Herald* and other dailies. By Greeley's own account, he sought to establish a journal "removed alike from servile partisanship on the one hand and from gagged, mincing neutrality on the other." He sought "a happy medium," a position from which a journalist might "heartily advocate the principles and commend the measures of that party to which his convictions allied him, yet frankly dissent from its course" and "even denounce its candidates" when deemed necessary."[22]

Equally important, the newspaper offered Greeley a widely noticed forum that allowed him to promulgate his various interests
in literature, social reform, and politic activism. Particularly in a
redacted weekly edition, for decades the "*Trib*" (as it became known
affectionately) introduced and promoted his omnivorous interests
to a readership that stretched from rural Maine and Vermont
across the Mississippi to the Great Plains, thence over the Rocky
Mountains, and, eventually, to the West Coast. Within a few years
the newspaper became a monument to Greeley's dream that,
through the printed word, the United States would achieve its
destiny as the world's first true democracy. By the Civil War its
circulation reached a remarkable two hundred thousand.

Greeley and European Socialism

In large measure, Greeley's political positions stemmed from his
long engagement—at least since his teenage years when he had witnessed his family's struggle with indebtedness—with the relation
of labor to capital. Specifically, he was distressed that workingmen
and women seemed ever at the mercy of those who profited from
their work without performing any comparable labor themselves.
In particular, he hated the fact that willing and able workers often
found themselves without gainful employment. Following the
Panic of 1837, when he saw "pervading destitution and suffering"
everywhere he looked, brought on by the "paralysis of business"
and a "consequent dearth of employment," Greeley's concern only
deepened.[23]

He knew of such things firsthand because he lived in the notorious Sixth Ward of the city. So bad were conditions in this
neighborhood that at a public meeting in December 1837, residents
formed committees to visit residences in the district "to ascertain
the nature and extent of the existing destitution, and devise ways

and means for its systematic relief." Serving on one these committees, Greeley saw "extreme destitution more closely than I had ever before observed it." In particular, he recalled a single young man who confided in him, "We do not want alms; we are not beggars; we hate to sit here day by day idle and useless; help us to work,—we want no other help: why is it that we can have nothing to do."[24] Such confessions helped Greeley and many others make sense of the sight of young families in squalor struggling to feed their children, and guided their efforts to help.

Greeley's position as editor and publisher of the *Tribune* allowed him to speak to such injustice, which he did regularly throughout the early 1840s. Particularly important was a series of his articles in the winter of 1839–1840 called "What Shall Be Done for the Laborer?," which caught the attention of young Albert Brisbane.[25] For years thereafter, the lives and goals of these two committed reformers were intertwined.

Brisbane soon introduced Greeley to "three competing projects of social reform" that originated in Europe, and he made clear which he found most salient. There was that of the socialist Robert Owen, a successful manufacturer and founder of a utopian community at New Lanark, Scotland, who sought to "place human beings in proper relations, under favoring circumstances," so that they "will do right rather than wrong." Make their external conditions what they should be, Owen urged, and "filth, squalor, famine, ignorance, [and] superstition" will give way to "industry, sobriety, and virtue." Second was Owen's French counterpart, Henri de Saint-Simon, who believed that unbridled "love is the fulfilling of the law.'" "Secure to every one opportunity," he urged. "Let each do whatever he can do best; and the highest good of the whole will be achieved and perpetuated."[26]

By Brisbane's lights, these two offered only vague solutions to the problem of growing social disorder. There was, however, another

Frenchman, Charles Fourier, "a poor clerk, reserved and taciturn," who wrote in a detailed, "hard, dogmatic, algebraic style" and filled his books with seemingly endless facts and figures. It was he who Brisbane offered to Greeley as the answer to the nation's economic and social problems.[27] Fourier proffered what Brisbane believed to be a detailed, practical plan that promised to keep labor at work and content in their prospects, even as they played a central role in the transformation of human history. What is more, this transformation was promised precisely because it evaded direct confrontations with the existing state of affairs. Withdrawal from and redirection of the ills that plagued contemporary society rather than directly confronting them promised to be the engine of true reformation.

But to get to that point, Fourier's acolytes had to wade through hundreds of pages of dense prose that described his belief in a complex "theory of destinies," in which everything in the created universe was linked to everything else in an elaborate providential plan. Without being diverted or confused by Fourier's fanciful theories, Brisbane and Greeley wanted the American populace to ignore Fourier's often-wooly speculation and move right into consideration of how universal laws of analogy affected the social realm.

These were based in a stinging critique of capitalist society, for Fourier argued that the market as currently conceived amounted to nothing less than "organized rapacity." "Half of its force," Greeley wrote, redacting Fourier, was spent in "repressing or resisting the jealousies and rogueries of its members." The solution thus was to be a system of "attractive industry," the matching of individuals to tasks they would find enjoyable, making them eager to work and allowing them to find fulfillment in whatever labor they chose. Moreover, Fourier, Greeley explained, insisted that people should be guaranteed a "social minimum": "homes, employment, instruction, [and] good living," as well as "the fair and full recompense of [their] achievement."[28]

Crucially, for Greeley and many others, the French social theorist's wholesale condemnation of current capitalist society urged not confrontation and bloodshed, but separation. Fourier's vision of cooperative industry required the creation of an "association of some four or five hundred families in a common household, and in the ownership and cultivation of a common domain, say of 2,000 acres, or about one acre to each person living therein," a model that would be adopted all over the world when others saw its justness and the economic plenty it guaranteed. Brisbane and others picked up on that one word—"association"—and offered Fourier's blueprint as one that would steady the country's increasingly dangerous course. Although Greeley admitted that "in many respects" Fourier seemed "erratic, mistaken, visionary," he was the "most suggestive and practical" of the utopians.[29]

Soon after he introduced Fourier's novel ideas in the *Tribune,* Greeley began to lecture on these and allied topics. Later, when he published a collection of some of these talks, he explained his intentions and, by implication, how he understood Association. As in his editorials in the *Tribune,* in these public lectures he had sought to serve as "a mediator, an interpreter, a reconciler, between Conservatism and Radicalism," and to "elucidate and commend what is just and practical in the pervading demands of our time for a Social Renovation."[30] As this indicates, as much as Greeley's language could be strident and condemning, he was never a revolutionary. Instead, he sought the peaceful evolution of society through adherence to Whig principles of order and organization for the public good. Importantly, he wanted to rationalize the existing social order and make it more humane to the working class, whose fate he cared so much about. In Fourier's plans (through Brisbane's filter), he found a precise route to safe and promising reform.

But what were those "pervading demands" for "Social Renovation"? In his memoirs Greeley outlined them in detail. The cutthroat nature of the present economic system most upset him. "In the market, on the exchange," he wrote, "we meet no recognition of the brotherhood of the human race," for one man's necessity always became another man's opportunity.[31] This inexorably brought on the poverty in which so many of his fellow citizens were mired and often made them destitute. Greeley thought that those who controlled production "babble idly and libel Providence who talk of surplus Labor, or the inadequacy of Capital to supply employment to all who need it," for where labor stood idle, there was only a failure of "brains," not of capital. Further, Greeley saw too much inefficiency in current modes of production, coupled with a great waste in consumption. "A thousand cooks," for example, are required, "and a thousand fires maintained, to prepare badly the food of a township," Greeley observed, when a dozen fires and a hundred cooks could do it better.[32] Fourier's reorganization of labor addressed such absurdities.

Greeley also abhorred the atomized nature of work as it then was conceived, another result of an economic system that rewarded individual initiative at the expense of the commonweal. Overall, such isolation of the individual was greatly counterproductive. Why should one go into debt to buy land and supplies, and as a result not have that much acreage or adequate resources to work the land properly? How much better, Greeley believed, to live in large cooperative groups, to "unite to purchase, inhabit, and cultivate a common domain," and to work for the good of the whole.[33]

He also condemned the greater and greater accumulation of capital in fewer and fewer hands, another result of the current system that rewarded individuals at the expense of community in general. No one able to earn his bread, Greeley fumed, "has any moral right to eat *without* earning it," for the obligation to be industrious and useful was not "invalidated by the possession of wealth nor by the generosity of wealthy relatives," a dig at the country's lack of any laws governing inheritance.[34]

Here he also recurred to what the young man in the Sixth Ward had told him. Given the economic chaos in the wake of the Panic of 1837, Greeley wrote, when wages had tumbled and there were too few jobs to be had, everyone willing to work had "a clear and moral right to Opportunity in Labor and to secure fair recompense." In short, the question that always "occupie[d] and puzzle[d] the knotted brain of Toil," is why "Speculation and Scheming" should "ride so jauntily in their carriages, splashing honest Work as it trudges humbly and wearily by on feet?"[35]

Greeley discovered in Fourier a way to eliminate class struggle without overturning the principles embodied in his beloved Whig Party—indeed, in a way that reinforced them, for Fourier premised his plan on an increase in wealth, so that everyone's lot—owners' and workers' both—would improve. One needed only to discipline and regulate the pursuit of wealth, to initiate a program the Whigs would supply in their own way. In short, the French social theorist's ideas, which promised to reshape human nature through the imposition of much needed rational order, buoyed Greeley's spirits and, through the 1840s, remained the inspiration for his manifold reform efforts.

Whig or Socialist?

Good Whig that he was, Greeley sought a cohesive society based in class harmony, a goal that, in theory, an increase in production would encourage rather than threaten or destroy. Toward this end, the party with whom he was aligned urged selective government intervention into the economic sector—the establishment of a resilient national banking system, for example, and of a national system of roads to expedite transfer of goods—to strengthen the integrity of the extant system. On the more individual level, they championed an ethic of thrift and self-discipline that guaranteed self-improvement, and (by implication) eventual success in the marketplace, and thus acceptance of personal responsibility for one's future. By and large, too, Whigs were conservative with respect to moral values. In particular, they viewed family and religion as pillars of American society.[36]

Theirs was a conservative ethic tailored to refine, not overturn, a market economy already deeply woven in the nation's larger economic and social fabric. They did not seek a society in which all had the same things but in which all at different ranks had what they wished without crushing the aspirations of those below them. Whigs believed that it was within each man's reach to achieve financial competency and, if he wished, to become part of the property-holding class (mobility of the sort Greeley himself exemplified) without undue disruption of the social order. In a properly regulated society, capital and labor were complementary, not antagonistic, forces. Greeley moved to Fourier so readily because he promised just this kind of world, one in which various degrees of luxury, as befit a profitable, democratic society, were still compatible with virtue. For Fourier, "attractive" labor became the magical force, properly aligning all of what were now disparate economic interests, honoring all men and women equally, no matter what their labor, and thus eventually delivering them to universal harmony.

Brisbane and his selective presentation of Fourier in *Social Destiny of Man* were crucial to Greeley's ability to graft European social science onto this Whig ethic. For if one descends into the thick of Fourier's sociology, as Greeley himself attested, some of the Frenchman's speculations were "fantastic, erroneous, and pernicious."[37] Thus, as he promoted Fourier's system, Greeley eschewed potentially controversial topics as much as possible and focused instead—as did Brisbane—on Fourier's description of man's flawed economic arrangements. In his newspaper and frequent lectures, Greeley detailed a utopian alternative that centered on

Fourier's signal concept, the doctrine of Association, that is, economic cooperation among a large group of people in communities called "phalansteries." He conveniently ignored Fourier's larger cosmological and psychological speculations.

Ever respectful of the great variety in the human species, Fourier posited a system of "attractive industry," work tailored to an individual's personality and gifts and that satisfied that person's deepest urges. Through this, he sought to free Western society from the manifold waste and irrationality of wage labor and the personal alienation that attended it. But he also emphasized the progressive development of the "Harmonian Man," in whom every desire was gratified rather than repressed. Universal laws of "attraction" governed the universe, Fourier announced, and in aligning labor (as well as other aspects of man's social existence) with harmonious principles that respected this attraction, one was linked analogically to the innermost workings of the cosmos. Just as God had created and ordered the different genera and species of plants and animals, he had so conceived all creation, from the relationships of the stars and planets, to the multitudinous steps in the evolution of human society, to the variety of "passions" that marked each person's individuality. Indeed, to Fourier, the natural world, all visible creation, was nothing but a mirror to human beings, their loves and hates, needs and satisfactions.[38]

However, Fourier's thinking moved beyond the world as we know it and into more eccentric theory. He declared that humanity would move through thirty-two different stages of evolution, from Eden at the beginning, through Savagery and Barbarism, to the "perverse" Civilization where it now sat, on its way to ravishing Harmony, when sixty thousand years of creativity and happiness would commence. He offered a detailed description of the changes to come. When the planet Earth entered its eighth phase, for example—it now was only at its fifth—Fourier predicted, among other things, that "men will grow tails, with eyes on the tip," dead bodies would turn into perfume, six new moons would appear, the sea would turn to something akin to lemonade, and all fierce and poisonous beasts would become sweet and gentle.[39] Men and women would live to be 144 years old and be assisted in their labors by wonderful creatures like "anti-lions" and other now-docile beasts that had evolved from their more ferocious predecessors.[40]

Knowing that their countrymen and women were nothing if not obsessed with practicality (as Alexis de Tocqueville and other European visitors to the United States contemporaneously observed), Brisbane and others, in their translations and redactions of Fourier's extensive writings, disguised, trimmed down, or eliminated his more fanciful notions, to present more quickly and convincingly what they took as the meat of his plan. They also shied away from the details of his doctrine of "passional attraction." For while Ripley and others in his Transcendentalist cohort saw the indwelling spiritual capacities of individuals, Fourier believed that the human passions themselves reflected the mystery of the law of universal attraction.

Greeley would have nothing to do with such matters. Like other Whigs, he insisted on the centrality of the marriage vow and the importance of the nuclear family for raising children. Later, he would be embroiled in debates that found him on the side of those who resisted any liberalization of laws governing divorce.[41] Fourier thought differently. According to him, "Passions" were instinctual urges—he identified twelve—that marked peoples' deepest selves, and that reason, duty, prejudice, or repression should never subdue, let alone eliminate. If mankind ever was to achieve promised Harmony, people had to acknowledge and satisfy these passions through the proper arrangement of social relations.

Fourier parsed these passions carefully. They comprised, he wrote, the "luxurious," which pertained to the five senses; the "affective" passions of friendship, love, ambition, and parenthood; and the "mechanizing" or "distributive" ones, like a penchant for

intrigue, variety, or contrast; and for combining and mixing plea-
sures in different ways (what he termed the "Composite"). Individuals possessed these in various degrees and combinations. To
form a truly harmonious social unit—the "phalanx"—there had be
enough people to balance such various urges and their combinations in any one person so that no one would be threatened or
harmed by anyone else's gratification of any of them.

Obsessed with numeracy, Fourier counted 810 such possibilities,
and thus derived his ideal community, a phalanx of at least 1,620
people, so that potentially each individual might find his or her
gratification with at least one other. To enjoy happiness as the Deity
intended, society had to reshape all its institutions—not just those
governing labor—to accommodate its population's complex, passional needs. All the world's pain, suffering, and anxiety, Fourier
believed, arose from the continual frustration—the repression—
of these deep-seated urges, whose various combinations composed
each person's individuality.[42]

Godwin, one of Fourier's most loyal American acolytes, condemned his countrymen's timidity on these subjects. In a chapter
on "Manners and Customs" in his *Popular View of the Doctrines of
Charles Fourier* (1844), Godwin stressed that "the passion of Love,"
too, must "undergo a similar organization [to labor] by series, to
meet all the wants of all the natures that God sends into existence,"
another way of saying that one's sexual urges, no matter what form
they take, should not be denied.[43] But Brisbane and Greeley, still
seeking to attract more converts to full allegiance to Fourier's
system, continued to downplay the Frenchman's psychological radicalism.[44] Greeley, a card-carrying Whig with conservative moral
principles, insisted that the economic, not the psychological, implications of "attraction" were the key to Association.

With Fourier, Greeley believed that work, to be satisfying, had
to be "attractive," that is, organized to allow for peoples' different
capabilities and needs. Practically, this meant offering everyone the

possibility of a variety of occupations and (if one so desired) a system
of periodic rotation through them, as well as different pay scales,
depending on the importance of the work undertaken, and the skill
and diligence with which it was accomplished. In this way, no single
economic function came to define a person. One maintained his
individuality because his work complemented his deepest urges.
It "attracted" him. He did not labor from duty or a compulsion that
family, society, or religion engendered. Variety in and freedom of
work guaranteed more effective production.[45]

But even here, Greeley parted company with Fourier. Fourier's
vision aimed higher than just the satisfaction of an individual's
deepest urges. His way offered nothing less than a path to universal
Harmony. This is what was truly utopian, not merely pragmatic,
about him. Yes, Fourier promised variety in and freedom of work,
but behind the veil lay the utopian promise of initiating the greatest
happiness man hitherto had known. The stakes could not have
been higher: he did not just foresee a better society; he promised
its regeneration and the subsequent elevation of all mankind
through it.

As Fourier's closest readers understood, this utopian result could
be realized only by embracing all the implications, including the
sexual, of Associative attraction. Stuck in his Whiggish principles,
Greeley disagreed, which in time left him open to a two-sided critique, from more hardheaded economic critics like Orestes
Brownson as well as those like Godwin, more willing to buy in to
Fourier's entire program. There is no denying, however, that a majority of Fourier's American disciples followed Brisbane and Greeley's pragmatic course and chose to ignore the full implications of
what Fourier proposed.

Fourier's criticism of contemporary economics was easily applied
to the recent financial debacle, however, and this accounts for Greeley's rapid adoption and promotion of them in his newspaper. But
his obfuscation of the more problematic aspects of the system was

a widely acknowledged fact. That he had little interest, for example, in Fourier's radical critique of monogamous marriage was clear from any number of his writings on the centrality of family life, something that did not accord well with Fourier's wish to allow individuals to act on their "passional" urges. Here Godwin was correct when he wrote to a friend that Greeley "plays coward on this question of marriage."[46]

Prominent American proponents of Association followed Greeley's suit: in 1844, for example, the American Union of Associationists, an important umbrella group in New York City, announced that it advocated only Fourier's theory of "the organization of labor," not its larger psychological or mystical speculations.[47] Greeley and other Whigs correctly understood the potential repulsion of such topics to moralistic Americans. Those who read in Fourier's complete (though untranslated) works understood, however, that matters of human sexuality were central. Brook Farm resident and Ripley's second-in-command, Charles A. Dana, for example, confided to Godwin that he believed Fourier's sexual speculations "essential" to his system.[48] By 1848, Fourier acolyte and Swedeborgian C. J. Hempel let the cat out of the bag, describing in his *True Organization of the New Church* Fourier's "four corporations of love" as they would exist in the phalanx. Henry James soon followed suit, translating from the French Victor Hennequin's *Love in the Phalanstery.*[49]

Greeley believed that such matters unnecessarily diverted Americans from an important truth: although few of them realized it, in many aspects of their lives they already had experience with the kind of cooperation that genuine, large-scale Association required. Such beneficial arrangements already were found, for example, in banking and insurance companies, and in other, similar enterprises in which the number of stockholders was large; in mercantile houses, with their many co-partners; and in large manufacturing establishments like the Lowell, Massachusetts, textile mills. This

partial articulation of Fourier's ideas, however, could barely support
Association's universal harmonizing hopes and expectations, a point
not missed by Greeley's more severe critics. Emerson recognized
this when he observed caustically that Associationists were not true
reformers but "only the continuation of the same movement which
made the joint stock companies for manufacturers, mining, insurance, banking, & the rest."[50]

Criticism, however, was drowned out by the self-evident need
of the nation to recover from the economic debacle of the late 1830s
and early 1840s, and to put in place a more equitable and just social
program. From his perch of popular and political influence, Greeley
answered the call and offered his watered-down socialism. Brisbane did, too. The longer Americans resisted the Associationists'
promise of order and precise social planning, he believed, the
more the capitalist market would produce "a collision of individual
efforts, tending to evil," as it had been doing for decades.[51] The selfishness and greed of undisciplined and unregulated people had led
to the Panic of 1837, and their detritus was everywhere evident in
the Sixth Ward and elsewhere in the city where laborers lived and
worked.

Greeley and Brisbane also understood that the current monetary system, with decentralized banking, contributed greatly to the
tyranny of capital over workers. This was particularly so in the
United States, still reeling from the adverse effects of President Andrew Jackson's dismantling of the Second Bank of the United States
and his meddling with the regulation of specie deposits. "The creating of banks, the extension of credit, the conjuring up of the representative of labor and production under every form," Brisbane
observed (and Greeley would second), marked what Fourier termed
the phase of "perverse" Civilization in which humanity now found
itself. Why, for example, should a paper dollar, so easy to make,
buy a bushel of wheat, which was so difficult to grow? The answer
lay in the capitalists' shell games, for "the shrewd and scheming"

in the population always worked to multiply the bank note or the instrument of credit instead of producing the "reality," which required much more effort.[52]

Brisbane's damning assessment rang true because to those who looked closely, a patent fiction lay behind the current monetary system. Even though many people sanctioned and even "applauded" the extended circulation of paper money because they believed that through it the nation's collective wealth was increased, in reality the seemingly endless proliferation of bank-issued notes overinflated an already-bloated credit system. "A restless money-making spirit, and the cupidity and selfishness which arise from the action of isolated individuals and companies has taken the field," Brisbane lamented, and "the schemes and artifices, which have been invented to issue and give circulation to a representative of production" were now "as numerous as the frauds, which have grown out of them."[53]

Although the overproduction of banknotes and the bloated credit system had many causes, real corruption existed. It arose from a misguided wish for self-aggrandizement at the expense of one's neighbor. The most egregious examples of this self-serving ethic occurred in the nation's cities, where there was "a *cut-up* system, in which every thing is reduced to the measure and selfishness of the individual." There, "riches are the leading wish of man," and wealth, "the all absorbing object of desire," so that "no one had any concern for the commonwealth."[54] This was why the American ship of state was foundering.

As the nation's economy grew exponentially, Americans, including Whigs, had naively continued to believe that a system of representative government could identify and correct any such abuses of the public interest and trust. The Panic of 1837, however, had revealed that the Jacksonian Democrats and their heirs had no interest in changing a system that they could manipulate in their favor. Despite their "strong protestations of devotedness to the cause

of the people," Democrats, their critics charged, viewed their con-
stituencies only "as tools to get into power." They also distributed
"all offices among the leaders" and proposed "no useful and positive ameliorations," leaving those who elected them to suffer the
consequences. The result was predictable: "the energies of the people
are so absorbed in personal or party interests, that their attention
is withdrawn from the real, that is[,] social progress."[55] But could
the Whigs repair the system if they replaced the Democrats in national office?

Greeley and other Whigs welcomed Fourier's theories because
the doctrine of Association was congruent to Whig principles. It
did not, for example, prohibit private ownership of goods but only
its perversion in the process of production, in "Industry." While
the Frenchman advocated the right to private property, Fourier also
thought it should be conditional on the right to work for all those
who wished to do so.[56] What elevated this above a political slogan
for a party out of power like the Whigs was Greeley's commitment
to put these principles into practice, allowing the successful example
to answer critiques and reform economy, country, and countrymen.

Transforming Brook Farm

Because of Greeley's many connections to the New England Transcendentalists (including Emerson and Margaret Fuller, whom he
eventually hired as book reviewer and correspondent for his paper),
he learned of Ripley's experiment at Brook Farm and viewed it as
an important step in the reorganization of social life. He made his
first of several visits to West Roxbury in 1842 and thereafter touted
the community as the sort in which true Association might soon
be realized. The farm's "Projectors," Greeley later wrote, "were cultivated, scholarly persons, who were profoundly dissatisfied with
the aims, as well as the routine, of ordinary life, and who welcomed
in theoretic Socialism a fairer and nobler ideal."[57]

But Greeley also recognized some of Brook Farm's endemic problems. In addition to its members being "deficient in capital, in agricultural skill, and in many needful things besides," he lamented the all-too-noticeable "cant of exclusiveness." In other words, having added but a few people truly from the more destitute classes of the region, Ripley had not really made a genuine effort to leaven the assemblage with people of different backgrounds and needs. Greeley worried, too, about Ripley's lack of organizational acumen, which, coupled with his naive faith in his members' "angelic natures," might prove Brook Farm's downfall.[58] Quite simply, the experiment needed an overarching social architecture like Fourier's to create "a rampart of exact justice behind that of philanthropy," that is, to contain and direct the centripetal force of those whom Sarah Ripley herself described as "so many unbridled egos wrapped and swathed in selfism [*sic*]."[59]

On his initial visit, Greeley found a sympathetic ear in Charles A. Dana, who subsequently read widely in Fourier's works and then proved instrumental in moving Brook Farm toward Association. Another member supportive of Fourierist principles was Greeley's fellow New Yorker, cordwainer Lewis Ryckman, a member of the New York Fourier Society who had arrived early in 1843. Then, beginning in May 1843, Brisbane blew on the flame. Now penning his weekly columns promoting Association in the *Tribune* (which he subsequently collected and published as a widely circulated pamphlet), he began to visit the community regularly, usually for a few days at a time but once for a few months, when he was "occupied," as young resident John Thomas Codman recalled, "in the study and translation of Fourier's works."[60] Before long, Brisbane emerged as Ripley's chief advisor for the implementation of selected parts of Fourier's system.[61] He was "an enthusiast," Codman noted, "and saw the full-blown phalanstery coming like a comet and expected every moment." He "loved to talk of the good things to be—of social problems worked out by science and by harmonic modes," and to flatter himself that "without great sacrifice, the world was to be regenerated."[62]

Greeley, too, was genuinely excited by what he saw at West Roxbury and continued to suggest that Brook Farm was ripe for a transition to Fourierism to serve as the chief beacon for other utopian ventures. For his part, Brisbane "labored hard with the society to change its name to Phalanx," all the while with Greeley and other New Yorkers encouraging artisans of all types—some who were still out of work or who had failed in their own ventures, fewer who had left lucrative positions—to cast their lot with Ripley.[63] Knowing that he needed more financial support to keep Brook Farm afloat, Ripley understood the wisdom of forging more formal ties to New York's Fourierist wing so that he could solicit its wealthy backers before they committed to other such communities, most importantly, the nascent North American Phalanx in neighboring New Jersey.

Matters in West Roxbury came to a head in December 1843, after Brook Farm sent representatives to a four-day convention of the Friends of Social Reform in Boston. Joining delegates from Adin Ballou's Hopedale, the Northampton Association of Education and Industry, and the Skaneateles Community in rural New York (like Northampton, founded by abolitionists but distinctive in prohibiting private property), were many other of New England's prominent reformers. Ripley and his contingent played a central role in the proceedings. They returned to West Roxbury convinced that the community's success depended on adoption of Fourier's economic principles, a transition which Brisbane and Greeley assured them should not prove that difficult.

Things moved rapidly. Early in 1844 the community approved a revised constitution and articles for what they called the Brook Farm Association for Industry and Education that in many respects reflected Fourier's scheme for the reorganization of labor. The new organization plan included a General Direction (that is, a committee of oversight), a Direction of Finance, a Direction of Education, and a Direction of Industry, with extant units of Domestic Economy and Agriculture now subsumed into this last and termed "Series," the word for subsets of the larger grouping. With this reorganization of labor into Series and "Groups" (Fourier's terms), Brook Farm's members signaled their commitment to Fourier's ideal of "Attractive Industry."

Significantly, all members were still guaranteed the right to private property, as Fourier allowed, but, if they wished, they could live in individual family units, an option he would have eliminated. In his scheme, children were separated from their parents at a young age for socialization and education, one of whose benefits was the further liberation of women from domestic chores if they so wished. When a prospective member asked about the reasoning behind this, Ryckman, now one of Brook Farm's de facto spokespersons, explained it in language that Brisbane might have used and that was fully concordant with the ideas of the good Whig Greeley. Brook Farm allowed private property, Ryckman explained, because it was an "extension of the individual" and its acquisition a "fundamental trait of character" and thus something that had to be respected and not repressed.[64] He might have added that Association, as they had begun to practice it, was very much in line with contemporary American values.

When Ripley announced the community's reorganization, he also issued a call for new members. Interested parties poured in. Six months later, eighty-seven applicants joined the community on a trial basis; and, after the two-month evaluation period stipulated by the bylaws, fifty-eight, primarily laborers and artisans (rather than farmers and intellectuals) were formally admitted and placed in various Groups and Series. In the following four months, Brook Farm received inquiries from another one hundred applicants, the

variety and geographical representation of which were truly surprising. Almost all reported having heard of the community through
Greeley's newspaper or Brisbane's book and pamphlets.

One inquiry came from a recent college graduate, looking for
an alternative to the paths that society had cleared for him; another, from a New York clerk tired of humdrum work in that metropolis—he lamented that he could not become a stockholder in
Brook Farm, but all his money had "gone to Davy Jones' locker in
the recent wreck of the commercial world."[65] Another applicant was
a minister who, like Ripley, found himself more and more at odds
with his ministry.[66] Yet another was a father who wanted better
schooling for his three children.[67] One applicant even wrote from
distant Alabama. He confessed that he was "weary and worn with
the heartless folly, the wicked vanity and shameful iniquity which
the civilized world everywhere presents." He had decided that he
wanted "to live, labor, and *die* in Association," and ended by as-
suring Ripley that he kept "no negroes."[68]

Although Ripley never intended Brook Farm to have more than
about four hundred residents, the lower limit of what Brisbane (already significantly revising Fourier's estimate downward) thought
feasible for a legitimate phalanx, Brook Farm's growing population, then a little over one hundred, still necessitated new physical
space. In early spring 1845, Brook Farm members began to build a
"Workshop" to house new crafts and industries and that would contain a thousand-dollar steam engine beneath it to power its machinery, replacing a horse-driven mill. Even more ambitiously, the
farm commenced construction of a large building, a "phalanstery,"
that would augment the community's primary living quarters and
meeting halls, with room for fourteen families, in addition to more
space for workshops.

During this period of expansion, again financed by loans, Ripley and other members continued to play prominent roles in Associationist meetings throughout the Northeast and thus frequently

crossed Greeley's path. Brook Farm's importance to the American Fourierist movement only increased when, again with Greeley's backing, the New York contingent moved the monthly journal of the American Union of Associationists from its base in New York City to Brook Farm. Renamed *The Harbinger,* it was first published at Brook Farm on June 14, 1845. Ripley's editorial notice spelled out its mission: "the advancement and happiness of the masses" and war "against all exclusive privilege in legislation, political arrangements, and social customs" as it strove to "promote the triumph of the high democratic faith."[69] The words might have come straight from Greeley's *Tribune.*

Encouraged by increasing national attention, in the spring of 1845 Ripley urged and received approval for yet another revision of the community's principles. This time, he renamed the community the Brook Farm Phalanx, signaling wholehearted commitment to Fourier's economic, if not all his social, ideas. Not everyone approved. Transcendentalist fellow traveler Convers Francis distrusted the new direction. Fourier's system, he complained, would quash spontaneity; it seemed "too much like applying mathematics & mechanism to a free soul."[70]

Writing in the *Dial* to introduce an essay by Brisbane, Emerson agreed. Fourier's system "was the perfection of arrangement and contrivance," he noted, and its merit was that "it was a system; that it had not the partiality and hint-and-fragment character of most popular schemes" (exactly what had doomed Brook Farm in its first incarnation). But, Emerson added, Fourier "skipped no fact but one, namely, Life," for he treated man "as a plastic thing, something that may be put up or down, ripened or retarded, moulded, polished, made into solid, or fluid, or gas, at the will of the leader." Member Amelia Russell complained that, after Ripley's embrace of Fourier's ideas, "the poetry of our lives" vanished.[71]

Soon enough Ripley had other problems. In a community in which the purported goal was an ideal of social harmony, he was chagrined to find that class friction increased because the new contingent of artisans and laborers soon resented what they viewed as some of the original Brook Farm members' patronizing attitudes. And more stress inducing yet were the community's faltering finances. Not only were some of the community's creditors—including Nathaniel Hawthorne—pressing for payment or return of their original investments, but Greeley and the New York Associationists, beginning to worry about Brook Farm's long-term viability, rebuffed Ripley's request for significant financial assistance. Instead, as Ripley had feared, the central organization began to funnel money to the ambitious North American Phalanx in New Jersey.

Greeley and other Associationists never learned whether Ripley's latest reorganization would work, for Brook Farm's fate was sealed on March 3, 1846, when sparks flew from a stove carelessly left burning in the nearly completed phalanstery. Within a couple of hours the large building was reduced to ashes. Begun a year and a half earlier, the edifice had consumed seven thousand dollars of Brook Farm's labor and supplies. Three stories tall, with a first-floor dining room for a few hundred people and a large lecture hall, the building had symbolized the community's conversion and was intended to be a monument to Fourier's influence. Ripley's dream had literally gone up in smoke.

Association after Brook Farm

Brook Farm's demise did not derail Greeley's ebullient optimism that Association held the key to the nation's future. He joined the Reverend William Henry Channing's recently established religious society of Christian Union (later, the Church of Humanity) in New York City, where this clergyman, late of Brook Farm, united his interest in Fourier with long-standing social concerns as a liberal Christian. Greeley also generously supported other phalanxes, directing his attention and financial support especially to the North American Phalanx, located in Red Bank, New Jersey. Over its ten-year history, he served as its vice president and then trustee, and was always one of its largest shareholders. Growing produce for the nearby metropolitan market, the North American Phalanx, unlike Brook Farm, generated considerable profit for its investors. After Brook Farm's failure, the Red Bank community became the showplace for American Fourierism. Strangely, however, there too a disastrous fire on the premises sent the project into a death spiral. In December 1854 flames destroyed a large, new "fruit house" where the workers had planned to store produce before bringing it to market. After brief flirtations to recapitalize, the members reached the decision to sell off remaining assets, disperse proceeds to the stockholders, and bring the experiment to an end. Later, Greeley acknowledged that the fire was what had "discouraged" some of the "best associates"—he among them—and encouraged them "to favor a dissolution."[72]

Greeley continued to try to apply Association as a salve to the nation's wounds. The problem in the United States, he believed, was not individualism per se but individualism without community. This was the allure of Fourier's theory as sanitized by Brisbane into something that could appeal to the country's entrepreneurs. Finally, it posed no severe threat to the current economic system and actually would help undergird it. For while always wishing to help workers, Greeley, unlike Brownson, say, thought much more about redeeming laborers intellectually and spiritually than about improving their lot economically. Association promised to do just that, for it was congruent with Whiggery's wish to improve man's lot through imposition of rational order; hence, the fascination with Fourier's insatiable numeracy, his many categories and correlations between man and nature.[73]

Through the 1850s, Greeley continued to insist on adequate reward for work well done; and here, too, in its insistence on the reorganization of labor and reward for it, Association fit his bill. For Greeley was not averse to using the lure of gain to stimulate production, and he insisted that profit from any such sincere effort should remain one's own. A particularly skilled or ingenious worker, for example, should not be compelled to share it with others who did not achieve as much. For Greeley, as for Brisbane and other of Fourier's American followers, Association never threatened modernization but was instead a peculiarly intense form of it. It supplemented market capitalism but was never intended to replace it.

Loyal to the movement because of his belief that in these and other ways Association could rationalize a seemingly chaotic economic system, Greeley continued to serve the cause in other ways, too. In 1850 he became president of the American Union of Associationists, a perch from which he continued to work to steer capitalism into channels he believed would induce harmony—again, not necessarily equality—among the classes. Greeley never wished to eliminate capitalism—after all, it had made him what he was—but only to make it more humane, open to upward mobility, and sensitive to the worker's social, cultural, and economic needs.

What did this mean for Greeley's politics? Ever loyal to Whig ideals, into the 1850s he continued to work to smooth relations between labor and capital. This poor boy made good wanted to help workers secure better wages and working conditions, and increase employment as well as opportunity for self-culture. He favored workers' cooperative organizations and urged the adoption of a ten-hour workday. He remained suspicious of an unruly competitive individualism that created too many losers; but through the nation's various political crises, including war with Mexico and the passage of the Compromise of 1850, he remained strongly wedded to free market capitalism.

Thus, even after Greeley became enmeshed as a major force in Whig Party politics, he urged American citizens to consider that some variant of Association could alleviate, if not eliminate, the economic disruption and psychological anomie that still marked the nation's economy. Even with the specter of sectional disunion staring him in the face, he recurred to Fourier's vocabulary and categories to work out his political allegiances. In a popular lecture that he later published in a collection of writings on social and political issues, he insisted, parsing the master, that "All needful Labor may be rendered Attractive" and that "The Right to Labor, and to the fair reward of Labor, inheres in all Men."[74]

But Greeley's long dalliance with Association also allowed more conservative members of his party to paint him as someone whose ideas might easily lead to nothing less than the nation's moral dissolution. Typical of such threats to his credibility as a stalwart Whig was a series of bitter exchanges in 1846 about Association's purported "socialism" and the immorality to which it might lead. The attack came from none other than Henry Raymond, who had worked for Greeley but now was editor of the rival *Courier and Enquirer* (and in 1851 founding editor of the *New York Times*). The extended verbal warfare, carried on in their respective newspapers, marked a pivotal point in Greeley's intellectual development, for Raymond was challenging him to show his cards, to see whether at this point Greeley would defend Fourier's system entire, throwing all his influence and money behind such European socialism.

Raymond represented a more conservative wing of the Whig Party, composed in large measure of nativists and Southern sympathizers. He mistrusted more progressive members of his party who paid more attention to the cause of labor, immigrants, and antislavery. For this latter group, Greeley had become a kingpin. For his part, Raymond was suspicious of Fourierism in general and particularly disliked Brisbane—he called him a "flippant,

brainless jackanapes."[75] He thought that Greeley's other pet
causes—vegetarianism, say, as well as Association, were all fine and
good as long as he kept them private but was incensed when Greeley
used the *Tribune* to urge them on Whigs more generally.

Raymond had long been concerned about socialism's threat to
private property rights but was most upset by Fourier's radical theories of sexuality and family life, which he now brought front and
center in an attempt to tar Associationists as immoral. The exchange
between the two went on for many months, with each party publishing twelve letters before the acrimonious discussions ended with
the approach of spring of 1847. The topic captured public attention, and the exchanges were collected and issued as a pamphlet,
Association Discussed.[76] Greeley continued to insist that adoption
of Associationist ideas would not drag the Whigs from their
core values of thrift, full employment, and stable family life nor
limit their commitment to the expansion and protection of the
American economy. Thus, *contra* Raymond, he reiterated that
under Association each family could still maintain the domestic
privacy and sanctity of its own apartments, and that individuals
were free to live more or less "sumptuously" according to ability
or inclination."[77]

Why? Because, despite Raymond's attempt to paint Fourier as
a fire-breathing, immoral radical, unlike "every other Social archi-
tect," Greeley explained, Fourier was wholly averse "to communism
or the denial of individual property as utterly subversive of justice,
not merely, but of individual freedom." He reminded readers that
diversity, not uniformity, was the "fundamental law to which all
human regulation must conform." In short, "Give every one the
work for which he is best fitted, give him knowledge and skill, and
guaranty [*sic*] him the full reward of his exertions; but disturb not
the foundations of Property, nor transfer to any one, save in charity,
the earnings of another."[78]

Greeley and the Problem of Slavery

In the late 1840s and early 1850s national politics more and more consumed Greeley, and that meant inevitably an engagement with the problem of slavery. Not surprisingly, given his commitment to Association at the national level, he continued to trumpet the notion that, if citizens would only see Association in the proper light, the nation might avert its seemingly inevitable sectional crisis. It would be difficult to convert the country as a whole to Association, mainly because for generations his fellow Americans had been under the sway of "self, the master-spirit" and lived by the maxim "'look out for Number One.'"[79] But he also knew that that there was "no probability that the mass of the well-placed and comfort-girded thousands will desert their happy homes to accept any which Association may offer them." Undeniably, capitalism worked for some, but what Association offered was a way to control it for the good of all.

Individuals satisfied with their lot denied that any structural economic change was necessary. Greeley let these people be. Let all "who are satisfied and useful where they are remain so," he counseled. "We need not disparage the old in order to commend the new." But to the others—and their numbers continued to increase—"to whom the old ways, the old purposes of life, have become impossible of pursuit—who must breathe more freely or be stifled—who can live no longer to merely personal ends—let these be lifted by the promise of Association and the labor and reward attendant on it."[80]

Greeley's idealism was well and good for the cause of Northern workingmen, but what specifically did it say was to be done about chattel slavery, deeply embedded in American culture? Did Association, with its curious allegiance to both the sanctity of the individual and his needs, and the good of civilization as a whole, offer a way to resolve this seemingly intractable problem?

Since Greeley's youth, when he had witnessed a New Yorker's attempt to reclaim a runaway in Vermont, he was an antislavery man, a position that had only hardened after the killing of Illinois abolitionist and newspaper editor Elijah Lovejoy by proslavery zealots in 1837. But like so many other Whigs, devotees of order and moderation, he also believed that the best way to approach the problem was slowly and deliberately, through the support of the Whig platform and, in particular, the presidential aspirations of Henry Clay.

After the public debate with Raymond in the mid-1840s, though, Greeley became much more pragmatic, which helps to explain his subsequent interest in the emergent Free Soil Party and, eventually, his role in the formation of the new "Republican" Party. The Mexican War got him to his feet in this direction, for to Northerners like Greeley it seemed obviously a trumped-up conflict so that Southerners and their sympathizers could increase the numbers of slave states, because the disputed territory was below the Mason-Dixon Line. But rather than uniting the Whig Party, the war initiated an internal crisis, dividing them.

From one wing there emerged the new, "Free Soil" Party. These disenchanted Whigs were adamant in their demand that Congress prohibit slavery in all of the territories ceded from Mexico. During the run-up to the pivotal election of 1848, however, Greeley distanced himself from the new organization and—his candidate had been Henry Clay—tepidly supported Zachary Taylor, a military man as Harrison had been, instead of ex-President Van Buren, nominated by the Free Soilers. Greeley, who thought Taylor a weak, ill-suited candidate, still endorsed him because he feared that a third-party, single-issue candidate like Van Buren could not garner the vote. Taylor won; but Greeley remained noticeably unenthusiastic about the new administration.

In 1852, although pained by and ambivalent toward prominent Whig Henry Clay's role in crafting the Compromise of 1850, he again supported the party's candidate—General Winfield Scott—the Whigs had passed over their incumbent, Millard Fillmore, who had succeeded Taylor in office. The Democrats ran Franklin Pierce, a dark horse, and he soundly defeated Scott. Before long, Greeley realized that there was a need for yet another new national party. Two years later, he finally jumped aboard the bandwagon for the new Republican Party, even though his erstwhile friend William Henry Seward urged him to stay with the Whigs. But for Greeley, by now fervently an antislavery man, there seemed no other way. It now was more and more apparent that, despite the decent return on his investment in the Associationist scheme, American Fourierists were not going to deliver on their most vaunted expectations. Slavery stubbornly persisted, driving American politics and economics and eventually threatening disunion. From that point, Greeley advocated outright abolition.

He did so because he knew that slavery was unjust and immoral, and now realized that it also was economically inefficient, a drag on profitable production. Hitherto, he had avoided any effort for immediate abolition, fearing disruption of the nation's international trade, which would be disastrous for the laborers who always were uppermost in his mind. Like other "Conscience" Whigs, Greeley had hoped that eventually the world markets for cotton and textiles would self-regulate to force the end of this moral evil. Ever the optimist, Greeley had been loath to put antislavery front and center in the *Tribune,* a reluctance that did not endear him to abolitionist leaders like William Lloyd Garrison and Wendell Phillips, but that kept him in favor with a majority of Whig politicians.

On this topic, too, Greeley and his friend Brisbane remained strange bedfellows. Like many other Americans, particularly Democrats, Brisbane worried that, in debates over slave labor, the North's "religious zeal" against the institution would ever remain at loggerheads with the South's zealous "spirit of property." Indeed, these two sentiments seemed irreconcilable because, as he put it, they had already become so "inflexibl[y] fixed in the human mind." While hitherto a "thousand other interests of the day" had tempered the two sides' convictions, they recently had grown so combustible that Brisbane could easily see them "grow[ing] to fanaticism," a situation that could lead to the breakup of the nation or even to civil war.[81]

Seduced by Fourier's overarching plans, the ever-slippery Brisbane—sculptor Horatio Greenough termed him a metaphysical "whirlwind"—sidestepped the question of slavery's morality and insisted that the institution was just one egregious abuse of capitalism among many.[82] Slavery was not itself "the foundation of social evil," he wrote, but merely "a defect of the current economic system," "accidental in character" and only "the worst side-effect of the nation's obsession with individual gain." Therefore it "should not be attacked first, and above all not separately." True to his Associationist principles, he argued that reformers should not address it apart from the insidious system of "isolated households" that gave rise to and reinforced it in the first place. Brisbane also could not restrain a swipe at self-righteous Northerners—Whigs included—wondering (as Brownson had in his widely circulated essays on the laboring classes) why "the strong philanthropic feeling, which exists for a few negroes of the South," was not "extended to the white laboring populations of civilized countries, which are so much more numerous" and suffered equal privation.[83]

Greeley concurred, but with less enthusiasm. He traced slavery back to the greed inherent in capitalism as it presently was practiced. "One man's necessity being another's opportunity," he wrote, "we have no right to be surprised or indignant that the general system culminates, by an inexorably logical process, in the existence and stubborn maintenance of Human Slavery." Yes, he continued, sad as it was, slavery was "a logical deduction from principles generally accepted, and almost universally accounted sound and laudable."[84]

So here, too, as he stumbled his way into the Republican Party, Greeley mouthed Associationist rhetoric. His comrade-in-arms Brisbane proposed to solve the problem of slavery as he would the problem of labor in general, by following Fourier and properly aligning the passions, which, when redirected toward "industrial occupations, instead of war and political controversy," were natural and healthy. Slavery had arisen because man had repressed parts of his passional nature in the belief that this was "the only means of obtaining order and justice." Instead of inquiring "whether some social mechanism could not be discovered, which would make use of ALL those passions as they were created," humanity persisted in "a vast system of compression [i.e., repression]" of its innermost needs and desires, "the principle levers" of which were "scaffolds, prisons, gibbets, exiling, branding, and fines," that is, the technology that supported slavery.[85] When these invidious mechanisms were dismantled and people truly liberated, Brisbane thought, chattel slavery would vanish.

Like the majority of his countrymen, Greeley had learned the hard lesson that the Whigs'—and by implication, the Associationists'—arguments against slavery, which had seemed reasonable and measured, finally were specious. Here he could have taken a page from the work of the Democrat Godwin, who observed, that "the Whigs, by the system they propose, would only consecrate by law those abuses and distinctions which are the evidence and result of our rapid tendency to a commercial feudalism."[86] Eventually, Godwin gravitated to the more practical utopian plans of Fourier's disciples Victor Considérant and Hippolyte Renaud than to Fourier proper. Greeley understood that only seeking reform that cut to the heart of the nation's slave-based economy, not the Whigs' continued commitment to middle-class liberalism, could halt the coming war.

But Greeley could not easily shake his infatuation with the Associationists' grandiose plans for society's renovation, pale as they did aside Fourier's true intentions for that transformation. As Greeley put it, "Every effort to achieve through Association a less sordid, fettered, groveling life, will have a positive value for the future of mankind, however speedy and utter its failure."[87] To his credit, Greeley finally realized that, at bottom, the nation's crisis of confidence could not be addressed simply by individual acts of conscience nor by tinkering with what amounted to middle-class socialism. Slavery was systemic and held the nation's economy in a stranglehold. By the end of the 1850s, its eradication required different, more decisive action, by a new party and a new president. Once again, Greeley would be a player in the action, but now on very different terms, his pipe dream of Association remaining just that.

3

William B. Greene and the Allure of Mutualism

In the wake of the Panic of 1837, George Ripley and his friend Horace Greeley were among scores of utopian dreamers who sought to present to their fellow Americans examples that would encourage them to initiate what they thought was meaningful reform of society's inner workings. Again and again, reformers and would-be reformers posited a universal, usually God-given harmony within and among their fellow citizens that for diverse reasons had been perverted, obscured, deadened, and / or thwarted. However grotesquely American society, politics, and the economy had been contorted, and many reformers were damning in their critiques, proffered solutions were ameliorative.

Sometimes demanding great personal and communal effort and sacrifice, reformer after reformer conjectured that individuals and, more broadly, the nation possessed an inherent indwelling goodness that was waiting to be called forth. Proper alignment of God-granted interests within and among individuals would ensure that acquisitiveness within the market would never become selfishness. Opportunities would descend on the just, and be acknowledged as just. Social inequities, most prominently the rights of women and labor, and most egregiously chattel slavery, would cease. Far from challenging America's guiding nineteenth-century liberal ideology, these reformers sought, by way of example, ways to perfect it.

A subset of these reformers fixed their attention on specific parts of the existing economic order. If only its most problematic components could be fixed or eliminated, the promised perfection would assert itself, even as its enshrinement of an ethic of self-reliance was preserved. A chief issue for some of these individuals was what money was and how it should circulate, particularly in light of what many viewed as the abuses of the myriad state-chartered banks that arose in the wake of President Jackson's veto of the Second Bank of the United States in 1832. The eventual collapse in the late 1830s of this complex monetary system had, in the opinion of many, brought on the subsequent financial debacle.

Financial reformers clearly saw the relationship between inadequate supervision of a decentralized banking system and the panic, when those who sought to redeem their paper banknotes quickly decimated inadequate specie deposits. If capital was more widely and easily available and accessible in some other form, these reformers argued, the national economy would flourish. A significant side effect, they argued, would be that more Americans could attain the happiness that the Founding Fathers had envisioned.

One such reformer was William Batchelder Greene. Almost unknown today, Greene was one of the antebellum period's most original social theorists, launching himself on an intellectual journey that continued through a military commission during the Civil War and ended with his position as a philosophical anarchist. In the 1840s, reform luminaries of every stripe predicted great things of Greene. He was one of the young men whom Ralph Waldo Emerson remembered as having "knives in their brain," so intent were they on dissecting all inherited systems of belief.[1] By the end of Greene's life, though, by almost every measure, he had accomplished none of the great things expected of him.

The Transcendentalist and feminist Margaret Fuller, who no one would accuse of having a soft spot for dilettantes, described Greene as "the military-spiritual-heroic-vivacious phoenix of the day."[2] Annie Fields, wife of Boston publisher James T. Fields and renowned salon-keeper, recalled Greene as "a man of mark in his own time, a daring thinker, and one who possessed of much brave originality." His "deep thoughtfulness," she continued, "was always planting seeds of thought in others." He "never [could] be forgotten by those who were fortunate enough to be his friends."[3] Graduating from Harvard Divinity School in the mid-1840s, Greene began his career as a clergyman in a tiny Massachusetts town seventy miles west of Boston. His heartfelt religious beliefs, a unique combination of Calvinist orthodoxy and liberal Unitarianism, eventuated in a sharp critique of Transcendentalism as well as of America's compromised economy.

In large measure, he came to this through his association with Ripley's close friend Orestes Brownson, by 1840 one of the nation's most vociferous champions of the laboring man. Brownson fostered Greene's interest in the principles of French philosopher and political economist Pierre Leroux and his countryman, the sociologist and politician Philippe Buchez. Greene's intellectual odyssey was indicative of the continuing appeal of European solutions to the nation's economic problems, for, from them, he found his way to the economic reforms of anarchist Pierre-Joseph Proudhon. By the late 1840s, Greene mounted an elaborate program for economic and social reform based particularly on Leroux's and Proudhon's ideas, but fertilized as well by those of the American businessman and self-taught economic thinker Edward Kellogg. Greene urged his countrymen to adopt a radically new way to organize capital, around the concept of what he termed "mutual banks." Greene went so far as to petition the Massachusetts legislature to incorporate such institutions. Because of the opposition of many businessmen and particularly of the state's major banks, his efforts there failed, even though many of his countrymen in rural Massachusetts, where he had first broached his ideas in local newspapers, eagerly signed his petitions.[4] For a few more years he tried to raise interest in his plan, more concertedly after the Panic of 1857, but still without success.

One of his eulogists noted that Greene "could not but wonder at the fatality which prevented him from making that mark on the public mind which he had made on all the individual minds that came within his sphere of influence." The fault was placed in Greene rather than his historical moment. "He was indeed a great man," this writer continued, "but some subtle element in his nature prevented him from realizing the distinction to which his powers evidently pointed."[5]

The nation's problems, Greene believed, from class inequality to the horrors of slavery, rested, on the spiritual development of each individual. This, in turn, required reform built atop the sanctity and rights of the individual. Competition conducted under the influence of the better angels of our nature, something that mutualism would ensure, would by definition be fair. As he traveled from orthodox Calvinism to Transcendentalism and beyond, he never doubted that those angels existed.

Orthodox Roots

Greene was born in Haverhill, Massachusetts, in 1819, the son of Nathaniel Greene and Susan Batchelder.[6] His father was a newspaper editor who established the *Boston Statesman*, a leading Democratic Party journal, and whose political involvement secured him the position of Boston postmaster, which he held for two decades. He also wrote prolifically and translated some works from the French, one of which, the priest and political activist Félicité de Lamennais's *The People's Own Book* (1839), was instrumental in awakening his son to the plight of the disadvantaged. Such writings also account for Nathaniel's friendship with Transcendentalist and reformer Brownson, who befriended Nathaniel's son.

Believing that a sure way to preferment lay in military service and good connections in politics, early in 1834 Nathaniel wrote to prominent Democrat Lewis Cass, secretary of war, requesting his son's admission to the U.S. Military Academy at West Point. William had prepared at several academies in Massachusetts, study punctuated by a several months' stay in Paris with a relative and tutor. He attended West Point between 1835 and 1837, but poor health prevented him from completing his studies.

He returned to Boston to convalesce but within a year resumed his military career. He volunteered for duty in the Second Seminole War (1835–1842) then being waged in Florida. His commission supported by prominent Massachusetts senator Daniel Webster, Greene was made second lieutenant in the 7th U.S. Infantry and in July 1839 sent to Florida, where he served for two years under General Benjamin Bonneville. He abruptly resigned, again ostensibly because of ill health. His own testimony, however, indicates that during this time he went through a profound spiritual crisis, the resolution of which pushed him first toward a career in the ministry and then into social reform.[7]

Greene was unique among those whom the Transcendentalists influenced in having been raised in an orthodox Trinitarian faith.[8] This explains why when he left the army he joined the Charles Street (Boston) Baptist Church. Perhaps at the prodding of Brownson, however, Greene began to find his way into the world of the "New Thought," as Transcendentalism then was often termed. He visited Ripley's Brook Farm experiment and browsed regularly at Elizabeth Peabody's foreign-language bookstore on West Street in Boston. In this young man Peabody immediately noticed "a different cast and method of thought" from that to which she was accustomed.[9]

Impressed, she soon introduced Greene to her friend, prominent Unitarian clergyman the Reverend William Ellery Channing, whom she served as amanuensis. Before long Greene—again presumably through Peabody's goodwill—made the pilgrimage to Concord to visit Emerson himself. Likewise impressed, Emerson facilitated the publication of one of Greene's essays in the Transcendentalist periodical, the *Dial*. Eventually, Greene was even invited to some of the "conversations" Ripley hosted at his Boston home as he began to formulate his plans for the Brook Farm experiment.

Although increasing exposure to the radical ideas of his new Unitarian friends greatly influenced him and began to unsettle his orthodoxy, Greene still decided to commence study at the conservative Newton Theological Institution, a Baptist seminary near Boston. He candidly confessed to the administrators his growing doubts about Trinitarian theology—as Greene put it, he felt it "his duty" to be making some preparation for the ministry but was "not settled in regard to the particular course which he ought to pursue."[10] Fortunately, they offered him the latitude to pursue his studies in whatever manner he wished. For a year and a half Greene essentially was a special student, taking courses of interest and in spare hours reexamining the scriptural proof-texts for a three-person God.

After much in-depth exegesis, studying relevant passages "in their connections, and in light of the original language in which the New Testament [was] written," Greene found that most of his cherished Trinitarian beliefs "vanished like the morning mist before the rising sun." He become a Unitarian and in 1844 crossed the Charles River to attend Harvard's Divinity School. Given his evident theological sophistication, he was enrolled as a senior and quickly made his mark. His classmate, later clergyman and editor Thomas Wentworth Higginson, recalled Greene in that period as one of the "most interesting men in the Divinity School."[11]

Soon enough Greene published his first book, *The Doctrine of Life: With Some of Its Theological Applications* (1843), a revision and extension of what he had published in the *Dial,* as well as essays in the *American Review,* devoted to Whig principles.[12] These works displayed a growing independence of thought, for in them he was somewhat critical of Transcendentalism, and of Emerson in particular. Greene also preached in the Boston area as a substitute for his friend and mentor Brownson and other Unitarian clergymen, and held a temporary position in a liberal church in Methuen, Massachusetts. In the summer of 1845 he married acclaimed Boston belle Anna Shaw, the daughter of Robert G. Shaw, one of the city's merchant princes.

That autumn Greene accepted the call of a new Unitarian church in the South, or Third, parish of rural Brookfield, Massachusetts, and twenty miles west of Worcester, where his divinity school classmate Higginson and others were at the center of various reform movements, including abolition. The young Unitarian James Freeman Clarke, Transcendentalist and feminist Margaret Fuller's close friend, preached Greene's ordination sermon; and Dr. Francis Parkman from nearby Worcester, one of Unitarianism's elder statesmen, gave the minister's charge.

Greene remained in this pulpit until 1850, when, in a gesture reminiscent of Emerson and Ripley, he requested the termination of his pastoral relation. His marriage provided him with financial independence to pursue a career as a writer and reformer, the endeavors into which he now fully threw himself. Greene stayed in the Brookfield area for at least three more years. In addition to having collected his essays from the *American Review* and published them as a separate pamphlet, *Transcendentalism* (1849), he displayed his liberal credentials in two sermons in defense of the Unitarian interpretation of scripture; a refutation of Jonathan Edwards's treatise on the freedom of the will; and a lengthy autobiographical account of how he had settled on his eclectic religious and philosophical principles.[13]

Before his resignation, he also had waded deeper and deeper into economic reform, first bringing out a tract titled *Equality* (1849) in which he proposed solutions to the imbalance he saw between the worlds of capital and labor, and then a lengthy, original treatise called *Mutual Banking* (1850). These last two derived from his immersion, at Brownson's instigation, in French social thought and, coupled with his reading in American currency reformers, represented his heartfelt attempt to turn the nation from what he believed to be its headlong rush into greater social and economic chaos.

From Religion to Economics

From an early point in Greene's intellectual development, at the least following his return from the Second Seminole War, the young man drank deeply at the well of French economic and political philosophy. In the 1840s he admired particularly Buchez's *Introduction à la Science de l'Histoire* (1812; 2nd ed., 1842) and Pierre Leroux's *De l'Humanité* (1840), favorites of Brownson. Both Greene's essay in the *Dial* and his first separate publication, *The Doctrine of Life*, for example, depended heavily on Buchez's elaborate, schematized notions of mankind's moral and spiritual development and, concomitantly, on his belief that human progress was predicated on certain spiritual revelations—progress recapitulated in the spiritual development of each individual.[14]

More important, in both authors Greene found strong condemnation of the class divisions that marked nineteenth-century free-market society—especially visible in the United States in the aftermath of the Panic of 1837—and that Leroux believed were based primarily on inequalities of property ownership. From Leroux's analysis and discussion of artificial distinctions among men,

Greene began to consider that human happiness was attainable only through solidarity with the whole race—that is, through a profound identification with and commitment to a classless society. Further, he endorsed Leroux's and Buchez's beliefs that acquisitive capitalism, rather than marking the height of civilization, displayed willful capitulation to mankind's baser instincts, something for which the poverty and allied distress that followed the Panic of 1837 offered powerful evidence.[15]

An overwhelming, lengthy conversion experience pushed Greene in this direction, eventually leading him to combine his religious principles with a program for economic reform. His dark night of the soul had begun in the spring of 1839, well before he became a clergyman. He was still in Florida but had become disenchanted with a war that he came to consider unjust, a feeling that was shared by increasing numbers of Northerners aghast at the federal government's treatment of Native peoples. As he described it to Peabody, one evening "I was walking, about a hundred yards in front of the house in which I lived, when suddenly upon turning to go back, I fell—I felt no pain, no sickness of any kind, and immediately rose again to my feet." He fell again, though still for no evident reason, and this time found it difficult to rise. "I then crept," he continued, "as well as I could, on my hands and feet, into the house, and went to sleep."

A doctor came and bled him, thinking that Greene had contracted malaria in Florida's wetlands. Confined to bed for several days, he was completely prostrated, his physical and mental energies drained. He eventually recovered, and in his restored health resolved to carry on "that education of the will which [now became] the main occupation of [his] life." He yearned to understand, he told Peabody, the relationship between his own seeming independence and God's omnipotence. Greene tried to imagine himself, for example, "suffering the torments of hell, and rising superior to them through the forces of spiritual energy." But he discovered that

his mental energies were too weak for him to maintain such a position of "unflinching defiance" to God, whom he still regarded as
a "tyrant" in whose grasp he struggled to maintain a sense of his
free will.

All his efforts in this direction, though, proved futile, and he
finally capitulated and accepted God's utter and complete sovereignty over him and the universe as a whole. Greene finally understood that he was foolish to think that he was capable of any
"independent action." God, he concluded, "is behind everything,
including the complex laws of Nature,—a self-acting, free, supreme,
infinite Person, to whom all finite persons are responsible."

Now, Greene's spiritual pilgrimage would take the form of trying
to discover the means by which he might obtain "communion with
the FATHER." He eventually realized that he could achieve this
only through tireless devotion to his neighbors' plight in the aftermath of the nation's severe economic disruption.[16] Like the
French reformers whom he admired, including the Catholic priest
Lamennais, who had so moved his father, Greene tried to align
his life with God's wish for the solidarity of the race.

Throughout his intellectual development, however, Greene faced
one other problem: the difficulty of squaring his conservative religious background with the heady liberal religious ideas he had encountered at the Harvard Divinity School and then among the
Transcendentalists. Importantly, however, Emerson, the group's de
facto leader, had never convinced Greene to enter his fold.

Higginson, for example, remembered Greene as "mercilessly
opinionated" about even his closest friends and acquaintances. Similarly, Peabody frequently was struck by Greene's "unexpected and
oracular remarks, often quote piquant in their expression."[17] Brook
Farm member Ednah Dow Cheney perhaps put it best when she
observed that, when Greene debated, whether on religious or economic matters, he "almost rivaled Socrates in winding an adver-
sary up into a complete snarl."[18] In short, for Greene, seductive as

Transcendentalism was, in light of his religious convictions, born out of the evidence that he saw as a revelation, the movement finally provided only a way station on a long intellectual journey. In particular, Greene's forthrightness about Transcendentalism's tendency toward self-serving egotism early on marked him as an outlier, aligned more with Ripley and Brownson in their regard for social reform than with those in the ever-expanding Emersonian circle. Peabody, for example, recalled hearing Greene claim that "the Transcendentalists of Boston are the extreme opposite of Kant; they do not see the transcendental objective . . . but it is they themselves who transcend." Greene was offering a veiled criticism of the Transcendentalists self-centeredness. And as much as Greene admired Emerson, he found in him "a gospel addressed to the philosopher and theologian," not "to the poor, for that must address the heart and will rather than the intellect."[19] From his own pulpit, Greene attacked ever more strongly the egotism that he associated with Transcendentalist philosophy as he sought ways to work toward the social millennium that the French socialists envisioned.

Rejecting Egotism

This is the background to Greene's two essays in the *American Review*, which, with very few changes, he republished as a pamphlet, *Transcendentalism* (1849), in the same year in which he issued a call for a radical reconsideration of Americans' concept of equality. The essays show his opposition to the movement's elevation of the individual to almost godlike status, a belief he had held before his conversion experience. To follow Greene's wrestling with how to square the rights of the individual with the interests of the community under the umbrella of God's design for humanity is to see antebellum reform think itself into a dead end.

Those who took as their point of departure God alone, Greene began, most often became Pantheists. And those who started in nature became Materialists. But others started "with man alone," and ended as Transcendentalists. Here lies simple selfishness. When a man has cut himself off "from every thing which is not himself," Greene explained, he finds "the reason of all things in himself." But "the reason of God and the universe are not to be found in man."[20] To make such an extravagant claim was the height of self-delusion.

Greene also objected to Emerson's proposition that each individual soul "creates all things." "Build therefore your own world," Emerson had counseled in *Nature* (1836).[21] But, Greene countered, this amounted to "an identification of man with God" and thus to a *"Human Pantheism,"* the *"absorption of God in the human soul."* In his pamphlet, as elsewhere in his religious writings, Greene sought to preserve a notion of majestic divinity. Man, he declared, "is dependent, for the continuance of his life upon that which is not himself." Anyone, particularly the Transcendentalists, who thought otherwise "deified the ego in an illusory manner."[22]

True to the lessons of his mentor Brownson, rather than adopting what Peabody termed the Transcendentalists' "egotheism," Greene encouraged communion with all humanity, low as well as high, an ethic to which Horace Greeley's embrace of Universalism had brought him as well.[23] Greene's study of the New Testament convinced him that therein was taught "the great doctrine of the mutual solidarity of the members of the Christian Church, and by implication, the solidarity of the whole human race." And by "solidarity," he meant, that connection of things with each other "which makes it impossible that one should be influenced without the influence being transmitted, through that *one,* to *all.*"[24] Greene viewed humanity as an organic entity that remained healthy, in accordance with God's intent, only when all of its parts worked in concert for the whole.

Greene derived his understanding of the story of the Fall of Man from this notion of each person's linkage—and thus responsibility—to all others, and its most striking evidence, the rapacious capitalism that worked against this principle and ravaged the United States. God first created man, Greene explained, so that "all his passions, feelings, sentiments, and aspirations, were in harmony with the course of universal nature." But as soon as each person made "his own private enjoyment the main end of his life, the harmony of the universe was broken, the unity of the human race was shattered into as many fragments as there were individual men, and each cared for his own, and not for the common good," a situation that led inexorably to economic and social catastrophes like those that followed the Panic of 1837. The remedy was to make men *"one in the bond of charity"* and *"one in the unity of a common Life,"* a goal similar to what reformers like Ripley, Greeley, and others sought in their various ways.[25]

But Greene also knew that such Christian charity was often compromised in a society in which an individual's inalienable right to life, liberty, and the pursuit of happiness (and profit) was protected by law and sanctified by tradition. To direct such a destructive, self-serving ethic into a more charitable channel, Greene articulated what became the main theme of his life and work. He championed the unity of all people, as Christ had demonstrated in his tireless work among them; and, concomitantly, attacked what one of Greene's inspirations, Leroux, had called monopoly of "the property caste."[26]

Borrowing an analogy from mesmerism, a popular pseudoscience, Greene described what he saw as his own role in this coming reorganization of society. While he knew "but little of the truth or falsehood of mesmerism," this popular science offered an apt metaphor to express man's relation to God. "As one man by prolonged and earnest gaze," he continued, "can obtain control over another, transmitting his thoughts and feelings into the mind of the other, bringing the will of the other into complete subjection to his own, so the Father, by the might of the overpowering

effulgence of his glory, magnetized our Lord [Christ], bringing
him into conformity with the perfect image of his own infinite ho-
liness." In turn, Christ "magnetized" his disciples, and they, still
others, until the succession reached the present day, when these
followers of Christ were able to transform "the unconverted into
the form and image of Christ, through the magnetism of a holy
life."[27] Here, then, was a means of reform before which no national
sin or personal failing would be unaffected. Greene saw himself
in this apostolic succession, and considered his calling to be to right
his nation's economic (and, thus, moral) course before the United
States wrecked on the shoals of egotism and attendant selfishness.

The Challenge of *Equality*

Greene would set out to demonstrate his commitment to an ethic
of Christian "mutualism" in his own backyard of Brookfield and
its environs. But first, he publicized his humanitarian message in
Equality, a seventy-four-page pamphlet issued by West Brookfield's
printer.

This work clearly illustrates Proudhon's influence, particularly
in Greene's embrace of cooperative local associations of independent workingmen rather than reliance on any nationally organized
economic system. But Greene also drew on the work of American
economic theorist Edward Kellogg (1790–1858), who had published
a small pamphlet, *Usury, the Evil and the Remedy* in 1843 and, a year
later, a longer version, *Currency: The Evil and the Remedy,* under
"Godek Gardwell" (an anagram of his name). *Labor and Other Capital,* yet another revision and extension—now it was 300 pages
long—appeared in 1849; Greene drew directly from this version in
his own section on excessive interest rates in *Equality.*[28] He would
also revise and make his own Kellogg's proposed uniform national
currency secured by real estate and with an absolutely fixed rate of
interest.

Prompted by an ever-increasing number of state banks chartered to support Massachusetts's burgeoning industrialization—Brookfield's neighboring town of Ware, for example, would within a decade be transformed from a sleepy agricultural hamlet to a booming factory village—Greene's pamphlet was a weighty broadside against poorly regulated and usurious financial institutions.[29] Such monopolies on capital prevented healthy competition, raised interest rates on local loans, and contributed to increased acrimony between capital and labor. Every blow aimed at competition, he explained, is one "aimed at liberty and equality," for competition was but another name for that liberty and equality that "ought to exist in every manufacturing and commercial community." As then constituted, however, banks allowed qualified lenders to escape their fair share of the general competition and thus conferred "exclusive privileges upon a certain class"—those who had money and could borrow more.[30] Fair competition was not the problem: a skewed monetary system that favored bankers and property owners rendering competition lopsided and unfair was.

Much of *Equality* consists of examples of unfair advantages that state bank incorporation makes possible. Its larger interest, however, was linking Greene's opposition to banking to universal questions of "Equality, Justice, and Charity." Not surprisingly, given his contemporaneous religious writings, he argued for respect for each individual, rich or poor, based on Christian obligation to one's fellow man. Like his mentor Brownson, he deplored the increasing distance between labor and merchant and capital. He approvingly cited Proudhon's phrase, "Property is theft," and went on to note that the sudden disappearance of a thousand capitalists "would cause a sentimental evil only, without occasioning any serious inconvenience to society," unlike, say, the death of fifty of the state's best surgeons.[31]

In the second part of his pamphlet, Greene turned to the plight of contemporary labor. He dissected what he saw as the three main economic systems through which man related to nature and, ultimately, God: communism, capitalism, and socialism. Recycling his recently published thoughts on Transcendentalism, Greene noted that, "*The man who denies the rights of capital, is a transcendentalist in political economy.*" For what is capital, he asked, but an "outward object [to] which man is related, which man labors upon, which man transforms." But Transcendentalism is "the denial in the most unqualified terms of the very existence of capital, that is of things which are not man, and with which man is related."

The materialist is no better, Greene averred, for if the Transcendentalist "denies the existence of capital, and therefore denies its rights," the materialist "affirms [capital's] existence and denies the existence of the laborer, and therefore denies the rights of the laborer." Thus, while the Transcendentalist is "a fanatical radical," the materialist is "a bigoted conservative." And what of the socialist, who advocates state intervention in men's private affairs to replicate what they suppose to be a "Divine Order"? Influenced by Proudhon's suspicion of any centralized economic order, Greene described socialism as the philosophy of a "Theocracy" that wanted the state to intervene in men's private lives and, as such, was destructive to both liberty and equality.[32]

Because none of these explanations of man's relation to God and nature was fully satisfying, Greene championed an unusual combination of the three systems so that they would "limit, modify, and correct" each other. Only "in their union and harmony," he declared, is the truth to be found. It is formed in equal parts of the liberty of the Transcendentalist, the equality of the materialist, and the fraternity of the socialist.

To Greene's dismay, however, current events indicated such a union was far from being realized. Because "*the division of labor, and the increase of artificial wants*" have "*revolutionized our social condition,*" and, further, because "*the principle of the DISTRIBUTION of the values produced, is divorced from the principals of the production of those values,"* men were being led *"with gigantic strides, towards—*SOCIALISM!" The blame for this fell squarely on the Commonwealth of Massachusetts, which had effectively reshaped society by granting banks an exclusive privilege to monopolize capital. In so doing, the state had intervened in society *"for the distribution of wealth in some order other than that which would follow from the prevalence of* FREE COMPETITION."[33]

Greene's reaction to the evil tendencies of such evident "socialism" and his championing instead of a free and fully transparent market economy with a level floor for competition was strident. It also was aimed directly at social theorists like Fourier and his increasing number of American followers, about whom Greene heard much from his friends on the Boston/Concord axis. Socialism, Greene declared, "gives us but *one class, a class of slaves,"* and but one master, the state. Further, the worst evil of this system lay in its proclivity to pantheism, which "already was beginning to prevail extensively in the community," something he knew firsthand from his visits to Ripley in West Roxbury. And as for the "fullness of pantheism," which is "requisite for the completeness of a system of socialism," Greene observed caustically, it would be furnished by "the first Phalansterian who might happen to present himself."[34] So much for the communitarian promise of Brook Farm!

"Love" as proclaimed in the Gospels was the only answer to the inevitable social strife that the current perversion of market capitalism had engendered, love extended to all individuals, high and low, borrower and lender, owner and worker. Recurring to scientific metaphor, he wrote, "We all gravitate toward the same God." This upward gravitation "toward the same spiritual Sun, toward the same common Father" is "the revelation of our destiny." Rejecting any accommodation of the sort offered at Brook Farm or other intentional communities that smacked of socialism, Greene argued that people needed to be centered fully on "INDIVIDUALISM," which he believed was "a holy doctrine." "He that contends against the

rights of the individual man," he concluded, contends against
God, for the indwelling of God in every individual soul was "the
origin and foundation of all human rights." On the flag of every
republic, he argued, should sit "the mystical triangle" that had at
its points liberty, equality, and fraternity, "a sacramental formula"
that guaranteed not an "absolute democracy" in which individuals
cared primarily for themselves but rather a "Constitutional Democratic Republic" based firmly on Christ's principles and that
preserved individual rights and private property.[35]

In *Equality* Greene clearly enunciated a unique, radical individualism that thereafter informed all his thought and helps make
sense of his later philosophical anarchism. He did not base his arguments on Transcendentalist egotism or Greeley's quasi-socialist
"Association," but on appreciation and acceptance of all peoples'
basic humanity, what he termed their "individualism," as the Gospel
announced. Although Greene conceded that Emerson's thoughts
"radiate always in right lines," most of the Transcendentalists he
knew—save a few like Brownson—seemed incapable of grasping
how people were related to and in need of one another. For a nation whose soul was lost in the marketplace, he proffered a radically egalitarian Christian humanism. The destructive worm of
self-interest that had so contaminated antebellum America would,
in Greene's vision of universal harmony called forth by mutualism, be held in check by no less a power than God. However,
he left the implications for society of his being proved wrong
unexplored.

The Anti-Bank

Transcendentalism and *Equality* provided the religious and philosophical underpinning to Greene's chief practical effort at social
reformation, which he offered an explanation of in *Mutual Banking*
(1850), sought to realize through petition of the Massachusetts leg-

islature, and advocated through the 1850s. Perhaps stimulated by former Brook Farm member Charles Dana's introduction of Proudhon's ideas in a series of articles in the *New-York Tribune* in 1849, Greene clarified and refined the notion of mutualism for his countrymen.[36]

Gone now were the elaborate schematics on usury and other topics so evident in his other two publications. Now Greene focused squarely on what he took as the chief form of inequality, that which was founded on "the false organization of credit." He sought nothing less than a "new social state" based on the fact that Christ had come to "LEVEL UP," that is, to "confer nobility on the whole human race" through a "Christian communion," a harmony to be realized only through significant economic reform.[37]

Predictably, given what he had proposed in *Equality*, Greene's reforms originated in the Bible. On his title page he blazoned Ezekiel 18:7–9: "He that hath restored to the debtor his pledge." And in his introduction he displayed his knowledge of ancient history by discussing the concept of equality as it had arisen in Sparta, Egypt, and Israel. But hardheaded and deeply researched economic theory underlay his attempt at a solution to the nation's economic malaise. Greene began *Mutual Banking* proper, for example, by reviewing (and dismissing) two other recently proffered reforms of the banking system, that proposed by William Beck in his book *Money and Banking* (1839) and Proudhon in various of his works. In both systems, Greene found too much room for the partiality and corruption that marked the contemporary economic order.[38]

Greene was clearly impressed with Beck's sincerity, if not by the details of his proposals. In this work, self-effacingly written "By a Citizen of Ohio"—the publisher's notice identifies him as Beck—the author seeks to eliminate money as a circulating medium, be it in specie or bank notes, and to replace it with an elaborate accounting system that a "United States General Balancing Office" would oversee. "Money," Beck observed, was nothing more than "an accredited claim and counter with society, possessing certain convenient qualities" that recommend it "as a medium of exchange and as a transfer of credit."[39] Unfortunately, however, the form in which money circulated made it easily hoarded and manipulated, often with disastrous effects, particularly for the laboring classes.

Further, Beck explained, while the current system of exchange allowed satisfactory discharge of a debtor's obligation, it proved much less satisfying for the creditor. The person who had discharged his debt by repaying with money possessed the purchased good or service. The creditor, or the person who had provided the good or service, had in turn received a mere "medium" that he still had to redeem to attain his own "object of desire." The gap in time between the payment of one's debt with money and the recipient's use of that money to buy something, Beck declared, had provided the opportunity for the ubiquitous corruption of the nation's monetary system.[40]

Beck's solution was to institutionalize and tightly control the "circular route" money followed. He would accomplish this through the creation of a nationwide accounting system that made any circulating medium unnecessary and in which one could easily distinguish peoples' various obligations. Essentially, Beck suggested, this would take the form of a kind of superaccountant—"an account kept by a presiding power"—that recorded and maintained all debts and credits. He anticipated establishing financial offices throughout the country where such transactions would take place. There, subscribers, for the cost of $1.00, could open accounts to begin discharging and receiving debts, the tiny fee to go into the office's operating funds, as did a minimal 1–2 percent commission charged on transactions. As Beck proposed it, the system was essentially medium free. It existed only on paper, in accounting ledgers.

Greene pointed out that the problem with Beck's system lay in how to convince the entire population to relinquish their attachment to gold or silver, or to bank notes, and place their faith in abstract accounts. He also wondered whether Beck's scheme could include the sorts of transactions necessary for the maintenance of lucrative international trade.

Greene had similar reservations about comparable parts of Proudhon's reforms, particularly his projected plan to standardize payment on drafts or "bills of exchange."[41] Drafts, Greene explained, were essentially "a means by which a debt due one person may be made available for *obtaining credit* from another." When trading goods, a buyer often gave a certain term of credit, a note stipulating that he would pay the seller of the goods a given sum by a given date. Typically a note was due in sixty or ninety days. The seller receiving such a draft could discount the bill at a bank—that is, he could redeem the note immediately for a lesser amount. This enabled him to access money immediately. Later, when the note became due at par, the bank redeemed it for the full amount, thus making its profit.

Proudhon wanted to create a large-scale Bank of Exchange or "Bank of the People" in which such transactions were carefully regulated, particularly with an eye to preventing excessive discounts that were unduly punitive. In short, Proudhon wanted to constrain the bank's ability to take advantage of a note holder's need of immediate cash. Greene, though, still saw no way to prevent or punish "arbitrary conduct, partiality, favoritism, and self-sufficiency" on the part of a bank's officers, nor to get around the fact that a draft for goods initially issued could, after being discounted, continue to be sold and circulate widely, even though it no longer represented real goods but was just a paper obligation.[42] If one of the parties failed to be able to honor the note, one was left with nothing but a worthless piece of paper. Again, the door remained open for unscrupulous speculators to abuse a system purportedly based on good faith.

Greene borrowed from Leroux's own criticism of Proudhon when he summarized his problems with this plan. Nor could Greene guarantee a way to prevent scheming members from "caballing" to obtain control of the bank's direction and operations. "Mr. Beck thought out a Mutual Bank by generalizing credit in account," Greene concluded, and Proudhon, "by generalizing the bill of exchange." Neither system sufficiently reined in selfish individualism. Some other kind of financial reorganization, Greene believed, was necessary.[43]

His solution was simpler than either Beck's or Proudhon's, and crucially, Greene was convinced it was more immune from the machinations of rapacious capitalists. His projected mutual bank was to be based on that most important commodity, "REAL ESTATE."[44] How would it work? Any person who pledged real estate to the bank became a member of a mutual banking company and could borrow paper money from it on his own note to an amount not to exceed three-fourths of the value of the property he pledged. When the member paid this debt, the property was released from his pledge with no further obligations to the bank.

Most importantly, each member bound himself legally "*to receive in all payments, from whomsoever it may be, and at par, the paper of the Mutual Bank,*" that is, with none of the discounting in which conventional bankers engaged. The rate of interest on such loans was minimal—Greene suggested 1 percent—just enough to cover the institution's operating expenses. He also insisted that none of the mutual bank's money could be loaned to anyone who was not a member. Finally, the bank would never redeem any of its notes in specie nor would it accept specie from its debtors, except at a discount of a mere one-half percent, a rule that would prevent the kinds of monetary abuse that had overrun the country prior to the panic.[45] This was so different from the way that contemporary banks operated that Greene termed it nothing less than "a bank turned inside-out, or rather turned bottom side up." One came nearer the truth, he observed, if one understood it as "the positive negation of a bank, and designate it as an ANTI-bank!"[46] Little wonder, then, that when he lobbied the Massachusetts legislature to organize such an institution, his efforts fell flat.

Greene anticipated resistance from skeptics as well as those whose profits depended on the existing system. Some might object, he wrote, that thereupon the price of land would rise because it was now the basis for issue of money and capitalists with adequate funds could dive in to monopolize real estate. Greene countered, even if this occurred, another effect would mitigate the result. For an added benefit to his plan was that the price of labor would also rise. With so low a rate of interest, "all capital would rush to the market, there competing with all other capital for the employment of labor" for new jobs created. Workers would benefit because wages would increase; but the price of produce would not, because it was tied to supply and demand, not to bankers' manipulations. If a speculator bought land with the goal of monopoly, Greene explained, he soon would be ruined, for he would have to pay three or four times as much for labor. Thus, the effect of "real estate mutual banking," Greene concluded, was to benefit the person who worked his own land and ruin the employer who refused to. Another presumed positive result was the redistribution of land, its "cutting up" into small farms that would give "a comfortable support to the families that actually labor upon them." Greene hoped to see the day when every laboring man in New England would own real estate and thus be able to take advantage of the mutual banking system.[47]

Why did Greene think this would work? The goal was utterly sensible: to abolish the use of "hard" money and the paper currency based on it. This would eliminate the unpredictable currency fluctuations that caused economic hardship and led to financial panic. To be sure, at present some individuals had no real estate to pledge. But what did the existing banks do for individuals without adequate security, Greene asked? The answer was, very little. Under a mutual banking system, however, if a propertyless man had a land-owning friend who was willing to pledge for him, he could obtain money at the mutual bank's low interest rate, not at the exorbitant one available in the current banking system, if he could even secure it. Greene asked readers to recall that a mutual bank's main task was not to seek profit off of investors but to *decrease* the interest rate on the medium of exchange, making more money available and causing wages to rise.[48] The key point was that "mutual money is not itself value"—like, say, a silver dollar—"but a mere medium for the exchange of values,—a mere medium for the facilitation of barter."[49]

To emphasize the safety and good sense of such a mutual system, Greene, once more borrowing from Kellogg, contrasted it to the operation of the contemporary banking system in Massachusetts. In 1849, Greene observed, state banks had issued nine and one-half dollars of paper for every dollar of specie in their vaults. Thus, if for any reason there was a call for specie—a "run" on the bank—the institutions never could fulfill their obligations. Paper currency issued under this system was not only worthless and thus unfit to serve as a medium of exchange, it created the potential for the kinds of runs on banks that had started the Panic of 1837. What was more, such a banking system was patently un-American, for it engendered the very kind of aristocratic society that Lamennais condemned and that the United States purportedly had left behind in 1776, with bankers having ascended to the position of a new nobility.[50]

Comparatively, mutual money had many advantages. One could not monopolize it the way one could specie. And its establishment would "be the signal for the immediate transformation of the relations of capital and labor." Why? Because under the influence of mutual money, the market value of commodities would tend rapidly to coincide with their "natural value." Labor, too, would finally receive its just reward, as the supply of capital became commensurate to the supply of exchangeable commodities. Finally, no variation in the supply of money would affect the value of the mutual banks' money: it would never rise because of scarcity or fall through an excess of issue. Thus, Greene concluded, the great problem of social science will be practically solved, for "money will become—no longer a commodity, but—a mere medium of exchange," as it was intended to be. Mutual money, he declared, "transcended" the law of supply and demand.[51]

The inequality that current "merchandise-money" sowed, also a chief complaint of Kellogg, was grotesque in its own right, and an insult to something more transcendent. "The Silver Dollar," Greene declared disgustedly, had become "the god of this world," whose worship he linked to his fellow citizens' propensity to think of society only as an abstraction rather than a collection of individuals with specific needs and desires. But the proper "movement of money," he explained, should be "the realization, the concrete and material expression, of the—as it were—mystical interdependence of men on each other." When the medium circulated as it was meant to do—that is, in exact and regular exchange of products for products—"the mutual dependence of man upon man will be organized, labor will be definitively regulated," and just wages guaranteed. It would be the realization of a utopian dream.[52]

Greene also explained that, to the unfeeling, acquisitive capitalist, money signified not just a medium of exchange but also what enabled him, without labor on his part, to participate in the results of the labor of his neighbors. As a result, the working community became the "property" of the moneyed class. As a consequence, the country's political economy had become the "science of the means and methods whereby men of capital are enabled to bring the rest of the community under tribute." In America, the restricted circulation of money had become nothing less than a means to ensnare labor, insure inequality, and thwart God's intentions. The circulating medium had to move absolutely freely if mankind was to achieve the "Social Unity" Christ intended.[53]

Summarizing his plan, Greene returned to his religious roots. What is the Kingdom of God? he asked. What but "Communion, Fellowship, or, as the Socialists say, Mutualism." Just as Americans, he reminded his readers, already were pledged, as citizens of a democratic republic, to believe in mutualism in social relations, so they should accept the "mutualism of production, consumption, and exchange." God intended man to live in mutualism, for when someone isolated himself from others and "excommunicate[d] his brother in production, consumption, and exchange, [and] destroy[ed] mutualism by scission," he lived in an unnatural, sinful state marked by suffering and distance from God.[54]

Unsurprisingly, the consequences of adopting mutual banking would be immense. Quite simply, there would follow "the creation of order, and the definitive establishment of the due organization of the Social Body." If adopted widely, the system eventually would cure the evils that flowed from the present incoherence and disruption of the relations of production and commerce, and thus end the economic disruptions that had plagued capitalism. Mutualism would initiate the Kingdom of God on earth.[55] It was that simple.

In 1850 and 1851 Greene enlisted townspeople from Brookfield and the neighboring towns of Palmer, Warren, and Ware to sign a petition to the Massachusetts legislature to establish a mutual bank in their region. He sought to obtain for the "farmers, mechanics, and other actual producers," whose names appeared with his, a "just reward for their labor," something impossible under the present organization of currency. The petition included a redaction of the banking rules and emphasized that bills issued by such a mutual bank would never be redeemable in specie but only in services and products, and at the "stores, mills, workshops, and other places of business" of the members. The key provision, of course, was that the notes were to be secured by mortgage of real estate.[56]

Engendering opposition from entrenched business and banking interests, nothing came of Greene's efforts. As he later wrote, "Upon all the petitions, the Committee on Banks and Banking [of the Massachusetts legislature], after hearing the arguments of the petitioners, reported simply, *"Leave to withdraw!"*[57] Then and thereafter, Greene failed to win wider public support for what he regarded as so simple and promising a solution to a seemingly intractable problem.

Aftermath

Greene did not give up. In reaction to yet another economic downturn subsequently labeled the Panic of 1857, he published *The Radical Deficiency of the Existing Circulating Medium,* in which he recycled various arguments from *Equality* and *Mutual Banking* in another attempt to move people to mutualism.

By this time, Greene had become more widely known in the state's political circles and for his interest in other aspects of reform, including women's rights (an interest that he shared with Horace Greeley), which dovetailed with his arguments in *Equality.* Even as he was making his appeals to the General Court in favor of mutual banking, for example, he served as a member of the Massachusetts Constitutional Convention as a delegate from Brookfield. His speech to the convention in 1853 in favor of women's right to vote—in this case, on proposed changes to the state constitution— was so powerful that William Lloyd Garrison reprinted it in his widely circulated *Liberator.*[58]

Greene moved through arguments based on political theory in favor of women's right to participate, but then recurred to his deep-seated religious feelings. Dismissing a fellow delegate's argument from Aristotle to the effect that the state is not founded on right but on interest, Greene further countered that "interest" was nothing other than "egotism," which "as [Emanuel] Swedenborg, [Jakob] Boehme, and other spiritual writers affirm [is] the centre and essence of hell." This delegate had forgotten that Christ came

explicitly to break egotism's hold on mankind. "Modern democracy" was based "upon a divine principle, not upon egotism."[59]
Greene displayed a similar dedication to the cause of liberty in general when in 1852 he met the great Hungarian freedom fighter Louis Kossuth, then in Springfield, Massachusetts, as part of a national tour to raise money for his fellow patriots' cause.[60] Greene traveled the forty miles to present him a purse of one hundred dollars raised in Brookfield for Kossuth's Hungarian "fund." Greene also delivered a letter from the town fathers (in all likelihood penned by him) for Kossuth to read and consider before his scheduled visit to the North Brookfield train station.

The town fathers' missive was a ringing defense of the quest for liberty that Kossuth pursued and that earlier had animated Americans when they broke away from England. Greene's proposals for financial reform were also everywhere evident. "Amid the glare of material interests," the letter read, Americans were in danger of forgetting "the high destiny" to which they had been called by Divine Providence. "No man can isolate himself from other men," the letter continued, and "no nation can isolate itself from other nations." The nation that wrapped itself "in its own selfishness begins to suffer moral death," the letter read, as the United States clearly was doing.[61]

Greene never relinquished his belief that every individual citizen's well-being—not just that of a member of the moneyed classes—mattered most in any meaningful reform, political or economic. Likewise, he remained committed to a religious, almost mystical, faith in the indwelling, God-made goodness in men and women. This enabled him and so many others to square the circle of how arch-individualism could lead to social harmony. God would solve the thorny problem of selfishness, while human reformers performed the labor of addressing the social, economic, and political perversions that thwarted mutual cooperation. Greene's operative word continued to be "mutualism," based as it was in an ethic of compassion and as well in full acknowledgment of each individual's rights, whether of a Hungarian overthrowing the yoke of aristocratic tyranny, a female factory worker seeking the right to vote, or a Brookfield farmer having equitable access to capital in order to compete in the market economy.

Following the Panic of 1857, as the Civil War approached, Greene left New England for France, where he remained for several years and whose political and economic theorists he so admired. But his patriotism brought him back in 1861, when he joined the Union army as colonel of the Fourteenth Massachusetts Infantry (later, the First Massachusetts Heavy Artillery).[62] A year later, General George McClellan assigned him to command an artillery brigade in General William Denison Whipple's division. In 1862 Greene resigned, but he subsequently assumed other pivotal roles in the war.

He remained friendly, for example, with General Benjamin Franklin Butler, whom he had known as a fellow member of the Massachusetts Constitutional Convention of 1853. In 1864 Butler named him his civilian military aid and the same year asked if Greene would be interested in assuming command of a regiment composed of "transfugees," Confederate prisoners from the Point Lookout (North Carolina) prison camp who had declared their loyalty to and willingness to fight for the Union. Greene accepted the position.

Interesting personal details emerge from his response to Butler, particularly about Greene's antislavery stance. He had become "a radical anti-slavery man" in 1850, he admitted, when the fugitive slave law had been passed. In a gesture reminiscent of Henry David Thoreau's refusal to pay taxes to a government that was waging war with Mexico over territory that would enlarge the slave-holding South, Greene's "democratic and anti-slavery principles," he explained to Butler, had made him refrain, "for many years past, from voting," something he planned to continue "so long as slavery is, in any way whatever, guaranteed by the Constitution of the United States." For some reason, Greene was never called to lead the regiment of "transfugees," and he was otherwise left alone to till several acres of land and occupy himself "superintending the education of his children." He also returned to his writing and lecturing on economic and social matters.[63]

Throughout the 1860s and 1870s Greene's thought widened and deepened. In 1872, still a religious seeker, he published *The Blazing Star: With an Appendix Treating of the Jewish Kabbala.* Continuing to insist that true freedom was guaranteed only if one recognized the significance of each individual, Greene now drew sustenance from the Jewish mystical tradition, which similarly reinforced a sense of the centrality of man in divine creation. The world, Greene observed therein, "is in one aspect a poem; in another, it is a logical argument." But "in every aspect, the universe is a work of art," Such mysticism originated in Greene's immersion in American Romantic thought—the writer Edgar Allan Poe claimed that "the universe is a plot of God"—but eventuated in an ever more inclusive faith that sustained him after his failure to reform the nation's damaged and seemingly unfair economic system.[64] He never lost faith in the individualist ethos that had sustained him during his efforts to establish true equality through mutualism.

In 1875 Greene published a collection of earlier pieces under the title *Socialistic, Communistic, Mutualistic, and Financial Fragments,* a work whose topics ranged from his favorite hobbyhorse, the mutual bank, to the plight of the laboring classes, to the (for him) new issues of free love and the institution of marriage.[65] He gave time, too, to politics. He became vice president and chairman of the executive committee of the progressive Labor Reform League and supported the anarchist platform proposed by Ezra Haywood, to whose journal *The Word* he frequently contributed.[66] At Greene's death in 1878 he was known as one of the country's most prominent philosophical anarchists.[67]

Perhaps the most fitting statement on Greene's influence came when his old friend and mentor Brownson reviewed his *Remarks on the Science of History; Followed by an A Priori Autobiography* (1849). Brownson pointed out the incongruity of Greene's seemingly always being caught between the poles of self and society. In particular, Brownson was exercised over what he called Greene's "autotheism," what he regretted as well in his friends Emerson and fellow Transcendentalist Bronson Alcott. For these people, Brownson noted, all that is or exists is "I or Ego," a philosophical position that presented the same difficulties as pantheism.[68]

In other words, Brownson thought that, despite Greene's frequently stated concern for linking all humanity in a bond of mutualism, he still placed too much stock in the rights of the individual soul, a carryover from his long struggle to maintain belief in man's free will in the face of God's absolute power. In so doing Greene opened a crack for the selfishness he deplored. In minds less subtle, this concern for individual rights in turn could lead, seemingly inexorably, to self-interest. But Greene believed that everything, from wealth inequality to the horrors of chattel slavery, was best addressed by calling forth man's conscience. This left repeatedly, however, two urgent questions: first, how to encourage man's best nature to express itself; and second, what to do when, despite being given every opportunity to give that expression, society remains mired in selfishness, cruelty, and perversion.

After Emerson first met Greene, he observed that the young man seemed "an answer to a special prayer."[69] But the prayer went unanswered because Greene, undeniably earnest, could not shake the liberalism that already was woven deeply into the fabric of American thought and culture, particularly the belief that equality of opportunity for each individual remained not only the defining characteristic of American democracy but evidence of its citizens' better angels. Solving the nation's social, economic, and political problems could demand elegant solutions—like phalanxes or mutual banks. But the possibilities and opportunities for reform differ fundamentally when you presume, as Greene did, that most people are inherently good rather than inherently selfish. Inherently good individuals need systems that allow that goodness to express itself and examples of mankind's better angels to emulate.

To this, however, there is a harsh corollary. The longer an individual or society thwarts God's intentions, the more deserving are they of sterner, harsher reprimands. Greene's commitment to what he believed a salutary individualist ethos, expressed in his call for mutual banks, indelibly colored his activities and finally worked against the cooperative venture that he urged. So too did his neglect of the problem of chattel slavery, evidenced by his refusal to cast his ballot as the sectional crisis escalated. It was almost beyond his ability—as it was for many reformers—to imagine a different, more ameliorative, more pragmatic approach to the nation's problems. Slavery wasn't an economic problem, any more than inequality was. For these reformers, it was a moral indictment; slavery was simply a sin. This same theology underlay Greene's attempts at monetary reform. His dream of mutualism—like the reform efforts of so many of his contemporaries—was among the last pure expressions of American liberalism when those who sought to change the nation's course still uncritically assumed that God backed their efforts.

4

Orson Squire Fowler: Reading the National Character, for a Price

Horace Greeley's first residence in New York City was in a simple boardinghouse devoted to the dietary principles of health reformer Sylvester Graham. Graham urged a vegetarian diet and temperance, and counseled frequent and vigorous exercise, exposure to fresh air and sunlight, and strict sexual hygiene, including continence before marriage.[1] His industrious followers found many ways to market such ideas; city boardinghouses operating according to the principles of health reform were among them.

In Grahamite boardinghouses like the one in which Greeley stayed, boarders received two vegetarian meals daily, eschewed stimulants like coffee or tea in favor of cold water, and were shaken from bed at five in the morning to exercise. And the Graham diet—Emerson wittily termed its originator "the prophet of bran bread and pumpkins," a reference to Graham's animus against "white," overground flour as well as to his vegetarianism—was only one of a wide and extravagant range of reforms through which individuals sought to regulate and improve their lives in the face of the moral complexities arising from the market economy and the new urban spaces it created.[2] In addition to his attention to diet and physical culture, Greeley sampled a large number of these technologies of self-discipline, and, in the pages of the *New-York Tribune,* he frequently urged them on others.

He was particularly interested in phrenology, the wildly popular "science" of deciphering a person's character through the study of the shape of the skull, which was itself the outward form of the brain and what phrenologists identified as its many discrete activities. After European advocates introduced phrenology to the United States in the early nineteenth century, within twenty years practitioners were everywhere, setting up offices in cities and towns—sometimes even moving from community to community in traveling wagons that doubled as salons. What attracted droves of eager paying customers was not just the opportunity to learn about themselves but the promise phrenology held out of explaining how they might improve.

At heart, phrenology was a theory of body and mind, about how anatomical and physiological features were related to mental attributes. Phrenologists believed that the brain was "the organ of all our instincts, propensities, sentiments, aptitudes, intellectual faculties, and moral qualities." Further, it was not unitary but composed of more or less four-score faculties localized in certain regions, which were manifested in the shape of the skull. By examining these protuberances or bumps, an adept in the science could ascertain "the dispositions, and intellectual and moral character of any individual," and advise on their development and behavior.[3]

Not one to miss any chance at self-improvement, in 1847 Greeley sat for such an examination, the results of which appeared shortly thereafter (presumably with his blessing) in the *American Phrenological Journal,* a widely circulated publication that popularized the science. Because Greeley was a well-known national figure, the journal's editors believed that its readers would want to know what made Greeley so successful, something a phrenological analysis would reveal in great detail.

The phrenological analyst described Greeley's skull as very large and high and his body and brain as uncommonly active. This was "abundantly evinced by his light, fine hair, thin skin, light complexion, and general delicacy of structure," even though his physical constitution was not strong. The phrenologist also noted that not only was Greeley's brain large but it also was "in the right PLACE," not wide, round, or conical, but narrow, long, and high, developments that indicated anything but "selfishness or animality." Greeley's "reading" supported the fact that, although he was of humble origins, he had developed the character traits he had been given and thus could not help but succeed as he had.

Recurring to the specialized vocabulary of phrenological analysis, the examiner also noted that Greeley's "controlling organs" were "Benevolence, Adhesiveness, Firmness, and Conscientiousness," and these were seldom found in larger form than in his example. This clearly accounted for "that high moral reformatory, and progressive turn which he gives to even his politics," and made him "advocate the RIGHT, both on its own account" and because it furthered the cause of humanity. Similarly, Greeley's great "Benevolence" and "Adhesiveness" (love of fellow man) coincided perfectly with his "Associationary views" as well as for his principled opposition to the Mexican War. The phrenologist went on in this vein for several pages, cycling through scores of markers on the skull and measuring Greeley's head against them. The conclusion was inescapable, if to most Americans finally unsurprising: "This summary of his organic condition renders it apparent that he is no ordinary man."[4]

Few pseudosciences were better suited to nineteenth-century American liberalism, with its faith in an individual's unimpeded talents rising to deserved merits, and, before the Civil War, countless Americans sought the knowledge and advice phrenology proffered. How it attained such widespread popularity is traceable largely to, Orson Squire Fowler and his younger brother,

Lorenzo Niles Fowler. As the editors (and owners) of the *American Phrenological Journal*, the Fowlers lured Greeley and thousands of others to examinations in their "offices" in New York City. For almost half a century the Fowlers were the premier purveyors of all things phrenological. First at Clinton Hall, on the corner of Beekman and Nassau Streets in New York, and then at 308 Broadway, they displayed a gallery of the heads of prominent Americans, living and dead, and sold plaster and porcelain busts, charts, skulls and the tools for measuring them as well as a plethora of their own pamphlets and books issued in scores of editions. Their acolytes spread throughout the country, and in turn they analyzed thousands, who also proved eager to buy the merchandise the Fowlers sold. From their headquarters in New York, the Fowler brothers oversaw a financial empire that served phrenology's practitioners and the ever-increasing number of patients who flocked to phrenology to learn about and better themselves.

Early Success

Orson Squire Fowler was born in 1809 in Cohocton, New York, a mountainous region near the headwaters of the Oswego and Genesee Rivers.[5] His parents were farmers in this newly settled landscape, and their children, Orson, Lorenzo (b. 1811), and Charlotte (b. 1814), were expected to contribute their share of work, even as their father, Horace, a deacon in the local Congregational church, insisted that they learn to read and write and to follow a strict religious path. Orson's mother died of consumption in 1819, and Horace's second marriage brought three half-siblings—Samuel, Almira, and Edward—into the Fowler family.

The two older boys were earmarked for the ministry. For poorer though ambitious families in that region, that meant study at the newer, smaller colleges such as Williams, in the Berkshire Mountains in Williamstown, Massachusetts, or recently founded

Amherst, on the eastern edge of the Connecticut River Valley in the same state. Both prepared young men for further study for the ministry, usually in Congregational churches in the region. To ready himself for entrance exams, Fowler studied with clergymen in small towns in western Massachusetts, one of whom, Moses Miller of Heath, was instrumental in Amherst's founding. Unsurprisingly, in 1829 Fowler entered that fledgling school. Soon thereafter, his brother Lorenzo enrolled at nearby Amherst Academy.

Amherst College already had a distinguished faculty overseen by the college's president, Heman Humphrey, a prominent Congregational clergyman. Humphrey instilled in his students a passion for emerging reform movements, including temperance, of which he was an early and strong advocate. Another influential teacher was prolific author Edward Hitchcock, later the state geologist, who taught natural history and chemistry, and who whetted the Fowlers' interest in physiology.

Fowler particularly enjoyed the college literary and debating societies—the Athenian and the Alexandrian—and quickly excelled in the frequent competitions they sponsored. One such debate became the stuff of legend and directly led to Fowler's interest in phrenology. Students had become interested in the new "science" but doubted many of the claims advocates made for it, so they assigned a skeptical classmate to take the negative on the question of whether it was a bona fide field of study. The student, sophomore Henry Ward Beecher, would subsequently rise to extraordinary renown and influence.[6] His path crossed Fowler's in western Massachusetts, however, because it was where his father, prominent clergyman Lyman Beecher, had sent him when it became apparent that Yale College's curriculum was too demanding for the high-spirited young man.

To prepare, Beecher sent to Boston for all the latest books and pamphlets on the subject, and even purchased a phrenological bust. To his amazement, the more he read, the more he was convinced of what phrenologists argued; and when he rose to speak, he declared himself a convert to what he had intended to ridicule! Beecher's about-face fueled interest throughout the college, and soon Fowler asked if he could read the materials Beecher had acquired. He too was won over and soon found himself in demand as an amateur practitioner, with students and even some curious faculty paying two cents each to have him analyze their characters.[7]

Fowler later recalled this formative time. When he entered upon the study of "mental philosophy," he wrote, he soon found phrenology superior to what he found in his assigned textbooks on the Scottish "Common Sense" philosophy. The proponents of phrenology whose works Fowler read were intellectuals such as George Combe. They presented phrenology in scientific but also philosophical terms, seeing the shape of the skull an aspect of the link between one's physical body and one's inner nature. Their theories drew on sources like the eighteenth-century scientist and mystic Emanuel Swedenborg's work, and they inspired Fowler eventually to declare that phrenology was proof of an individual's free will.

While Fowler pored over the theory of phrenology, he also "learned the location of a few of the organs and Faculties, from inspecting the heads of fellow-students," among whom he soon became noted for "making correct 'hits,'" that is, accurate assessments of their mental faculties as well as their general character traits. Soon his classmates "flocked" to him, "all curious to hear what [he] would say about themselves individually, and each other."[8] His brother Lorenzo's conversion to phrenology quickly followed. Shortly after that, his sister Charlotte followed suit. Within a few years the threesome had made phrenology a family business.

In 1834 Fowler gave the college's commencement address—on "Temptation"—and continued his plans to enter the ministry. He was admitted to the Lane Theological Seminary (overseen by Beecher's father Lyman) in Cincinnati, Ohio, but in the few months between his graduation and matriculation continued to develop his interest in phrenology. When he was asked to give a series of lectures on the subject in Brattleboro, Vermont, he prepared diligently. He printed handbill announcements, penned a brief pamphlet of the science's chief principles, and "ordered a bust, and thirty-two dollars' worth of works on Phrenology" from Boston. His presentations were a great success, as were his sales. After each lecture, he offered phrenological readings, filled out on printed charts, for twelve and a half cents each, half that price for women and children, and sold books and pamphlets that explained phrenology and its merits. Fowler was astonished to clear forty dollars.[9] He soon realized that he could make a better living as a professional phrenologist than as a clergyman. What was more, as a phrenologist he would continue in the work of helping people to know themselves better, assisting them just as he might from the pulpit.

When Fowler set out for his next lecture engagement, in Saratoga, on the Hudson River in New York, he asked his brother, still a student at Amherst Academy, to join him. This marked the end of Lorenzo's schooling, for soon the pair decided to go on the road full time and work the hinterlands as a well-organized unit. Lorenzo offered practical explanations of the science's principles, and Orson prophesied how the self-knowledge phrenology promised would initiate a new era in human relations. To convince skeptics, after each presentation they invited an audience member to the stage to demonstrate their skills. They measured and commented on the subject's skull, and from this "read" his behavioral propensities. Eager customers then lined up to pay for a similar experience.[10]

Although the Fowlers might have truly believed that they were reading character traits from their customers' skulls, there is of course no medical basis for phrenology; it is altogether a pseudoscience. However, Orson and Lorenzo earned a reputation for accuracy. It is likely the brothers were merely astute at assessing a subject's personality through minimal interactions, such as the way a customer responded to being called onto the stage, and through clothing, facial expressions, body language, and small talk. Flush with success, the brothers extended their lecture circuit. From New York they traveled south to Baltimore; west to St. Louis, Missouri; and on to Nashville, Tennessee, and then back northeast, sometimes working in tandem, occasionally separating and going in different directions, to meet on the road later. In the mid-1830s they reunited in Washington, D.C., and set up their first office. Lorenzo begin to make plaster casts of some of the heads and skulls they examined, including those of well-known politicians, to display to the curious. Soon they needed more space for their ever-growing collection and relocated to Philadelphia where, in addition to having examination rooms, they could more readily display their specimens.

Orson's gift for rhetoric (and for the printed word in general) served him well. In 1836 he published *Phrenology Proved, Illustrated, and Applied,* soon the chief manual on its subject.[11] In October 1838, he started the *American Phrenological Journal,* for the next seventy years the chief source of information about the science for practitioners and eager subjects. Following the Panic of 1837, with so many Americans eager to know how and why their fortunes had been so readily lost, and assuming that personal character flaws were the chief contributing factors, interest in phrenology, which promised just such explanations, exploded. In 1842 the Fowlers left Philadelphia for New York, the country's largest city, and established their office, in Clinton Hall, in a busy commercial district. For the next two decades, their location in this city landmark was the center of all things phrenological.

The seriousness with which Americans took phrenology and its promises is visible in part in the names of those who consented to be analyzed by the Fowlers or their close associates in one of the chief eastern cities. They included sculptor Hiram Powers; daguerreotypist Mathew Brady; authors William Cullen Bryant,

Lydia Maria Child, John Greenleaf Whittier, Oliver Wendell Holmes, and Walt Whitman; reformers Thomas Weld, Isaac Hopper, Arthur Tappan, Lucretia Mott, and, of course eventually Greeley; Red Cross founder Clara Barton; the impresario Phineas T. Barnum; ballerina Fanny Elssler; singer Jenny Lind; and clergyman Henry Ward Beecher, of course.[12]

Over time, the Fowlers extended their work and offered their readers analyses of the characters of other prominent Americans not necessarily taken from life but from careful study of their heads as presented in woodcuts, engravings, or daguerreotypes. These readings not only offered the general citizenry new ways to understand why certain individuals became so famous, they also provided inspiration to those who believed that they possessed some of the same relevant traits and propensities. What was more, phrenology as it was practiced in the United States made it clear that individuals could work to develop those traits—and to curb unfavorable ones—in the hope of achieving comparable success—financial, intellectual, and political.

Phrenology, History and Method

As with so many other antebellum reform efforts, in phrenology the onus was on the individual. One's true self, the best that one could be, was available, but the hard work of calling that self forward fell to each individual, at best to a community of individuals like those in a phalanstery or a Grahamite boardinghouse. Thousands upon thousands of Americans looked out on a world in need of reformation, and then they set about improving themselves and their neighbors in the belief that this was the most efficacious way of solving the world's problems. Phrenology allowed one the deepest view into one's character, its strengths and flaws, which one then could strengthen or ameliorate to allow one's God-given character most fully to emerge.

Phrenology thus posited the malleability of human nature, and consequently its proponents also saw themselves as educators, roughly akin to twenty-first-century therapists. After they helped a person identify his strengths and weaknesses, he could work to modify certain inherited faculties or tendencies and through appropriate exercise purge destructive or problematic tendencies or develop positive ones. To know one's self phrenologically, the promise went, was to become aware not only of what one was but what one might be.

Phrenology offered a way to initiate and direct healthy behavior as well as to analyze and improve character. It placed in each person's hands implicit directions for how to change himself, eliminating any excuse of ignorance after someone had sat for a "reading." One example, and one not lost on phrenologists like the Fowlers (or advocates like Greeley), was the direct relation of an individual's general physiological health to his or her mind, and, by extension, of the tendencies that flowed from it. Diet, temperance, exercise, and clothing, even the shape of one's home, all affected the brain, and thus mattered more and differently than people thought. Eating vegetables wasn't solely good for longevity and health, but by these lights it promised to improve character, and could theoretically improve society, indeed the world.

An Austrian physician, Franz Joseph Gall (1758–1828), was most responsible for the initial flowering of this new kind of quasi-psychological analysis. From careful observation of certain psychological and mental traits—selfishness, say, or the ability to memorize—he developed the theory of brain function outlined above. To some degree, his was an extension of the work of Johann Kaspar Lavater (1741–1801), who had developed the field of physiognomy, based on the premise that a trained observer can infer much about a person from his facial features and, to some degree, the form and carriage of his body.[13] Lavater insisted, however, that such

things reflected profoundly interior and finally intangible characteristics. They offered nothing less than a window on the mysterious, immaterial soul. By contrast, Gall developed a much more
materialist science. He came to believe that the *physical* organization
of the brain was utterly determinative of character.

Austrian authorities rightly surmised that such overt materialism
as Gall posited might undermine religious belief, and he soon
thought it prudent to emigrate before he received formal censure
or punishment. Subsequently, he lectured throughout Europe, including in Germany and the Low Countries, where his ideas were
received enthusiastically. By 1807 he had found his way to Paris and
there published his definitive treatise, *Anatomie et physiologie du sys-
tème nerveux en général* (1810–1819). Accompanying him during these
years and assisting him in the preparation of this magnum opus
was his pupil Johann Gaspar Spurzheim.

Before Gall completed his multivolume work, Spurzheim departed for England and there began to establish phrenology on a
slightly different footing. Spurzheim, who coined the word "phrenology"—literally, "science of mind"—was more moral philosopher
than scientist. As such, he was more in tune with the optimistic spirit
of the Romantic age than Gall, who never escaped the Calvinism,
with its ironclad emphases on original sin and predestination, in
which he had been raised. To the contrary, Spurzheim believed
that, as defined by their psychological attributes, men and women
had free will. They were naturally good and had only properly to
balance their intrinsic predispositions to achieve personal and social harmony. Phrenology enabled precisely this happy outcome. By
indicating what needed improvement, it showed its practitioners
how they might attain it. From such individual applications,
Spurzheim eagerly moved phrenology outward to address larger, more
social questions, specifically, its potential effects on such matters
as education, penal reform, and treatment of the "insane."

He soon learned enough English to translate his and Gall's works, and in 1814 toured England and Scotland, where in public debate and in print he convincingly refuted many detractors' objections to the new science. In Edinburgh, a young attorney named George Combe heard him and, with his brother Andrew, became a fervent convert. Combe, too, began to write on phrenology's application to social problems. He soon developed a sophisticated method of "crainioscopy" to measure with new tools the skull's bumps and depressions, the better to assess the brain's outer manifestations. As a result of George Combe's lectures and publications, phrenology became immensely popular in Scotland. Flush with this success, he decided to visit the United States for a lengthy lecture tour to promulgate the new science.

Spurzheim and Combe in the United States

Phrenological ideas had circulated in the United States as early as the 1820s, brought by Americans who had traveled to Europe and become inspired by new scientific and philosophical ideas, Gall's among them. In the Unitarian *Christian Examiner*, sometime Transcendentalist Frederic Henry Hedge reported with some surprise and disgust the rapid spread of phrenology, particularly among medical practitioners. Throughout the Northeast, he wrote, "this theory of man [has] obtained a speedy and signal triumph," so that "all the higher principles of our nature [are] in danger of being entombed in the little tumuli of the brain."[14] Through the early 1830s there was among select Americans curiosity about phrenology's therapeutic possibilities, but not yet widespread interest.

Spurzheim visited America in the late summer of 1832. His trip sparked further interest and appreciation for the science. He delivered a series of eighteen lectures in Boston to crowds so large that the venue had to be changed, from the elegant Athenaeum to the more capacious Masonic Temple. As an indication of the respect in which he was held, he was asked to repeat the series in Cambridge for the Harvard College community, and he lectured as well on the brain's physiology to the Boston Medical Society.[15] Sadly, this exhausting regimen debilitated Spurzheim, and he died in Boston in November. After his autopsy (much discussed in the press), his Boston acolytes, following his directive, preserved his brain and skull, placing them at the Athenaeum (they now reside at Harvard), where his visit had commenced. Three thousand people attended his funeral services at the Old South Church, where Professor Charles Follen, Harvard's first professor of German, eulogized him and attendees heard the Handel and Hayden Society sing an ode composed expressly for the occasion. It was as though one of the country's first citizens had passed: Spurzheim's canonization was sealed with interment at the new Mount Auburn Cemetery in Cambridge, the nation's first rural cemetery.

Despite the unforeseen brevity of Spurzheim's stay, it marked the commencement of broad interest in his science, a consequence as much of his much-remarked benevolent personality as his compelling lectures in physiology and phrenology. A subsequent flurry of publications and lectures fueled wider interest in phrenology, including at Amherst College where Fowler and Beecher first encountered Spurzheim's ideas.

Spurzheim had unwittingly set the American stage for the visit of his erstwhile disciple, who would prove phrenology's even greater publicist, George Combe. Having won over the British Isles, he soon made his own visit across the Atlantic. He arrived in the fall of 1838 and circulated through the eastern seaboard on a grueling eighteen-month tour, delivering over 150 lectures—a series at each venue usually consisted of sixteen such talks—to audiences of 300 to 500 people, as well as offering hands-on practical classes on cranial analysis for the curious. Combe formed friendships with such intellectual luminaries as William Ellery Channing, Samuel Gridley Howe, George Bancroft, and George Ticknor, and even met three men who held or would hold the presidency—John Quincy Adams, Martin Van Buren, and William Henry Harrison. On his return to Europe eighteen months later Combe published his three-volume *Notes on the United States of North America during a Phrenological Visit in 1838—1839—1840* (1841), a work that, like Alexis de Tocqueville's virtually contemporaneous *Democracy in America* (1835, 1840), offers a detailed eyewitness account of American democracy in the early nineteenth century.[16]

One unanticipated result of Combe's tour was the formation in many American cities and towns of numerous phrenological societies devoted to the study of the science. But he was disappointed when he realized that these discussion clubs were little different from the audiences he drew. They consisted primarily of doctors, clergymen, and other professionals who embraced phrenology's theoretical premises—its roots in and contributions to physiology and psychology—without necessarily having any interest in its wider promulgation. In Combe's words, most of his auditors made up "a phalanx of very superior persons, most of them belonging to the learned professions, who are excellent phrenologists so far as the philosophy of the mind is implied in the study." The problem is, he continued, "they are theorists."[17]

For phrenology to reach not only beyond "theorists" and America's intelligentsia, if it was to fulfill its promise as a means to reform not just individuals but also society, it required two additional elements: The transformational powers phrenologists wished to assert needed grounding in an even more utopian optimism which would be provided by the German physiologist Franz Anton Mesmer and the Swedish mystic Emanuel Swedenborg. The second necessary element was a more uniquely American genius: the entrepreneurial, passionate conviction of the Fowlers to inform, educate, animate, and profit from as many of their countrymen as possible.

Combe, Swedenborg, and Mesmer

In the Boston area, Combe's popularity among the intelligentsia was coincident with rabid enthusiasm for the theology of the Swedish mystic Emanuel Swedenborg (1688–1772). In that city, for example, members of and fellow travelers in the Swedenborgian Church of the New Jerusalem, whose adherents, though not greatly numerous but influential in the city's reform circles, enthusiastically embraced Combe's *Constitution of Man* (1828). It sold an astonishing 200,000 copies before the Civil War, trailing only the Bible and John Bunyan's *Pilgrim's Progress*.[18]

Unlike Combe's *System of Phrenology*, which describes in detail the new science's physiological foundation and chief principles, *The Constitution of Man Considered in Relation to External Objects* was a work of moral philosophy, successor to the works of Scottish Common Sense philosophers Adam Smith, Dugald Stewart, Thomas Reid, and Thomas Brown, as well as of ethicist Bishop Joseph Butler. The book's goal, Combe explained, was to indicate and develop the relation between man's "constitution"—that is, his physical being—and the general laws of nature. "We are," he wrote, "physical, organic, and moral beings, acting under the sanction of general laws," but there had yet been no convincing theory of the relation of the mind to the natural world. Phrenological principles supplied such a theory, Combe argued.

As we have seen, a dream of universal harmony, from mankind through nature to spirit, informed both Charles Fourier's utopianism and Emerson's Transcendentalism and undergirded Ripley's expectations for Brook Farm as well as Greene's faith in a mutual bank. In announcing the moral purpose of Combe's book—"to show how the human race may be as happy as the constitution of man allows it"—its American editor declared its principles were congruent to contemporary concerns in both liberal religion and social reform. For Combe explained how man's constitution was "designed to harmonize perfectly with itself in all its parts" as well as with "the whole of creation." Human happiness, the editor continued, thus consisted "in an exact accordance of all the laws which are in operation within us, and again of these with all the laws which govern the external world."[19] This explains why Emerson could write in his journal that he found Combe's work to be "the best Sermon" he had read "for some time." And Combe made the explicit connection to Swedenborg theology, another of Emerson's pet interests, which similarly promised the imminent realization of divine harmony.[20]

Emanuel Swedenborg was a remarkable figure who, like his near contemporary the American theologian Jonathan Edwards (1703–1758), attempted to reconcile Christian doctrine with Enlightenment science. For Swedenborg this came naturally, for (unlike Edwards) he had trained specifically in the natural sciences. He studied at Uppsala, Sweden, and then in England. There he encountered Locke's philosophical writings, which were transforming the understanding of the relation of consciousness to the outer world and eventually pushed Swedenborg in new directions as he sought to reconcile science and religion.

In the first phase of his career Swedenborg had written widely on metallurgy, mathematics, and physiology. All this changed, however, when, at the age of fifty-seven, he had a religious experience that reoriented his life. As he described it, after he finished a meal, "a kind of mist" spread before his eyes, and he saw the floor of his room "covered with hideous reptiles, such as serpents, toads, and the like." When the mist evaporated, Swedenborg discerned "a man sitting in the corner of the chamber who said to him, 'Eat not too much!'" This was no isolated dyspeptic dream, however, for the next night the strange visitor reappeared, with a more serious message. "I am God, the Lord," he told an astonished Swedenborg, "the Creator and Redeemer of the world." He had chosen the Swede "to unfold to men the spiritual sense of the Holy Scriptures," lessons He subsequently dictated to the erstwhile scientist, soon to turn mystic.

Swedenborg took his assignment seriously. For the next several years he professed to have had frequent communication with the world of spirits, from which he produced a plethora of theological works that form the cornerstone of the Church of the New Jerusalem. Central among its tenets is the doctrine of "series and degrees," links in the chain from the natural world to the spiritual. The "natural" series, for example, comprises the mineral, plant, and animal kingdoms, each of which can be traced to its first series or source, from whose simplicity stems the world's utter complexity and yet harmony.

Observers later connected this idea approvingly to the social analyses of Fourier, who parsed the various types of humanity into equally numerous, complex categories, and organized both work and social life around them. He, too, promised harmony would be the result. The similarities did not escape Emerson, who introduced Albert Brisbane's essay on Fourier to readers of the *Dial* by noting that "one could not but be struck with strange coincidences between Fourier and Swedenborg."[21] The difference was that, in Swedenborg's schema, each "series" everywhere announced in the created, physical universe culminated in God. Fourier's culminated in a harmonious society congruent with the universe's laws.

For Swedenborg and his followers the natural world corresponds perfectly to the spiritual. The New Jerusalem will arrive, Swedenborg claimed, when humanity uses his "key" to read properly the relation between the worlds of matter and spirit and progressively discovers this harmony and thus the truth of God's word. Swedenborg's doctrine of "Universal Correspondency," British disciple James John Garth Wilkinson wrote, claims "that bodies are the generation and expression of the souls, and that the frame of the natural world works, moves, and rests obediently to the living spiritual world." The "events of nature and the world become divine, angelic, or demonic messages, and the smallest things, as well as the greatest, are omens, instructions, warnings, or hopes."[22] American Swedenborgian Sampson Reed, whose work Emerson praised, put it more simply: "The very stones cry out, and we do well to listen."[23]

The central proposition that the body expresses the interior man, the soul, was what linked Swedenborg not only to proponents of phrenology but also to those of mesmerism. Franz Anton Mesmer was another Enlightenment savant who like Swedenborg believed in invisible fields of energy that moved in and through individuals. And like Swedenborg, Mesmer's ideas were also widely followed by America's intelligentsia, in greatest detail in the work of American scriptural scholar George Bush.[24]

Like Spurzheim, Mesmer had trained in physiology and so was not particularly interested in the theological implications of these invisible currents. Rather, he believed that the mysterious "electrical" or magnetic forces—"vital energy"—that flowed through people influenced their physical and psychological health, and could be adjusted by a skilled mesmerist. Occasionally, the invisible fluids were blocked in their circulation; at other times they flowed freely. Their movement determined physical and mental health. Through mesmerism, or "animal magnetism," usually with the use of iron rods or specially treated water, the practitioner sought to balance these forces, and thus restore physical and mental well-being.

For Mesmer's disciples, particularly Charles Poyen, a French expatriate and former sugar plantation owner on Guadalupe who made his way to the United States in the 1830s, such therapeutic work most often took the form of hypnotism. When a mesmerist placed a patient in a somnambulistic or hypnotized state, the patient was most pliable to the practitioner's manipulation of the invisible currents that determined health and sickness. Mesmer—and by extension Poyen—based his work (as did Swedenborg) on the notion that *outer* manifestations—in this case bodily or mental illness—had their sources in the *inner* being.

Bush, a Protestant clergyman who converted to Swedenborgian, devoted his lengthy work to the overarching premise that what had come to light through Mesmer and his disciples' investigations of access to the transfer of mental states undeniably corroborated Swedenborg's transformative experience when he had received divine illumination. "The main phenomena of Mesmerism," Bush explained, are *"mental"* and "involve the laws of *mental communication* between one spirit and another." This was, he wrote, precisely the same "sphere of phenomena which Swedenborg professes to unfold." Bush did not seek to "prove" mesmerism, but to show how it validated Swedenborg's theological system. Bush concluded, "the ultimate design, in Providence, of the development of Mesmerism at the present era" was "nothing less than to pave the way for the universal admission of Swedenborg's claims."[25] Not surprisingly, Fourierists, too, often found their way to Swedenborg, for he provided their system with what many saw as much-needed religious grounding.

Bush neglected to mention, however, a novel and all-important scientific corollary of Swedenborg's system that the mystic had also explored. After long study of the physiology of the nervous system, Swedenborg came to view the brain as the chief transfer point between the inner and outer man. This is how he understood (as scripture indicated) the interpenetration of body and spirit, and how the latter, through the brain to the nervous system, manifested in the body, allowing the spirit to do its work in the world. Swedenborg thus could locate the soul with utter precision, in the brain's cortex.[26]

Like other contemporaries, Swedenborg was also interested in the circulation of the blood, which he regarded as an analogue to the movement of spirit through soul. Consequently, breathing, too, fascinated him. Breath pushed the blood through the body and nourished the brain, just as the spiritual fluid fed the soul from the infinite reservoir that was God. To Swedenborg, all was linked in one elaborate, harmonious circular movement of which mankind too often recognized only small parts. The brain's cortex was the key point in this life-giving, divine exchange. There, the material and spiritual mingled and influenced each other. Early phrenologists only simplified his system and focused on the practical implications of the brain's influence on man's outer behavior.

Other American Swedenborgians besides Bush merit notice. In 1848, C. J. Hempel published *The True Organization of the New Church* in which, in addition to elucidating precisely what his title promised, he applauded Charles Fourier's view of different, more enlightened, sexual relations, the first American to do so. Like Fourier, for example, Hempel argued that people of different temperaments needed different sexual partners. Shortly thereafter, Henry James, another Swedenborgian enthusiast, offered a translation of French Fourierist and spiritualist Victor Hennequin's *Love in the Phalanstery* (1848), which made clearer the relationship between Fourier's psychology of sexual relations and the Swedenborgian cosmology.[27]

These connections that linked Combe, Swedenborg, and, later, Fourier, fascinated Emerson and his cohort, intent as they were on linking man to nature, and nature to spirit. Later, however, in his lectures on the "representative men" of the age, among whom he numbered Swedenborg, the Concord sage became more measured in his praise. Although he appreciated what Swedenborg had to say about the relation of nature to spirit, he finally found the Swede's system too severe and restrictive, much as he did Fourier's. The "vice" of Swedenborg's mind, Emerson complained, is "its theological determinism." The mystic "fastened each natural object to a theological notion," the Transcendentalist observed, but forgot that "the slippery Proteus [that is, nature] is not so easily caught."[28]

But couldn't the science of phrenology be simplified and so brought to a wider audience? Couldn't Americans jettison the admittedly complex philosophical and theological scaffolding that supported universal harmony, so that countless individuals, and then society as a whole, could reap the benefits of the heightened self-awareness it promised? Into this opportunity the irrepressible Fowlers, their eyes always on the main chance, stepped forward.

To "Phrenologize" the Nation

The Fowlers accomplished the popularization of phrenology by separating the practice from the science behind it and transforming it into a lucrative business. Lydia Maria Child recognized this achievement when she described phrenology as the Fowlers practiced it as the "democracy of metaphysics."[29] Previously, phrenologists saw themselves as participating in rigorous scientific investigation of the brain's physiology, but the Fowlers encouraged the practical application of phrenology's insights: every American's chance to better understand and improve him- or herself.

What were a person's predispositions? What might one accomplish in life if he overcame his known limitations? What kind of work most suited the individual, and what should he or she look for in a spouse? How might one decide whether to trust someone with whom one was about to do business or deal with in some other important way? How should one educate one's children or reform criminals? The practical phrenologist could answer these and other questions, all related to self-knowledge, and all for a price.

In the *American Phrenological Journal* Orson Fowler announced his populist ambitions. "Let *practical* phrenology be encouraged," he urged, for it would lay the foundations "on which those glorious superstructures of reform are now so rife—now sweeping into oblivion the evils that enthrall society, and placing man upon the true basis of his nature." He dismissed notions of man's innate depravity that still had wide currency in certain religious denominations. The mind was not a "single malign force," he reminded his audience, but instead a comprehensible set of faculties that could be altered for the good of the individual.[30] Man had free will, Orson Fowler believed, and so could mold his life. Why? The brain was a physical organ that could be modified and developed by proper exercise. Thus, one could eliminate one's faults and cultivate strengths.

Writing in the *American Phrenological Journal* in the 1840s, the Fowlers spelled out what they took as the relation between phrenology's growth and the nation's destiny. Their periodical's purpose, they crowed, was nothing less than "to Phrenologize Our Nation." The journal would "mould the Now Forming Character of Our Republic . . . [and help to] reform governmental abuses."[31] Forget Transcendentalist brother- and sisterhood, Fourierist association, or mutual banking. Self-knowledge through phrenological analysis was the panacea for a stricken nation. "I shall publish no work," Orson Fowler wrote, "which I do not think eminently *calculated to do good*," so that all, "especially the labouring classes," can learn "the comforts and happiness of a virtuous and healthy life."[32] When widely practiced, phrenology would produce the citizenry the nation needed.

But how did one start on this path of self-reformation? In the city, it was as easy as finding the nearest phrenologist's office. In the hinterlands, one sought an itinerant practitioner's temporary shop. The customer paid for a phrenological examination—by the 1850s a dollar was a common price at the Fowlers' offices, less in the countryside—that usually included some sort of written evaluation.

The phrenologist examined the patient, alert to the various regions of the skull where such traits—Gall listed twenty-seven, Spurzheim added eight more, and the Fowlers eventually settled on forty-two—as Amativeness, Adhesiveness, Philoprogenitiveness, Conjugality, Combativeness, Cautiousness, Self-Esteem, Sublimity, Acquisitiveness, Hope, Spirituality, Imitation, Ideality,

Mirthfulness, Benevolence, Comparison, and Language, among others, manifested themselves. The phrenologist noted an individual's predisposition to each, usually by numerals from one to ten, the higher the number, the greater the propensity. A pamphlet explaining in detail what each phrenological marker meant for one's development was often available for purchase.

The public could acquire its best understanding of the nature and extent of the business of phrenology, however, from a visit to the Fowlers' New York headquarters, which rivaled P. T. Barnum's museum as a spot that newcomers to the city had to visit. The curious found an extensive "Cabinet" that consisted not only of hundreds of casts of the heads of famous or interesting people, but also displays of stuffed animals, mummies, and paintings and drawings of humans and creatures, all related to salient lessons about the development and capabilities of the human mind.

Offering reproductions of some of these heads in plaster of Paris or porcelain, the Fowlers also sold all sorts of pamphlets and books, most issued by their own ever-growing publishing house.[33] In addition to carrying new editions of the works of Gall, Spurzheim, and Combe, they made good on their attempt to bring the science to the common man, a typical title such as *Phrenology, Proved, Illustrated, and Applied* (1837) selling thousands of copies in many editions.[34] They also carried scores of titles (many authored by themselves) on such subjects as vegetarianism, temperance, hydropathy ("the water cure"), and personal hygiene, staples of the contemporary reform movements. Titles included *Love and Parentage* (1846), *Self-Culture and Perfection of Character* (1847), *Education and Self-Improvement* (1847), and *Memory and Intellectual Improvement* (1847).

Admission to the Cabinet was free, but the Fowlers expected the visit would seduce visitors into paying for a phrenological reading. What precisely their money purchased can be seen in the assessment of the medical doctor, poet, and essayist Oliver Wendell Holmes, for whom Lorenzo Fowler himself completed a chart. Though skeptical, Holmes was enough interested that he returned a few days later for a lengthier, written analysis by phrenologist E. R. Gardner, helpfully filled out in the space provided in copies of the Fowlers' *Illustrated Self-Instructor in Phrenology and Physiology; with over One Hundred Engravings; together with the Chart and Character of* [the subject's name to be filled in].

"You have a full size brain," Gardner noted,

> which connected with your exquisite temperament gives you a fair amount of power to sway & mould the minds of others . . . You are constitutionally ambitious . . . You have excessive Conscientiousness & adhere very rigidly to what you think is right & you are disposed to bear down hard on those who are wrong. . . . Language is very large: & you are seldom at loss for words to communicate your ideas; are naturally copious in speech, & the outlet to your mind is most ample . . . You are firm & fixed in your purposes & quite tenacious in your will . . . You are somewhat wanting in Complacency & have not much dignity or pride . . . In summing up your character, I would say that you have great intensity of feeling & clearness of mental action; are very ambitious, very watchful, very rigid, & at the same time very liberal; are decidedly well qualified to amplify & magnify your theme; have great love of wit; have great powers to communicate; are quite original in your mode of viewing subjects, of understanding human nature & of adapting yourself to circumstances.[35]

Ever the skeptic, Holmes later parodied the experience in an essay included in his popular *Professor at the Breakfast Table* (1859). The experience began, he deadpanned, with "Mild champooing [*sic*] of head." Then, "Extraordinary revelations!" for the analyst noted

"Cudiphilous, 6! Hymneiphilous, 6+Paediphilous, 5! Deipniph-
ilous, 6! Gelasmiphilous, 6! Muskiphilous, 5! Uraniphilous, 5!
Glossiphilous, 8! And so on." He concluded, "Invaluable information.—Will invest in grammars and dictionaries immediately."[36]
One critic added that phrenologists were becoming expert at the
art of "pleasing" their customers. They were "keen enough to dis-
cern that flattery [was] a correct coin among their dupes," and thus
they were careful to "discover in the bumps so many good qualities, as to counteract the bad ones."[37]

Whether due to flattery, the Fowlers' tireless proselytization, or
the widespread desire on the part of Americans to understand and
improve their circumstances after the devastating financial panic,
from the 1840s on phrenological examinations occurred in mind-
boggling numbers. In a retrospective of his life, phrenologist
Nelson Sizer estimated that he personally had examined 200,000
individuals.[38] The Fowler family—the brothers' sister Charlotte,
too, eventually joined them, offering readings and writing tracts—
contributed at least tens of thousands more, and greatly extended
their influence through the practitioners they trained and those
who had prepared themselves for the profession through the
Fowlers' various publications. By the Civil War the Fowlers were
indeed well on their way toward their goal of "Phrenologizing"
the nation.

Although he then did not know it, one of the 200,000 heads
that Sizer examined was of someone soon to achieve laudable fame
or, others thought, terrible notoriety. One day in New York in 1858,
after Sizer returned to his office from lunch, a man asked for a phrenological analysis. There was bright sunlight in the room, and at
first the phrenologist had a hard time seeing his patient. Soon, however, he could make out a flowing beard and piercing eyes, and
began to take the client's measure. The man, he recalled, had a face
that showed "firmness and energy enough to swim up the Niagara
river [*sic*] and tow a 74-gun ship, holding the tow-line in his

teeth." He also had courage enough "to face anything that man may face, if he think it right, and be the last to retreat if advance be impossible."[39]

The man clearly wanted to know about himself, for this was his second phrenological reading. A little more than a decade earlier, when he was in New York from Springfield, Massachusetts, on business in the wool trade, he had sat for Orson Fowler. And in the early 1850s, one of his sons had worked in the Fowlers' New York offices, combining his belief in phrenology with the panacea of "Pure Cold Water."[40] Ten years before Sizer, Fowler likewise noted his striking, rugged features. "You are very active both physically and mentally," the phrenologist wrote, "are positive in your likes and dislikes, 'go the whole figure or nothing[,]' and want others to do the same." The client also showed much stubbornness— "firm as the hills when once decided"—and liked to think and act for himself. In 1847 Fowler, and a decade later, Sizer, had taken accurate measure of John Brown.

Phrenology and Wider Circles of Reform

That the violent abolitionist John Brown, as well as his oldest son, John Brown Jr.—the one who had worked in New York offices— were pulled into the orbit of the Fowlers' empire is not surprising. Little that touched on nineteenth-century reform escaped it. Phrenology's remarkable success was contingent on its connection to and support for an ethic of individual self-development that was central to nineteenth-century Americans' self-understanding. At the time, the appeal of and market for tools for self-awareness, self-improvement, and societal reformation was substantial.

Early on, the Fowlers took into partnership Samuel Wells to oversee their burgeoning publishing efforts that now included not only phrenology but also reform efforts in general. Before long they were issuing their own and other authors' works on a wide range of subjects pertaining to personal health and hygiene. The nation's mood was ripe for such things. As one humorist put it, its citizens had "taken the pills of foreign and domestick quacks by the thousand," and had "swallowed Maria Monk, abolitionism, and homeopathia." Now they were "busy in bolting down Phrenology and Animal Magnetism." "These several humbugs having been disposed of," he continued, "the same persons, and thousands more, will be prepared for farther experiments in gullibility, *ad infinitum*."[41]

Vegetarianism had been an early interest; and Graham, the derisively titled "prophet of bran bread," became a frequent lecturer in Clinton Hall at Orson's invitation. Graham's coworker in the field, William Alcott, one of the nation's most prolific of writers of advice literature for men, women, and children on many subjects, including diet—he advocated ass's milk to cure cancer—also appeared under the Fowlers' imprint.[42] In part through Alcott's leadership, a national organization, the American Vegetarian Society, was started, its membership united in their belief that, if the millennium was to commence, "we must, inevitably, give up our belief in animal food." In the Cabinet's rooms, too, one could depend on finding Orson, a longtime "frugivore" (one who eats mainly fruit), eager to dispense advice on proper diet.[43] The link to phrenology was obvious: one could curb or improve certain of one's propensities—gluttony, say—by practicing proper eating habits.

Another of the Fowlers' pet reforms was what John Brown Jr. followed, hydropathy, popularly known as the "water cure," whose precepts Orson, too, followed religiously. He frequently wrapped himself tightly in cold sheets to improve general well-being and applied wet bandages over his chest for relief from periodic heart pain. Like the vegetarians Graham and Alcott, the water cure's chief proponents, Russell T. Trall and Joel Shew, also frequently visited the Fowlers' offices. Trall prophesied social harmony when humanity was liberated from the machinations of the medical profession and its too frequent recourse to drugs. Instead, he argued, the sickly should drink plenty of water to purify themselves, along with adopting the wet sheets Orson favored, frequent douches, and complete submersion, whether in tubs, ponds and streams, or the ocean. Trall oversaw the New York Hygieo-Therapeutic College, a training institution for budding hydropathists that the Fowlers endorsed.[44]

When the Fowlers extended their empire into other areas of reform, they began with education. As Combe had indicated in his *Constitution of Man,* one of the most important contemporary fields of labor was education, and the basic premise of popular phrenology—through self-knowledge man could discover what God intended for him and improve himself accordingly—led directly and naturally to efforts at better instruction of youth. Tendencies to virtue and vice, phrenologists believed, were not inherent or permanent but related to the physical structure of the brain. Effective education thus depended on the exercise or restraint of certain faculties that the practitioner identified. Toward this end, Orson Fowler penned works such as *Education and Self-Improvement* (1844) and *The Perfection of Character, Including the Management of Youth* (1851), and Lorenzo's wife added textbooks, such as *Familiar Lessons Designed for the Use of Children and Youth in Schools and Families* (1854).

In these and other pedagogical guides the Fowlers argued that a sound mind is found in a healthy body, and this led logically to consideration of the incarcerated and the mentally challenged, two categories of individuals who in this period were frequently placed in novel institutional settings in the hope that they might be rehabilitated. With those considered "insane," enterprising phrenologists sought to identify the weakened parts of character as displayed in the afflicted brains' structure, and then urged proper exercise or restraint of these functions so that individuals might return to well-adjusted lives. This might be as simple as making available proper diet and exercise and plenty of fresh air or encouraging temperance, rest from strenuous mental exertions, and abstinence from masturbation. It also might involve prescribing drugs or laxatives, or selectively bleeding inmates (usually with leeches), to relieve the pressure of blood on certain organs. Directors of the spate of new state asylums that arose in this period—Amariah Brigham at the Retreat for the Insane at Hartford, Connecticut; Samuel B. Woodward at the Massachusetts State Lunatic Asylum in Worcester; and Dr. Isaac Ray at the State Hospital for the Insane at Augusta, Maine, among them—all endorsed phrenology as an aid to working with their patients.

Those incarcerated for crime constituted another population ripe for phrenological analysis and rehabilitation. As public opinion turned from a belief that criminals were inherently evil to viewing them as unfortunately deficient in mental and moral development, wardens at new penitentiaries—the word itself suggests that therein the criminal could recognize and lament his behavior as aberrant—turned to phrenology to understand their inmates. Many people no longer regarded incarceration as a way to make an inmate "pay" for a crime but as an opportunity to address whatever had turned him (or her) to antisocial behavior. Again, the phrenologist could discover the imbalance in the criminal's brain and suggest ways toward its correction.

Wardens at the Pennsylvania State Prison; the New York penitentiary at Ossining (Sing Sing), where Eliza Farnham, head of the women's department, enthusiastically embraced the Fowlers' insights; and the Massachusetts State Prison at Charlestown, looked to phrenology to help them understand a prisoner's unique history and opportunity for rehabilitation. A lively debate followed as these officials contested over whether reformation was best accomplished through extended solitary confinement and enforced silence, as practiced in the Pennsylvania system, or a "congregate" system like that used in the Auburn, New York, prison, where inmates mingled at meals and at requisite classes in religious and moral instruction.

But in both systems, phrenology was a common denominator. Popular practitioner Charles Caldwell's *New Views of Penitentiary Discipline* (1829) exemplified the genre of advice literature on this topic that was found on the Fowlers' shelves.

All such reforms circled back to the premise that, because the brain is an organ, *physical* well-being is essential to a healthy life. Thus, in addition to frequent testimonials on behalf of a vegetarian diet, the Fowlers advocated abstinence from all stimulants, like coffee, tea, and tobacco and, of course, from hard liquor. They also proselytized for dress reform, inveighing particularly loudly against women's tight lacing with corsets or belts, and endorsing the loose pantaloons developed by Amelia Bloomer, popular at radical communities like Brook Farm because it gave women more freedom of movement as well as the opportunity for healthier posture and respiration.

These reforms led naturally, and most radically, to the Fowlers' involvement with the crusade to improve relations—including physical—between the sexes. Lorenzo's wife, Lydia, for example, along with her friends Elizabeth Oakes Smith and Mary Gove Nichols, was among the first women to lecture to audiences of women (they excluded men from the audiences) on anatomy and hygiene, offerings much in demand. Nichols had come to the Fowlers' attention through her commitment to hydropathy. With her husband, Thomas Low Nichols, she operated the American Hydropathic Institute, where eager students trained in the water cure.

For Orson Fowler, such frenetic commitment to all aspects of bodily health eventually led to his final hobbyhorse, the built environment. Influenced by the great number of publications on rural homes and cottages, at Fishkill on the Hudson River he designed and built an octagonal home (from new construction material resembling grout or concrete) in the belief that the building's almost spherical interior offered the most comfortable and healthy configuration for a domicile. He became so enamored of the eight-sided house's implications for contributing to a healthy life that he penned *A Home for All, or the Gravel Wall and Octagonal Mode of Building* (1842).

His own version of the building was immense: with four stories and seventy feet high, topped with a cupola for a skylight, his home had such new inventions as water closets, a hot-air furnace, and speaking tubes to communicate between rooms and floors. Nor did Fowler neglect the need for proper exercise. Among the monstrosity's sixty-five rooms were a gymnasium and large dance floor. Eventually, the house served not only as his home but also as a venue for lectures and courses on all subjects relating to and emanating from phrenology. Termed "Fowler's Folly" because of its huge size and unorthodox floor plan, it was a monument to his sincere belief in the connection of all parts of man's existence.

The Fowlers' ascent over all things that promised a renewed United States of America continued through the 1850s, after they relocated to 308 Broadway, just below Edward Anthony's "National Daguerreian Depot," filled with photographic images of the nation's celebrities as well as of common folk. With Orson now more often off on lecture tours or offering courses at his octagonal retreat on the Hudson, Lorenzo kept up a full schedule of lecturing and publishing in the city. The firm of Fowlers and Wells expanded its display of heads, adding the more sensational by including those of different races as well as of known criminals, each day becoming more like P. T. Barnum's famous museum of curiosities.

The success of Fowlers and Wells (after Orson withdrew, Fowler and Wells) proved far more enduring than Ripley's Brook Farm or Greeley's faith in phalanxes. It touched and influenced lives to an extent these reformers could only dream of. Through the 1850s, undimmed by the Panic of 1857, during the Civil War and beyond, Fowler and Wells remained among the nation's most prolific and successful publishers of advice literature, a vast enterprise still rooted in the perceived insights afforded by phrenology.

Seductive Diversion

What does one make of this remarkable movement and its appeal to all segments of the American population? Frederic Henry Hedge, one of the original members of the Transcendentalist circle and a clergyman in Bangor, Maine, offered an early, if dismissive, answer. Phrenology "appeals simply and solely to the senses," and therefore was suited to "the humblest capacity and the coarsest taste." Because phrenologists laid out their premises in the form of "a map," any man, woman, or child who took the trouble to spend a few hours with the map and learned "the names of its different provinces, with their respective locations, may rise up a philosopher," just as the Fowlers and their myriad acolytes promised.[45] Hedge's critique was more right than he appreciated.

The change that phrenologists' customers sought so avidly had nothing to do with an overturned political or economic order but the "perfection" of the same one in which they lived. From Clinton Hall there thus never emanated any talk of a need for concerted group action or large-scale structural reform. The problems besetting America were in fact problems besetting individual Americans, and phrenology offered a quick and easy way to discover what precisely in one's constitution needed attention. Phrenologists did not view, say, the poverty and attendant crime that followed the Panic of 1837—or the horror of chattel slavery—as an economic matter. Instead, they sought to lift individuals—whether Northern mechanics or Southern overseers—from whatever pits into which they had fallen by addressing their individual bodily health: stop drinking, eliminate tight lacing, and eat more vegetables. These were the keys to healthier bodies and minds, and in turn the means of ending aberrant, antisocial behavior. And similar to so many other contemporary reforms, if the desired change did not come about, the fault lay with the individuals.

The secret to the Fowlers' success was how little was asked of individuals compared to how much was promised. Admittedly, by contemporary standards, many of the reforms with which phrenologists were associated were remarkably novel and some decidedly unorthodox. In 1840, it was unusual to throw open the windows in the dead of winter to let in fresh air; it was challenging to abstain from stimulants in an age of excessive alcohol consumption; and it was novel for women to attend lectures at which they heard about the intricacies of their reproductive organs. Phrenologists and innumerable reformers promised that through sacrifice and self-education, a person could learn to develop his or her character and discover guidance from the spirit within. Crucially, this was a promise with far-reaching consequences: not only could each individual realize his or her best self, but by extension the insane could cure themselves and criminals reform themselves. No less essential to the Fowlers' success and the wide appeal of the reforms they urged, book by book, was the promise of the new and improved world that beckoned and whose arrival demanded refining the individual rather than overhauling social relations.

A glance at what the Fowlers had to say in their *New Illustrated Self-Instructor in Phrenology and Physiology* about the trait of "Acquisitiveness" illustrates this point. Cognate characteristics, they noted, were economy, frugality, "the acquiring, saving, and hoarding instinct," a desire to possess and own, and a love of amassing property. If one's acquisitiveness was highly developed, they continued, a person was too eager to attain wealth, too "close" in making bargains. He gave his "entire energies to acquiring property," "palm[ed] off inferior articles for good ones," and bought more than he could pay for. At the other end of the scale, he whose tendency was little-developed neither heeded nor knew the value of money, was wasteful, spent all he had, lacked industry, and was always in need.

The point was, no one should want to reside in either category, rapacious or needy, but rather to strive to attain just the right balance of each trait. For this, the Fowlers advised what we might call judicious immersion in the contemporary market economy: to develop one's acquisitiveness one should economize his "time and means," engage in "mercenary" business, "determine to get rich, and use the means for so doing," save as much as one can to be able to buy real estate or get into business, and "do by intellect what you are not disposed to do by intuition."[46] In other words, one should pursue the kind of activities that make an individual economically independent. One should strive to become precisely the sort of businessman who increased the nation's prosperity, without interrogating its basis or asking to what end, other than the acquisition of more wealth and property, it led.

Through simple lessons like these a person learned to develop his character. But, again, as this example indicates, phrenology never challenged but rather supported and reinforced the American economic and political system in its general contours as it then functioned. But what did any of this have to do with the recent catastrophic economic depression or the ever more threatening sectional divide threatening to split the country?

Phrenology simply offered people an easy way to feel positive. It convinced them that they retained a high degree of control over lives that otherwise seemed to be spinning out of control, at the mercy of large, impersonal forces few understood. Phrenology thus aligned with other seemingly radical but similarly safe cultural shifts. Unitarians and Transcendentalists, for example, stressed an ethic of self-culture; Protestant denominations emulated Methodism's success and began to emphasize man's free will; the medical profession made the mind comprehensible as a physical entity whose functions could be understood like those of any other organ.

In *Nature* (1836), Emerson's seminal philosophical statement that became the fountainhead of Transcendentalism, he declared that the two key precepts of the age were "Study Nature" and "Know Thyself." Orson Fowler offered the same advice, without recourse to Emerson's elaborate philosophical apparatus. The brain, an organ like the heart or lungs, influenced behavior. Study it, a part of nature, and one could take the next step, to know one's self. It was that simple, that easy, and that seductive. Further, it allowed one to avoid hard questions about the deeper failure of a social and economic system that each year brought the nation closer to full-scale cataclysm, a tragedy looming on the horizon even as Orson Fowler built his octagonal mansion above the Hudson River. Tangible proof of that conflict had come in 1858, when Sizer had taken the measure of John Brown, just back from "Bloody Kansas."

5

Mary Gove Nichols: Individual Health and Sovereignty

While antebellum reformers turned inward to discover the well-springs of both personal and universal improvement, for most the point of that effort was publicly to declare, and demonstrate, realized benefits. Indeed, public demonstrations—whether by utopian community or new banking system—and public education—whether one-on-one in consultation with a phrenologist or in auditoriums filled with people awaiting a lecture—were understood to be a crucial means of realizing the better world beckoning. Some reformers, like Horace Greeley, were politically active, but a majority of the most vocal reformers did not turn first or sometimes ever to the slow gears of democracy with its promise of incremental improvements. What need was there for the corrupted and corruptible mechanisms of man when universal, God-inspired, and God-authored levers of change waited to be thrown? And if the world proved disinterested, or, worse, condemnatory, one choice was to retire from the world.

The life of Mary Gove Nichols exemplified this path. Her career as a reformer was unusual. The *New York Herald*, for example, did not know whether to label her "saint, *savante,* serpent, or whatever," but admitted that she was "an extraordinary woman."[1] And even though in these antebellum years her radicalism ended in a philosophical defense of extreme individualism, it derived from her espousal of women's rights and of a novel understanding of relations between the sexes that she and her second husband, Thomas Low Nichols, drew from none other than Greeley's champion, Charles Fourier.

Beginning in the 1840s, Mary explored and entered the wider world of reform in large measure through her association with other denizens of the Fowlers' offices, particularly erstwhile-daguerreotypist and then hydropathist Joel Shew, whose residence at 47 Bond Street was a meeting place for many of the city's more radical reformers and thinkers. There, for example, she met the eccentric Marx Edgeworth Lazarus from North Carolina, who combined interests in Fourierist harmony with Swedenborgian correspondence, and penned several books that openly broached "passional" affinities in ways that Brook Farm members and even the pioneering feminist Margaret Fuller, had never dared. Lazarus stressed what he called "passional hygiene," grafting Fourier's psychology onto vegetarianism and other health reforms.[2] Not surprisingly, Fowlers and Wells published his work.

In her late thirties, Mary met Thomas Low Nichols, who shared her interests in health reform and whom she eventually married. Here they were supported by yet another of the Fowlers' circle, Stephen Pearl Andrews, who with Josiah Warren started the unusual utopian community of Modern Times (now Brentwood) on Long Island and who, as an extension of his interest in the utter sovereignty of the individual, himself became a vociferous advocate of free love.

Mary Gove Nichols's belief that self-knowledge—in this case, of the whole physical being—was central to human happiness propelled her circuitous journey along these highways and byways of antebellum reform. Friends like the Fowlers, who analyzed the skull as an indicator of an individual's tendencies and motivations, or Shew and other hydropathists, who focused primarily on bodily well-being, operated on parallel courses, but their interest in and commitment to the more radical implications of Mary's writings always remained more theoretical than practical.[3]

From tragic personal experience, Mary gradually had recognized that true happiness depended on different, more equal sexual relations, including acceptance of women's desire for physical pleasure in them. Why? This central aspect of peoples' lives mirrored the patterns that the deity had established in nature, something that Fourier had stressed in his extensive writings on social reorganization, and that others following him mirrored or modified in various ways. Once Mary realized this and as well its relation to the sacred integrity of each individual, she challenged her contemporaries to confront and understand how in some cases marriage could become another kind of slavery. When such marriages led to debilitating emotional poverty and attendant bodily illness, she urged, again against the popular will, the remedy of divorce.

A Disastrous Marriage

Mary Gove Nichols was born Mary Neal in Goffstown, near Manchester in southern New Hampshire, in 1810, a decade or so before the construction of textile factories along the Piscataquog River transformed the area into one of the region's manufacturing centers. Her father, William Neal, was a farmer and locally notorious freethinker who exercised much influence over Mary's intellectual development: there was nothing he enjoyed more than having his daughter, whom he had taken pains to educate at an early age, read to him from Voltaire or Paine.[4]

William brought to the family three children from a previous marriage, and Mary was the second of the three children he would have with his second wife, Rebecca Neal. In some ways, Rebecca was more traditional than her freethinking spouse, particularly in her demands that from a young age her daughter Mary assume household duties. After the death of Mary's older half-sister of consumption, the family moved up country, to Craftsbury, Vermont. There, anguished by her sister's death, Mary searched for a faith whose consolation her father, ever the infidel, always had denied her.[5] In Goffstown, Mary had watched and listened as a Methodist minister attended the dying Emma; but in the tiny town of Craftsbury she found only one church, a Presbyterian one. Then, through her now-voluminous reading, she discovered the Society of Friends' ethic of self-denial and frugality, and soon became a believer, and the only Quaker in town. Later, she vividly described this trying period of her life as a religious seeker (as she did other parts of her youth and adolescence) in her autobiographical novel, *Mary Lyndon; or, Revelations of a Life* (1855).[6]

Severe economic woes soon engulfed the family. In the wake of a failed business partnership in which William Neal was a principal, the family's situation became dire. Cheated of his investment and left with nothing after an unscrupulous partner burned the company's warehouse, Neal fell ever more deeply into debt. The town forced him to work it off by chopping a hundred cords of wood, and his wife and daughters sewed clothes that they sold in the community. Even as she wished to assist her father, to escape this drudgery Mary decided to leave home and become a schoolteacher.

She first found work in a neighboring town, where through reading she also was able to continue her ever-broadening education. She was particularly interested in physiology and medicine, in part another consequence of her having watched the tragic death of her half-sister and trying to understand its cause. She had fallen ill after venturing out in the cold in inadequate, stylish clothes, including a tight corset. Typically, the lessons drawn would be of a coquettish daughter who ignored her parents' pleas and suffered the ultimate penalty. Mary, however, resolved to learn all that she could about the human body, even though most deemed the subject improper for a "lady" to study.

Eventually Mary began to meet other Quakers, who favorably impressed her. One, a woman who commanded her husband's respect and was the moral and spiritual center of her family, set an example Mary long remembered. Then, Mary's uncle, who also had found his way to Quakerism, introduced her to Hiram Gove, another Friend and a hatter by occupation. Aware that Quakers urged marriage inside the faith, and with few other prospects to consider, Mary precipitately, and soon to her profound regret, accepted Hiram's marriage proposal.

As Mary relates the story in her autobiographical novel, even before their vows she knew that she was making a mistake, for she never had really loved the man.[7] She tried to back out, but pressured by Quakers, neighbors, and family, she felt powerless to extricate herself.[8] The couple exchanged vows in the spring of 1831, and a long, terrible decade would pass before she was able to free herself from the hell this union created. "I was pledged to Death and Hell," she explained in *Mary Lyndon,* "driven back into the fire from which my spirit shrunk in every nerve."[9] In her first ten years of marriage, for example, Mary went through five pregnancies, with only one live birth.[10] Before the ordeal ended, Mary would entertain increasingly radical thoughts about marriage and, in particular, under what conditions women should be allowed to divorce. As the laws stood, a woman had virtually no rights. She could bring suit only for a husband's explicit act of adultery, not for any cruelty or abuse, no matter how excessive, toward her.

Not long after the wedding, Hiram began to coerce her physically as well as psychologically, again something she reported but did not describe with any specificity in her *Mary Lyndon.* The result was predictable—both deep depression and frequent illnesses brought on by unhappiness and her debilitated state. Then, slowly but inexorably, Mary began to attribute the horror and pain of her experiences with her husband to her lack of knowledge about how to control her sexuality. The only way that she could exercise a degree of control over the horrors he represented, she concluded, was to learn more about her body. During her marriage, this interest, originally awakened by her half-sister's untimely death, grew into an obsession. She decided to pursue, as much as she could, given her husband's tight control over her, her interest in physiology, and in particular to study female anatomy. The more she learned, the more she wished to share her new knowledge, particularly with other women. This inward search reflected, and soon fueled, nineteenth-century America's burgeoning health reform movement.

To realize her aspiration, Mary needed to establish a reputation for expertise. A child, an abusive husband, and mounting debt all stood in her way. Her first priority was her only child, Elma, who, given her disgust with Hiram, was her great solace. In whatever spare time she had, Mary struggled to make the family's ends meet, through sewing and other such domestic tasks. Soon, she was able to add a few more dollars to the family coffer by writing stories for periodicals, a skill that she would hone and use to very different purposes when she turned to questions of reform. Meanwhile, because of their still-straitened financial situation, Hiram became more abusive and paranoid, monitoring and restricting his wife's movements outside the home, reading her correspondence, and otherwise oppressing her. To make matters worse, to escape his violent temper Mary had to do virtually anything that he asked. As she later put it, again without saying exactly what he did to her, "He arrogated the rule over my soul and body, with the utmost confidence."[11]

On the cusp of the Panic of 1837, the Goves moved to Lynn, Massachusetts, the shoemaking capital of New England, where Hiram hoped that they could find decent-paying work. Here, in good measure because of the increasingly dire economic situation after the panic, Mary began to display an independent, entrepreneurial streak that would increasingly mark her relations with Hiram. Recalling her earlier success as a teacher, she told him that she wanted to open a school for girls, an idea that at first he resisted. But she persisted, and after she described the potential income such work would bring, soon enough the family had the benefit of the class's tuition. By law, however, all her earnings devolved to Hiram, who held them parsimoniously.

Mary Gove's next step was even more daring. Somehow she managed to elude her husband's pathological vigilance and attended a lecture by prominent health reformer Sylvester Graham. His counsel of strict diet and accompanying bodily self-control spoke to and inspired Mary, so much so that she soon began to operate her school on Grahamite principles, feeding her students on fruits, vegetables, and grains, and making sure that they got plenty of exercise. Dr. Harriot K. Hunt, who became one of the country's first woman physicians, visited the school in 1838 and, noting Mary's own ill health—she suffered from consumption—criticized her strict regimen. "This is frequently the case with downright ultras," Hunt wrote, "they ruin their own health, and then prescribe rules for everybody."[12]

Forging a Career

More importantly, sitting in a crowded auditorium to hear Graham inspired Mary Gove to think that she, too, might draw crowds— in her case, of women—on the topic of health, particularly as it pertained to their bodies. So, in 1838, married to a ne'er-do-well who provided little income for his family and whose needs were particularly pressing in the wake of the financial meltdown the previous year, Mary formally began her career in public speaking. Inspired by such women pioneers as champion of the working classes Frances Wright and antislavery advocates Sarah and Angelina Grimké, and mindful of Graham's recent success in Lynn, Mary decided to offer lectures on women's health in that city, even as she knew that she would have to endure the condemnation of

Friends and others who thought such public exposure unbecoming a woman.

To her relief, her initial lectures were well received, and Hiram tolerated her new direction because of the money her speaking brought in. Before long the Ladies Physiological Society of Boston, a group started a year earlier by health reformer William Alcott, invited her to repeat them. Alcott was yet another of the Fowlers' friends. Mistrusting the medical profession, he urged people to learn to care for themselves. He believed that women would prove keen to hear about their health from other women, and he generously invited Mary to offer a series of twelve weekly lectures on topics that ranged from basic descriptions of bones and musculature (as well as of the sexual organs), proper diet, bathing, and exercise, to the dangers of masturbation and too-tight lacing of undergarments.

Alcott's hunch was correct, for women flocked to hear one of their own broach such subjects. The series drew several hundred auditors eager to hear how they might better know and care for their bodies, whose unhealthy treatment—from improper drugs to ill-fitting and harmful clothing—Mary identified and explained as sources of illness and disease. Again, Hiram evidently allowed her to follow this novel career path because it guaranteed an income that he, as her husband, controlled.

One young attendee enthusiastically wrote her friend abolitionist Abby Kelley about the lectures. She noted Mary Gove's daring in speaking out as she did on topics little if ever discussed in public. Referring to press reports about the lectures, Anna Breed wrote, "She is censured, ridiculed, and misrepresented, of course." But Breed added, because Mary had "a pretty good share of independence," she would not be "much affected by the sarcasms inflicted upon her." Perhaps most tellingly, Breed also remarked on the audience: she had "never before seen so intelligent looking a company of Women together in this place" as she saw that night.[13]

A few months later, Mary repeated this series in Boston to equally
enthusiastic crowds. The daughter of Scottish phrenologist George
Combe, who was then on his famous American tour, heard and
raved about Mary to her father. His child's reaction so impressed
Combe that he subsequently defended Mary from increasingly
frequent detractors in the New York press. He was particularly
incensed at James Gordon Bennett's New York *Morning Herald*,
which could not decide if Mary was "more of heaven than of hell."
Bennett had sent a reporter disguised in women's clothes to her
lectures in the city in 1839 so that he could know exactly what she
was saying.[14]

Combe countered by condemning the paper's editor for publishing "what he pretends to be reports of her lectures, pandering
to the groveling feelings of the men, and alarming the delicacy
of the ladies."[15] Such publicity only fueled interest in Mary Gove's
talks. Earlier, in Providence, Rhode Island, she had filled all 750
seats of a lecture hall. She repeated her presentations with equal
success in Philadelphia, where, for the first time (and proof of the
city's much-vaunted liberality), she spoke, again approvingly, before mixed audiences. Women's rights advocate Lucretia Mott attended the series and wrote a friend, "much opposition has been
acted out here to Mrs. Mary S. Gove." She has been "disowned by
the Orthodox," she continued, and has been "slandered by others,"
but Mott welcomed her because of the need for "that subject [female
anatomy]" to be "properly presented to females."[16]

Jealous of his wife's newfound success, Hiram began to keep
closer tabs on her whereabouts. Given Mary's belief in the essential goodness of humanity, she continued—too generously—to
attribute Hiram's violent psychological and physical behavior to illness rather than to moral depravity. Understood in this way, Hiram
was amenable to reform, if only he would undertake the hard work
of self-improvement. From what Mary had learned of physiology,

she believed that from a young age he had been twisted into libidinous perversion, causing him to behave toward her as he did. Hiram, however, did not visit the local phrenologist. He showed no signs of self-awareness, let alone a willingness to improve. By the next year, 1839, Mary had had enough of his cruelty and began to plan what decisive action she might take to free herself and her beloved daughter from him. She did so knowing that the legal system offered her no protection and, further, that if she took their daughter against Hiram's will, she was technically committing a crime.

Breakout and Breakaway

As Mary considered ways to escape her plight, she had continued success as a health reformer. She placed her writings in various health journals throughout the Northeast and continued to expand her public engagements. In 1841 in Baltimore, she broached the subject of women's rights for the first time. Later, in Lynn, she spoke before a local debating society and repeated her effort on the sphere and condition of women.[17] In 1841, too, she escaped Hiram's clutches, if only temporarily, after she finally unburdened herself to her parents.[18] With their encouragement and support, she decided on the then-extraordinary step of leaving her husband and moving in with them, taking along Elma. By law, Hiram Gove could reclaim his daughter at any time; but he was considerably in debt to Mary's father, who threatened Hiram with civil action unless he left Elma and Mary alone. Hiram took the threat seriously, and Mary's life finally stabilized. But she knew that divorce was the only permanent answer to her situation, even though such legal recourse had been made virtually impossible by her having abandoned her husband. Hiram would have to bring the suit for divorce against her.

Soon Mary's life became even more complicated, for after she published her first book, *Lectures to Ladies on Anatomy and Physiology* (1842), derived from her popular public lectures, she met and fell in love with Henry Gardiner Wright, an attractive and compelling Englishman interested in all sorts of reform, including dietary—he was a confirmed Grahamite.[19] Wright had come to the United States with his friend Charles Lane and the American Transcendentalist Bronson Alcott, who had been visiting England. The latter was planning to establish a utopian venture, Fruitlands, upon his return to Massachusetts. Lane eventually signed on to what quickly proved an abortive attempt at plain living and high thinking in rural Harvard, Massachusetts; but Wright, disappointed in Alcott's lack of organization, demurred and went his own way.

In the autumn of 1842, entranced by Mary, Wright moved to Lynn, where, nothing if not forward, he boarded in her parents' home.[20] He was married and had a family in England; but it was clear, as Mary revealed in *Mary Lyndon*, that they became lovers. "Soothingly," she wrote, "his musical words fell on my spiritual ear. It was not a man or a friend who asked me to be myself, to be quiet and happy. It was the True Life in him."[21] The next year the two began to issue *The Health Journal and Independent Magazine*; and with Gardiner bitten by the utopian bug, they began to solicit subscriptions for their own planned community, in the West. Sadly, this idyll of like-minded souls could not last, for Wright grew seriously ill with some sort of abscess or tumor on his shoulder blade. "Six months at times of keenest anguish and pain, and again of unendurable suffering," she remembered. "Six months of living love, which heaven may parallel, but not excel; six months of teaching in the deepest wisdom earth has known, all gone."[22]

At first Wright tried the water cure, with which he was enamored and to whose theory he introduced Mary; but he finally had to submit to surgery. It proved unsuccessful; and, in great pain and obviously failing, he returned to England for further treatment. As he departed from New York, the couple, no doubt aware that they were whistling in the dark, made further plans for their projected community in the Ohio River Valley. Wright died that same year, before he could see his lover again. Compounding tragedy, late in the year Mary's father died, of consumption. Both her bliss with Wright as well as the protection from Hiram that she had enjoyed had vanished.

Hiram, seething from what he had heard of his wife's liaison with Wright, soon made his move. In the spring of 1845, when Mary was absent on a speaking tour in Ohio and Pennsylvania, he went to the Neal home in Lynn and took Elma.[23] When Mary returned, she was frantic. Despairing of reclaiming her daughter through any legal means, with help from a friend she took the remarkable step of kidnapping Elma and going into hiding.[24] By law, Hiram could not bring charges against his own wife. He thus sued her accomplice in the abduction, who eventually settled the case for damages, which Mary helped to pay. But she again had her daughter, if not still her full independence.

The Water Cure

Influenced by her paramour Wright's attempts at recovery through the water cure, Mary decided to visit a recently established facility in Brattleboro, Vermont, devoted to that treatment. She liked what she saw and decided to train as a water cure physician in order to add this science to her repertoire. The therapy, initiated and popularized in Europe in the 1820s, was still fairly novel in the United States. It had arisen on the Continent after the Silesian farmer Vincent Priessnitz successfully healed himself after his ribs had been crushed in an accident.

Doctors doubted that he could recover, but Priessnitz got the idea to soak a bandage in cold water and, after he had aligned his ribs, to wrap himself tightly with it to secure them in place. That wasn't all. Over the next week and a half he also drank much cold water, and he attributed his remarkable healing to this unorthodox treatment. He subsequently used similar methods on animals as well as patients who had heard of his success, and became convinced that he had come upon a new way of treating injury and disease.

In the late 1820s Priessnitz established the Gräfenberg Water Cure facility, which soon flourished. There, patients drank great quantities of water, were wrapped with various sized sheets and towels soaked in either hot or cold water (depending on one's malady), and had their bodies rubbed vigorously with towels or "flesh" brushes after they bathed. They also ate a bland diet, with no spicy, or even cooked, food, and had vigorous daily exercise, all toward the goal of purging their bodies of the causes of the various illnesses that they suffered. Mary became an eager convert. In 1845 at Brattleboro, where German-trained Dr. Robert Wesselhoeft had recently opened an elaborate spa, Mary engrossed herself in the cure's theory and practice.

At first the water cure was regarded as quackery advocated by a few eccentrics but soon became an integral part of the period's culture of reform. As such, it demonstrated that culture's guiding assumptions, most especially its all inclusiveness: through the transformation and redemption of the individual, it promised the entire society's reformation. How? In this it much resembled phrenology and its ability to both identify and address an individual's weaknesses. The water cure promised personal improvement through proper hygiene, itself based in better self-management. In turn, this spawned better-adjusted individuals who, having successfully cared for themselves, could extend such improvement to others. Thus, particularly in the United States, the water cure became yet another panacea perfectly tailored to people who considered individual sovereignty a bedrock value.

Although the benefits of fresh air, cold bathing, and soaking in mineral springs had been known for centuries, Priessnitz and his followers went further. They proclaimed water the universal panacea. Priessnitz's chief innovation had been to wrap the patient's entire body in a wet sheet and then in layers of dry blankets to induce sweating. Earlier advocates of "water cures" had just applied local compresses to particular injuries; Priessnitz's method laid claim to a more compete cure of physical and psychological ills. By the 1840s, his retreat in the mountains of Silesia catered to over fifteen hundred individuals a year, European royalty among them.[25]

Priessnitz's theory was simple. Health was the natural, positive condition of the body, and disease the unnatural, negative condition. Left alone, the body would heal diseases produced by external causes, except things like broken bones or conditions needing immediate surgery to correct. Water ingested and applied in various ways accelerated the process by disrupting and expelling any foreign matter that caused illness. Toward this end, Priessnitz sought to initiate in his patients times of "crisis," when the disease grew acute and manifested itself in sores, boils, rashes, fever, diarrhea, sweating, and the like. Such symptoms, according to his theory, indicated the beginning of the healing process. Water facilitated these effects, and to expedite healing, patients underwent the requisite wrapping and sweating, were harshly rubbed, and were subjected to strong streams of water, all to cleanse the body internally.[26]

In the 1840s in the United States water cure disciples Joel Shew and Russell Thacher Trall were most responsible for its popularity, the former its most effective publicist, the latter its most skilled theorist, enshrining it into a comprehensive healing philosophy, which Trall termed "Hygenic Medication." As he wrote in his *Hydropathic Encyclopedia* (1840), the sick individual usually suffered from some combination of impure blood, unhealthy secretions, obstructions in the blood's circulation, or imbalance in the proper working of various organs. There followed a concomitant loss of balance "in the circulation and action of the various parts of the vital machinery, producing a great discord in some portion of it, and more or less disorder in all."[27]

And what caused these imbalances? Bad air, improper light, ill-suited food and drink indolence or its opposite, overstimulation, and unregulated passions. Importantly, all of these were things subject to the individual's control. If one succumbed to disease, the hydropathist helped restore bodily harmony. Using water as a catalyst, he removed the patient's obstructions, rid him of impurities, supplied him with the proper food, and relaxed him into a state conducive for the body to heal.

Dead set against allopathic medicine as he was, the hydropathist also urged patients to abandon all medication and, instead, to effect hygienic reformation through self-reliance and attendant self-control. An individual's health was a matter of his whole being. Determined self-regulation was the key to restoring the body's proper balance. At first, a patient might enlist the hydropathist's guidance, but, because of the cure's simplicity, its principles could be practiced by any who had gone through the treatment or purchased one of the many self-help guides that proliferated in the 1840s and 1850s.

Mary went to Wesselhoeft's facility in Brattleboro just after it opened in May 1845. Catharine Beecher, a well-known female educator who took the baths there in 1847, left vivid testimony of the regimen. "At four in the morning," she wrote, she was

> packed up in a wet sheet; kept in it from two to three hours; then up, and in a reeking perspiration immersed in the coldest plunge-bath. Then a walk as far as strength would allow, and drink five or six tumblers of the coldest water. At eleven A.M. stand under a douche of the coldest water falling *eighteen feet, for ten minutes.* Then walk, and drink three or four tumblers of water. At three P.M. sit half an hour in a *sitz* bath

[i.e., sitting bath] of the coldest water. Then walk and drink again. At nine P.M. sit half an hour with the feet in the coldest water, then rub them till warm. Then cover the weak limb and a third of the body in wet bandages, and *retire to rest.* The same wet bandage to be worn all day, and kept constantly wet.[28]

Impressed, her sister Mrs. Harriet Beecher Stowe, who had not yet written *Uncle Tom's Cabin,* booked time at the facility.[29]

Usually, patients who came to facilities like Brattleboro or Gräfenberg and endured such a regimen complained of asthma, dyspepsia, gout, or nervous exhaustion, sometimes called neurasthenia. They remained from one to three months and paid from five to ten dollars a week for the treatment, including room and board, though they had to bring their own sheets, towels, and blankets. They left restored, rejuvenated, and able to meet the demands and pressures of the increasingly complex outside world, based as it was on the new market economy.

Mary realized that a central part of the experience involved just this sort of removal from the inordinate stress of everyday life. "The great trouble with Americans is that they are in too great a hurry," she observed, particularly, in a hurry to "eat and drink," and "to get rich." Then, "they get ill as fast as they can," she continued, "and they want a short cut to health," even though such "chronic disease that has been . . . induced by wrongdoing through half a lifetime, cannot be cured in a day or by any process now known."[30] Hence, the emphasis during the water cure on exercise and relaxation to effect eventual reinvigoration.

Mary trained at Wesselhoeft's spa for three months and then went to another, in New Lebanon, New York, to serve as resident physician. She enjoyed this experience but after another three months was, ironically, exhausted from overwork. She moved to New York City, where she and Elma boarded for a short while with Shew and his wife at 47 Bond Street. To help ends meet, she began to organize a new course of physiology classes for women. To support Elma in the art lessons she wished to take, Mary also wrote for popular periodicals as varied as *Godey's Lady's Book* and the *Democratic Review.* They remained in the city for the next six years.

Finding Fourier, Finding Love

Mary Gove also traveled farther into the world of utopian reform. She had considered Fourier's ideas as early as 1841–1842, when she wrote about them in a Lynn newspaper. She lectured on Association in 1842–1843, appearing on the same platform with Fourier's chief American disciple, Albert Brisbane, and in her western travels had visited the Columbia Phalanx in Ohio.[31] She even attempted to enroll her daughter Elma in Brook Farm's school and pay her tuition by giving a series of lectures but, for some reason—it may have had to do with the community's need for cash, much of which was brought in by the school—the directors did not take up her offer.[32]

With Brook Farm members John Allen and David Barlow, Mary edited the short-lived Associationist journal, the *Social Reformer* (1844), which was later absorbed into the *Phalanx,* the organ of American Fourierism, to which she also contributed.[33] She also wrote for former Brook Farm member and Association supporter William Henry Channing's *The Present.*[34] This periodical carried contributions from Transcendentalist and women's rights advocate Margaret Fuller as well as translations from the French of Fourierist Victor Considérant and of Pierre Leroux's *De l'Humanité,* a volume that had much interested mutual banking advocate William B. Greene.

At the Shews' home she met twenty-two-year-old Marx Edgeworth Lazarus, whose enthusiasm for what he termed Fourier's promise of "passional harmony" equaled that of Brisbane and Parke Godwin, another of Fourier's chief American proselytizers. And by "passional," Lazarus was to write, he meant "all the relations of our senses and our social affections, of our material instincts and our spiritual affinities."[35] "Characters are distributed in categories," the figure based on him in Mary's roman à clef explained to Mary Lyndon. "I flatter myself," he continued, "we may have affinity," although there is no proof that they became intimate.[36] When Mary left the Shews to find cheaper lodging, Marx proposed that he, Mary, and her daughter locate a large home and, with others whom they would recruit, begin to live according to Fourier's principles as much as possible.

For a few months, Mary and Elma lived on their own but then did move into larger quarters with Lazarus, who had the financial means to afford such a rental. Mary used parts of the space to offer physiology classes to women and set up the embryo for her own hydropathic institute.[37] In May 1846, she offered a series of twenty lectures to twenty women who paid five dollars each to attend. All the while, she continued to see Lazarus and was particularly influenced by his views of Fourier's radical vision of sexual relations. Using the language and logic of the era and their milieu, Lazarus explained, "It is only the discriminative attainment of the relations toward which the passional fountain of our life eternally wells up that life becomes divine, and we escape from passional blasphemy." The blasphemy presumably alluded to what Mary endured with her husband, and the rest gave license to what she had enjoyed with Wright.[38]

Fourier envisioned a society free from the repression that characterized Western civilization. In his ideal communities— phalansteries—marriages would cease to be patriarchal and tyrannical. He foresaw a healthy, fluid sexuality, with procreation not necessarily linked to permanent relationships. In the phalanstery, for example, children would be separated from their parents at a young age and raised in common with others their own age, freeing the parents to develop meaningful relations with other men and women, if they so wished. Obviously, Mary found Fourier's theories germane to her own situation: for years she had been trapped in a horrible marriage sanctioned and protected by civil law, and as well had had a lover in what was considered a clear flouting of the marital bond. In a Fourierist community, however, she could have left Hiram Gove as soon as his violent and abusive behavior became obvious.

With new buoyancy, Mary continued her lecturing and publishing on issues of women's health, and began as well to publish fiction, under the pseudonym "Mary Orme."[39] Literary circles opened to her. One Christmas eve at a soirée, she heard a guest named Edgar Allan Poe read "The Raven," a long poem he had just published, and at another met Horace Greeley.[40] Poe remembered her as "below medium height, somewhat thin, with dark hair and keen, intelligent black eyes." She also "converse[d] and with enthusiasm," he noted, and "in many respects" was a "very interesting woman."[41] At yet another such gathering, she encountered Thomas Low Nichols.

At that first meeting Thomas did not impress—indeed, he came close to repulsing—her because of his highly affected manner. Mary thought him foppish, for his speech and dress reeked of a Broadway dandy: he wore a white waistcoat and white kid gloves, "a coat of faultless Parisian fit," and had a figure "as graceful as a gymnast." Even though she tried to discourage him, he showered her with attention. "I did not like the speech or the speaker," she later wrote. "He was too finely cut—too manifestly a gentleman. There was an ultra neatness and fashion about his dress, and a fastidious formalism to his address." And when he touched her arm, "a strange fire shot" through her "nerves and veins too powerful to be pleasant."[42] When she saw him again a week later at a New Year's party, however, she found herself drawn to him and increasingly fascinated. That night, she remembered, Thomas's presence electrified her. To speak in the Fourierist terms both she and he knew, their "passions" seemed particularly "aligned."[43]

Thomas's costume and manner belied his recent circulation in an unusual segment of New York City's publishing world, for a few years earlier he had been very much involved with what was called the "Flash" press. "Flash" was a code word for a group of periodicals that, under the guise of presenting sporting news, actually catered to a clientele who sought what amounted to quasi-pornographic—or at best titillating—journalism.[44] One newspaper described Thomas's works as "simply licentious and immoral."[45] In 1842 Thomas had edited the weekly *New York Arena,* in which he had broached topics appearing in more notorious papers but that showed a different perspective: his concerns more those of the health reformer asking questions about sexual hygiene rather than those of the prurient gossipmonger. This well may have contributed to Mary's increasing interest in him.

In editorials in the *Arena,* Thomas justified rather than condemned prostitution because of how it satisfied certain men's sexual needs that, unresolved, might push them to vice or crime. As he put it, it was "madness to expect [men] to refrain from intercourse with the other sex." Thus, the public should not condemn wholesale such outlets as prostitution, given its important purpose in the human sexual economy.[46] Admittedly, in these and other matters, Thomas represented the sexual avant-garde of the city, his writings reflecting the same openness about relationships that made him attractive to Mary Gove.

Thomas Low Nichols

Like his future spouse, Thomas Low Nichols was born in New Hampshire, in the town of Orford in 1815, the son of a Baptist minister. After attending the local academy, he enrolled at the Dartmouth

Medical School but stayed only a semester. He took to the road, lecturing on phrenology and mesmerism. By his own admission, however, Thomas still had some wild oats to sow. He slid into bad habits, moved to Boston to indulge them, and supported himself through both lecturing and hack writing. For a couple of years, beginning in 1835, he there edited an anti-Catholic newspaper, the *Standard*. He also dabbled in mesmerism, for a report from 1836 places him as an assistant on a Boston stage to the French practitioner Charles Poyen, recently arrived in the United States and lecturing to large audiences. Thomas was described as "possessing the magnetic power."[47]

By 1837 he had wandered to Buffalo, where he worked for another newspaper and, in the wake of the panic, became embroiled in the furor over the bankruptcy of prominent local citizen Benjamin Rathbun, the area's foremost developer. When the economic meltdown reached that flourishing new city, Rathbun found his credit overextended and soon was reduced to forgery and bankruptcy. For reasons never made clear, in the *Commercial Advertiser* and also in another local paper, the *Herald,* Thomas persistently defended Rathbun, believing him wrongly accused, but soon found himself on trial for libel and then jailed (for four months) for having impugned the character of some of Buffalo's leading citizens. He recorded details of the tawdry episode in his entertaining *Journal in Jail.*[48]

By the end of 1841, Thomas had served his sentence and, after having spent some time in Rochester, he moved to New York City, where he worked for a variety of papers, including the *Aurora* and the above-mentioned *Arena*. He lived the life of a bon vivant, acquiring firsthand knowledge of some of the racy subjects he broached in his papers. He also published a novel, *Ellen Ramsay; or, The Adventures of a Greenhorn* (1843), in which he spoke to the various sexual relations, legal and not, that the metropolis made available. Herein, too, he demonstrated a radical openness on the subject of marriage.

Thomas's interests were well aligned with Mary's, and Mary eventually fell wholeheartedly in love with him. But what could they do while Mary Gove was still married? In Massachusetts, she wrote, their union would have been "a State's-prison offense, to be punished by years of incarceration and hard labor." Thus, she told readers, they saw how much freedom there was for "a true love and a true life in America."[49] Serendipitously, around the same time that Mary met Thomas, Hiram Gove found another woman he wished to marry.[50] He filed for divorce, on the grounds of Mary Gove's abandonment, and his plea was quickly granted. Mary and Elma finally emerged from the terrible shadow under which they had lived for so long, and Mary was now free to marry Thomas if the two so wished.

That they did in 1848, despite their experience of the ways in which a marriage was liable to go wrong. This was less hypocrisy than faith in the power of properly aligned passions, as Fourier had theorized them. In keeping with this broad understanding of how the world and God worked, Mary and Thomas invited a clergyman from the Church of the New Jerusalem, none other than George Bush, who wrote *Swedenborg and Mesmer,* to solemnize their vows.[51] By this point, as Poe noted, in addition to Mary's being "a mesmerist, phrenologist, a homeopath, and a disciple of Priessnitz, she was a Swedenborgian."[52] The choice was conscious and appropriate, for Emanuel Swedenborg's ideas about marriage—he believed in "conjugal love" based in a couple's spiritual union, and as well counseled divorce if they found that such proved not the case—meshed with their own. As early as the late 1830s Mary had requested of another Swedenborgian cleric exactly that title in which Swedenborg describes "spiritual" marriage.[53] Thomas and Mary Nichols now began a long, productive relationship devoted to health and marriage reform that only deepened over time, a truly "celestial" union, in Swedenborg's terms.

Thomas returned to medical school, at the University of the City of New York, and completed the course that he had commenced at Dartmouth many years earlier, and Mary continued her very visible educational lectures. In a spacious home at 89 West 22nd Street, she joined with her husband in offering medical services based on the water cure, to which she had converted him, as well as in more general principles of health and hygiene gleaned from Graham and others. The couple soon welcomed a baby girl, Mary Wilhelmina, born when Mary was forty years old and Elma, now a flourishing art student, eighteen.

Both Mary and Thomas were particularly influential through their sponsorship of hydropathy, described in Mary Nichols's *Experience in Water Cure* and Thomas Nichols's *An Introduction to Water Cure*, both issued in 1850. They saw through press other books, too. Mary, for example, never relinquished her wish to publish fiction; both her *Agnes Morris; or, The Heroine of Domestic Life* and *The Two Loves, or, Eros and Anteros* had appeared the year before, when Thomas published *Woman in All Ages and Nations*, a significant compendium about women's place in history and culture.

Their most ambitious joint undertaking was the opening of the American Hydropathic Institute, at 91 Clinton Place, in the late summer of 1851. There, over an intensive three-month period, in addition to being trained in hydrotherapy, students heard both Nichols lecture on anatomy, physiology, pathology, chemistry, surgery, obstetrics, and the like, offerings as rigorous as at any contemporary medical school, and were offered practicums in examination procedures. Guest lecturers spoke on such varied topics as phrenology, natural science, and moral philosophy. Significantly, the institute was coeducational, one of the first medical schools in the country to be so. "We want women," Mary told the first matriculates in words that might have been autobiographical, "who can break the bonds of custom, who are great enough to be emancipated from all that weakens, degrades, and destroys," and who will also teach other women "not to be independent of man, but that man and woman should be mutually dependent."[54] Their first graduating class included nine women, presumably with just such aspirations. Elated by their success, within two years the family relocated the facility to the country, at Port Chester, New York, where it continued to flourish.[55]

Esoteric Anthropology

In Port Chester, Thomas came into his own when he wrote his most important and controversial book, whose mysterious title, *Esoteric Anthropology,* he amply explained in the subtitle: *A Comprehensive and Confidential Treatise on the Structure, Functions, Passional Attractions and Perversions, True and False Physical and Social Conditions, and the Most Intimate Relations of Men and Women.* The 1850s saw other men with "M.D." affixed to their names who proffered coeducational advice about physiology and reproduction, but none with Thomas's particular bent, originating as it had in his interest in Fourier's principles.

In describing his intentions, Thomas was adamant that he did not write this work to lure in patients but in the hope that he would actually reduce the number of people who needed medical attention in the first place. And this was not an interest narrowly held in the physical health of the nation, but its health broadly understood. For "the material basis of all reform," he maintained, is health. Looking around him, what did he see? "Individuals are sick, communities are sick, nations are sick," and "the very earth" is now diseased. "All must be cured together," he acknowledged, even as "the work must be begun with the individual." Civilization's unfortunate situation could be rectified only when every man and woman purified and invigorated his or her life.[56]

In his first chapters Thomas detailed the anatomy and physiology of the human body, in text similar to what one could find in any popular medical book of the period. But when he moved on to the "Function of Generation," his radicalism emerged. Without embarrassment, he explained that, to do justice to this subject, he had to treat it with absolute freedom and, in so doing, introduce matters of human sexuality that other writers had not felt comfortable broaching.

For example, he was catholic in his understanding of men's and women's physical needs. Taking a cue from Fourier, who detailed hundreds of different personality types, Thomas explained how "the passion of love, or the propensity of Amativeness" (a phrenological term), varied between the sexes, and as well among individuals of each sex. As a consequence, "no natural passion, no healthy attraction of any being is wrong." Those who opposed any such because they believed it morally "wrong" produced only unhealthy "discord" in those individuals and, by implication, in society as a whole.[57]

Thomas was not afraid to follow this logic. It meant, for example, that homosexuality was as acceptable as heterosexuality. "I see no reason," Thomas wrote, "for punishing a man for an act which begins and ends with himself or with a consenting party." Moreover, "sodomy," he reminded readers, had been practiced "from the remotes ages, and is still so common in Eastern and tropical countries, as not to excite remark."[58]

Nor did he believe monogamy necessarily normative, for he saw it, too, as based in social convention. To make his point, he gave examples of people who indeed loved more than one person at the same time. "I knew one woman," he said, "who slept with two men on alternate nights, and she declared that she loved them both, and could not endure the thought of parting with either." Over three-quarters of the globe, he continued, "polygamy was tolerated, and more or less practiced." It was quite simply "absurd to suppose that no man ever loves more than one wife," and equally absurd to suppose that "European and American women, as long as they love their husbands, can love nobody else." In short, the whole notion of monogamy was insidious, "the parent of jealousy and all its tyrannies."[59]

Thomas also was very open and honest about the nature of sexual passion in women. Love between a man and a woman, he explained, was not based in mere lust but began in "spiritual attraction," then became "voluptuous desire," and finally found "its ultimate expression in sexual union." Women sought and experienced sexual pleasure as much as men did, and their virtue should not be impugned for doing so. Moreover, it followed that women also had the right to control when and how they sought such fulfillment.[60]

The worst came when two people never could achieve anything resembling "passional harmony" with each other. Mary's sad experience with Hiram Gove was a pressing case in point. Thomas explained that, while marriage was "the union of two persons in mutual love," adultery was, "perhaps, best defined as any gratification of mere lust, or the sensual nature, without the sanctification of a true love, and apart from the awful uses of marriage." Thus, he explained, "a true marriage may be what the laws call adultery, while the real adultery is an unloving marriage." The implication of such mismatches was clear. Those caught in unseemly relations had the right to leave them, to find true love. "A cursed despotism under the name of legal marriage, compels a woman to receive the embraces of a man she loathes, or, if she loves him, at the peril of her life."[61] This is what Mary had endured for years before she abandoned Gove.

Thomas also was equally frank in his section "Diseases of the Generative System," in which, among other things, he discussed masturbation. He was not embarrassed to reveal that it prevailed "to about an equal extent in both sexes," and that "probably not more than one person in ten, of either sex, entirely escapes it."[62]

Like other contemporary writers on the subject, he worried about its debilitating physical and psychological effects, but he then took his criticism in an unexpected direction. He warned that, by practicing this "secret licentiousness," women often became so *virtuous* as to hate the sight of a man, and abhor the idea of the holiest expression of mutual love," that is, regular intercourse. Thus, when a woman who frequently masturbated, married, she often was indifferent to her husband's embraces and "cold amid his ecstasies," yielding only to "his commands" to satisfy his passion and not from genuine love.[63] Thomas Nichols believed that sexual union's greatest delights were only attainable through reciprocity of feeling.

Moreover, to deny that a woman wished for and reacted to sex as powerfully as her partner greatly diminished any chance for true passional harmony. What was more natural, Thomas asked, than that a healthy passionate woman should give herself in love to a man whom she believed to be worthy of her? Concomitantly, men had to recognize and attempt to gratify a woman's wish—virtually never talked about in the literature—to achieve orgasm, and not leave her to attain it in the solitude of masturbatory fantasy. Once alerted to a partner's desires, a man who wished her to experience such pleasure might "resort to manipulation of the clitoris, with their fingers, etc., and to various novel . . . methods and positions," as long as they were not harmful.[64]

Finally, in his attempt to educate women about and give them control over their bodies—including their reproductive systems— Thomas discussed various methods of contraception. He mentioned condoms, vaginal sponges, cold-water douches, as well as the "rhythm" method, all toward the end of letting the woman determine when and with whom to conceive. From the importance of "passional" harmony, he extrapolated out to the health of all humanity. "Sexual congress," demanding as it does "the whole powers of the body and soul," confers "the greatest happiness upon the individual," he explained. Depending on how the individual conceives it, it might be either the basis of "social harmonies, or the source of radical discords." One thing, however, was certain: healthy sex is "of absolute necessity to the life of the race."[65]

Thomas's publication filled an important niche in contemporary medical literature, even as, predictably, it offended some people, even among the couple's friends. Fellow hydropathist Trall was so affronted that he closed the pages of his *Water-Cure Journal* to Thomas, even though Thomas and Mary had used it as an outlet for their essays for years. They thereupon decisively cut ties with Trall and founded their own periodical, *Nichols' Journal of Health, Water-Cure, and Human Progress,* whose title perfectly captured their large ambition. They also made plans to expand their new facility on Long Island Sound to include a "School of Integral Education" designed to develop the whole person, mind, body, and spirit.[66] Trall, resenting the Nichols' usurpation of his position as the country's premier promulgator of the water cure, was bent on discrediting the institution, specifically claiming that Thomas and Mary indoctrinated their students with their radical notions of "passional" relationships.

As if this negative publicity was not enough—it appeared in Greeley's *New-York Tribune*—the writer Charles Wilkins Webber, long nursing a personal grievance, finally took his revenge. Webber had lived at the Tenth Street boardinghouse where Mary had had rooms, and he had fallen in love with Elma, only to have Mary squelch his suit (he was a good deal older, an alcoholic, and quite erratic). Now appeared Webber's *Spiritual Vampirism: The History of Etherial Softdown, and Her Friends of the "New Light."* The roman à clef described Mary—"Etherial Softdown"—as a frighteningly egotistical and vampirish woman who threw away a fine, decent husband for "Mr. Narcissus," patently Thomas Low Nichols, and oversaw a nest of wild-eyed radicals. Published in 1853, it probably prompted Mary to respond in her own scarcely veiled novel, *Mary Lyndon,* as she sought to set straight the record of her horrendous years of marriage to Gove as well as her subsequent success as an educator and writer.

At Modern Times

Given the development of their thought on health reform, and with such controversy swirling around them, Thomas and Mary decided to move to Josiah Warren's utopian community, Modern Times, forty miles east of Brooklyn on Long Island, and easily accessible from New York City by a recently completed railroad.[67] On adjacent land, the couple planned to start yet another educational institution, Desarrollo, which means "development" or "unfoldment." It would sit literally on the border of the world and Modern Times and, Thomas and Mary anticipated, provide both a window on how individuals pursuing self-healing could be beacons to the world.

Their initial plans were grand: a four-story building with a sixty-foot tower holding a reservoir for the water for hydropathy instruction and therapy. It also would house a library, gymnasium, rooms for art studios, and lecture halls. Future plans called for a quadrangular arrangement with foundries, printing presses, kitchen and bakery, and a laundry, all run by an enormous steam engine. All this was reminiscent of the Fourierist phalanstery described in Albert Brisbane's *Social Destiny of Man* and a reflection of the Nichols' faith that Associationist principles held the key to meaningful individual and social reform.

They had the requisite funds to dig the foundation of the edifice's first phase, but the Institute of Desarrollo never came to be. Despite their best efforts, the Nichols failed to raise more of the necessary capital. The couple had to be content with living in and working from Modern Times, where they joined about sixty other "settlers" in a community that, while far removed from Associationist principles, offered a degree of individual freedom through which they could continue what had become a virtual program for the reform of domestic relations, set by their own example.

Modern Times was the brainchild of philosophical anarchist Josiah Warren and his friend Stephen Pearl Andrews, whose ideas about marriage were as radical as those of the Nichols. Warren and Andrews had started Modern Times in the spring of 1851 as a community based on individual sovereignty, that is, on the right of any individual to live as he wished. Warren explained it thus: "With regard to mere difference of opinion in taste, convenience, economy, equality, or even right and wrong, good and bad, sanity and insanity, all must be left to the supreme decision of each individual, whenever he can take on himself the cost of his decisions; which he cannot do while his interests or movements are united or combined with others."[68]

The community's other chief principle had been worked out by Warren when he was at Robert Owen's New Harmony, Indiana, community and then at another in Utopia, Ohio.[69] It was explicitly economic and, in shorthand, required that "cost was the limit of price." Warren abhorred the profit motive, believing it the root of the worst social as well as economic evils. His solution was to dictate that all transactions would be done without profit. If, say, you were purchasing a new barn, the cost would be materials and labor only. Profit, speculation, lending at interest, and, beneath all, greed, were the demons of the age and had to be exorcised.

William B. Greene had addressed the same issues in a different way through his mutual banking system, but Warren went farther. Agreeing that a rational and predictable circulating medium was central to any meaningful reform, he wanted this medium to represent a certain set amount of goods or labor, for the relation between these two was at the heart of his reform. Thus, in his system speculation was prohibited and all trade was deemed cooperative, with harmful competition left behind.

This eventuated in what Warren, in a much-reprinted pamphlet—first published by Fowlers and Wells in 1852—termed "equitable commerce," which he declared was "based on INDIVIDUALITY," and was clearly another attempt to blunt the harshness of the market-based American economy.[70] Unsurprisingly, Modern Times caught the eye of many of the nation's advanced reformers. Greeley, for example, still enamored of such castles in the air, even though they were not explicitly Fourierist, bought several plots of land on community grounds, though he never moved there. Oddly, Andrews did not either, remaining in the city two hours way, where he assiduously proselytized for the experimental community.

On a practical level, Warren's plan for commerce involved "labor-notes" that one received for work done for someone in the community and with which one could purchase items at a central "Time Store." These pieces of paper served as well as exchange for equal amounts of labor. Warren also deducted the time that any transaction took to complete—the storekeeper, for example, would subtract from one's labor note not only the cost of an item but how much time a clerk took to complete a certain transaction with a customer. The system was complex, and the worth allotted different sorts of labor—a carpenter's as opposed to a seamstress's, say—admittedly difficult to ascertain and standardize. That it was lauded let alone tried at all despite its impracticality suggests just how disenchanted some Americans were with the status quo.

Domestic Relations Debated

At Modern Times Warren also found himself drawn into an experiment in domestic relations, because of Andrews's influence as well as the arrival of the Nichols. Andrews did not rest with mere condemnation of the market. He hated not only the inequitable profit system that cheapened the intrinsic worth of labor but all governmental interference with individual rights. To him, Southern slavery was but another example of how tyrannical laws crushed possibilities for individual self-realization.[71] He extended this reasoning to the marriage bond as well, and here crossed paths with the Nichols. All three urged a concept of "free love," or, put another way, of individual sovereignty in "sexual intercourse."[72]

An interview with a resident yielded further clarification as to their intentions. He thought that people went to Modern Times as oppressed laborers and sought to transform themselves into "individual sovereigns." "We are not Fourierites," the informant said. "We do not believe in association," for that would have to answer for "many of the evils with which mankind are now afflicted." Neither were they "Communists," nor "Mormons," nor "Non-Resistants." Rather, "we are Protestants; we are Liberals. We believe in the *sovereignty of the individual.* We protest against all laws which interfere with *individual rights;* hence we are Protestants. We believe in perfect liberty of will and action; hence we are Liberals. . . . We have no compacts with each other, save the compact of individual happiness." In theory, neither law nor taxes had much of a place in Modern Times. Finally, there was the delicate subject of marriage. Here the influence of Thomas Nichols was clear. Some of the members did not believe in the concept of "life-partnerships," this resident opined, "when the parties cannot live happily." Everyone is supposed to know his or her interests best, and there is "no eavesdropping or prying behind the curtain."[73] Domestic relations, like all other matters, were left to the individuals themselves and thus, as Fourier predicted in his phalansteries, took various forms.

This was possible at Modern Times because law and religion had been discarded in favor of individual rights. "Inside my door I am lord and king," one resident noted. "What if I take a dozen wives? How these ladies choose to live, is for themselves, and not for you, to say. What business have you to take offence because they do not live according to your law?" There, "a woman who was fair and a

man who was discreet, had nothing to fear from the moral and religious passions of his fellow-settlers."[74] Women separated from
their companions when they wished, and the next week, or perhaps the next day, were living with other men. No one censured
them, except, of course, the outside world.

The residents of Modern Times were far more willing to match
the opprobrium of critics with disdain than Ripley and his followers
at Brook Farm. Among the former, the felt necessity of presenting
a defensible example that required approval, if not adoption, by the
wider world was muted at best. In the minds of the residents of
Modern Times, they were simply practicing what they believed,
the full sovereignty of the individual, confident that mature adults
would be able to make decisions in line with their happiness. That
the wider world failed to take notice and be suitably impressed only
condemned the wider world.

This prescriptive failure, however, could prove destabilizing even
within the confines of Modern Times. For the Nichols soon were
unwittingly at the center of controversy. By this point in their lives
they did not just believe in free love themselves, but were convinced
that all other people should live by its principles. The problem
was that they urged such behavior in a community where individual
conscience, no matter where it led, reigned. At Modern Times, no
individual had the right to speak for or impose his or her ideas on
others; but in their frequent writings on the subject of sexuality
and marriage, the Nichols began to do just that. Warren quickly
chastised them and centrally posted a reply to one of their published columns on the subject, in which they seemed to identify
Modern Times with free love, when in fact it was just one way its
denizens could order their relationships. Warren did not want his
community associated primarily with such radical sexual freedom
but rather with the sovereignty of individual rights. The Nichols
reined in their rhetoric, but they continued to believe that the
community offered a place where they might realize their utopian

visions. Eventually, they settled into an uneasy peace with the founder, which they proved able to maintain for the over two years that they resided at Modern Times.

Love vs. Marriage, in the Tribune

Through these years, however, the Nichols continued to be linked to Andrews and, thus, to the most radical efforts toward marriage reform. The main controversy that kept them in the public eye began when Mary's friend Lazarus published *Love vs. Marriage* (1852), a Fourierist-inflected indictment of the ways in which contemporary marriage laws trapped spouses in psychologically debilitating relationships. His remedy, not surprisingly, was the sexual freedom promised in the phalanstery, where each individual's sexual proclivity and need were respected and might be satisfied.

In Greeley's *Tribune*, where Lazarus could have expected a favorable notice, Swedenborgian and erstwhile Associationist Henry James gave the book a searching but negative review. He understood and approved of Fourier's analysis of the marital bond but insisted that Lazarus erred in his outright condemnation of monogamy, which James believed still suited most people. James's main criticism was of divorce laws that were too strict to allow the marriage bond to be terminated as necessary.

To his chagrin, James found himself lumped in the popular press with Lazarus and others whose positions were much more radical. James defended himself in the *Tribune*, where Greeley also printed a letter from Andrews. Thereafter ensued a lengthy exchange between Greeley—who defended monogamous marriage—James, and Andrews that the last eventually collected and published as *Love, Marriage, and Divorce, and the Sovereignty of the Individual* (1855).

In this book, Andrews condemned "the interference of the State in his morals" and proclaimed "freedom in love was . . . the culminating point, towards which all other reforms end."[75] He also included a letter of support for his positions from Mary that she had sent to Greeley but that he had not seen fit to publish. Mary, Andrews explained, was "a noble and pure-minded American woman, one to whom the world owes more than to any other man or woman, living or dead, for thorough investigation and appreciation of . . . all that concerns the sexual relations and the reproduction of the race." What had set off Greeley was that in her missive she offered the remarkable proposition that each woman has "a heaven-conferred right to choose the father of her babe," a position that the *Tribune*'s editor found outré.[76]

The exchange was archetypal of the entire antebellum reform era. Atop the most personal and individual of judgments—love—was constructed the most far-reaching of consequences—the culmination point at which all other reforms ended. Constructed from the theology of Swedenborg, the ideology of Fourier, and the science of water cure and phrenology, an argument over heaven-conferred rights touched on reform of marriage laws and women's health.

Andrews criticized Greeley for only a piecemeal appreciation of Fourier's principles, which he supposedly championed. The editor was "a man of statistics and facts, but not of principles," and so never saw "down into the center of things," that is, to the heart of Fourier's system, which included the sort of sexual freedom the men then were debating.[77] Mary realized this, too, and Greeley's rejection only stirred her to more action. She joined with her husband in the preparation of a lengthy, detailed work called *Marriage: Its History, Character, and Results; Its Sanctities, and Its Profanities; Its Science and Its Facts* (1854).

In addition to detailing marriage customs through many centuries around the world, the Nichols were not afraid to draw what to many seemed startling conclusions. "Love," they wrote, "with its ultimations [*sic*], enjoyments, and results, is the right, as it is the function, of every human being," and whose "deprivation" might well eventuate in "physical and mental diseases and miseries." When "what the law calls fornication," they noted, in fact came from "the union of mutual love," it well might be "the holiest action two human beings can engage in." The Nichols strenuously objected that such pleasure was closed to people who were not legally married, for they believed that such suppression of true emotions could lead to severe physical as well as psychological illness.[78]

Moreover, the marital bond as then constituted undeniably was patriarchal and implied ownership of the wife, as though woman was merely property. "For a human being to surrender up all right of choice and will, during her whole life, to another, to merge her legal, political, and to great extent, her social existence in his; to have no separate individuality or sphere of action" seemed "a sad lot" for any being whom God "had endowed with a human soul."[79] Those in favor of greater equality for women had to ask for "freedom in all the relations of life," and that meant first and foremost "in the highest and purest—the realm of the affections."[80] Any serious "Women's Rights" advocate, they continued, had to demand "the abrogation of civilized marriage." Mary explained that she was not pleading for "a plurality of love relations" but only "for freedom and truth" in relationships. In words as ringing as any of Margaret Fuller's, Mary proclaimed, "The age has dawned in which woman shall stand between God and man, the arbiter of her own fate and medium of inspiration, not to an owner, but to another self."[81]

This belief that neither church nor state, culturally biased as they were, should deny sexual pleasure, a God-given right, flowed as a natural consequence from Warren's understanding of the sanctity of each individual soul, male or female. Because of this sanctity, Warren and other emergent anarchists demanded the individual's sovereignty. But this sovereignty was of a piece with the entire development of Mary's commitment to reform. From her early days as a teacher of physiology, when she taught women to own and control their bodies, through her practice and promulgation (it would remain lifelong) of hydropathy, with its similar emphasis on an individual's assumption of control over that which promotes good health and then encouragement of others to do the same, to her discovery of the reciprocal, "passional" needs of both men and women that delivered her to the most advanced ideas about love and divorce—through her entire intellectual and emotional development—the passe-partout remained the centrality of the individual.

In this, she was exemplary of the vast majority of her contemporary reformers. The untapped possibilities inherent in each individual, the God-granted interests and strengths indwelling in each, were understood to be the engine of local, regional, national, even global reform. From this vantage point, the problems of the country were best addressed through a process of self-discovery that led to realigning individuals and then society with God's knowable intentions. Difficulties arose when that process somehow came up short, when one individual's discovery was society's collective fear, leaving that individual and her admirers confronting a nation impervious, perhaps willfully, to God's own intent.

The Civil War and Exile

While living on Long Island, the Nichols became enthusiasts for spiritualism, a belief that one can communicate with the spirits of the dead.[82] They held séances at their home, and by 1855 Mary believed that one of their circle was her spiritual guide. He encouraged the couple to move from Modern Times to Cincinnati, to a region that had seen several interesting utopian experiments and had a publisher, Valentine Nicholson, not afraid to issue the Nichols' work. From his press, for example, came Thomas's utopian novel, *Esperanza: My Journey Thither and What I Found* (1860) and as well his and Mary's *Marriage: Its History, Character, and Results*

(1855). Therein, the couple, at the prompting of "Heavenly Intelligences," urged nothing less than the establishment of "Progressive Unions" in "Harmonic Homes" all over the country. Therein each "family" would abjure meat, medicine, the ownership of property, and any personal gain, as well as have whatever sexual partners they wished.[83]

From Cincinnati, the Nichols moved to Yellow Springs, Ohio, where near fledgling Antioch College they re-opened an earlier hydropathic facility whose projectors had placed it on one of the region's mineral-rich streams. Here, Thomas again planned an ambitious educational institute, Memnonia, "a School of Health; a School of Progress; a School of Life." Despite animated local opposition to the school, Thomas prevailed, and for a few years Yellow Springs served as a proving ground for a whole range of the couple's reforms, including hydropathy.[84] But here Thomas also struck a new note. As part of one of his reports from the "Central Bureau of the Progressive Union," he explained that when one rose from the "plane of natural life" to that of the spiritual, "material union is only to be had when the wisdom of the Harmony demands a child," forgoing his hitherto wholesale commitment to free love and the enjoyment of sexual relations for their own sake.[85]

During this period, too, the Nichols continued to be devotees of spiritualism, Mary in particular now believing that she could communicate with the spiritual realm. But this interest, based as it was on a set of harmonies for which Swedenborg had set the foundation, proved only preliminary to their last conversion. On the cusp of the Civil War, the family, again on the advice of one of their trusted mediums, converted to Roman Catholicism and joined St. Xavier Church in Cincinnati.[86] They then spent several months at a nearby Ursuline convent before moving back to New York City, now full communicants. Thomas's recent redefinition of what sexual intercourse was best fitted for—procreation—obviously fit with the church's teachings on the subject. Perhaps Mary herself believed such an understanding of chastity offered women yet another way to control their own bodies and lives.

Thomas thereupon lectured about Catholicism through the Midwest and South and ended up in New York City, defending his new faith. He eventually published some of these offerings and as well became the New York correspondent for the *Boston Pilot*, chief organ of the Boston Catholic community.[87] Of Mary's activities in this crucial period we know little. Under the cloud of war, the couple moved to England, where Mary again published fiction under the pseudonym Mary Orme. They spent the rest of their lives there as advocates of health reform and the water cure.[88]

That Mary and Thomas Nichols never made abolition the priority they did other antebellum reform activities stemmed naturally from their preoccupation with another kind of bondage closer to home. They were not callous to the plight of African Americans, but rather they were sensitive to the need for everyone to be free, whether or not one knew he or she was in chains. In their view, slavery was among many terrible forms of subjugation that pervaded their world. After Harriet Beecher Stowe's *Uncle Tom's Cabin* (1852) appeared, for example, Mary Nichols opined, "Everywhere are fetters and chains. African slavery is the simple, external type of the more oppressive and crushing institutions of civilization," including the financial, itself a vicious "scheme of oppression and slavery." Indeed, she continued, "there are few civilized institutions, upon which we could not write an 'Uncle Tom's Cabin.'"[89]

Mary even told abolitionist William Lloyd Garrison to his face that "the Northern wife is worse off than the Southern slave, for her moral cultivation gives her a keenness of anguish that the want of spiritual culture saves her Southern sister from." Subsequently, she admitted that "chattel bondage is the lowest of all," yet "those who are oppressed by marriage, and find no escape but by the loss of name and fame, food and children, may well be excused for seeing a parallel to the institution of marriage in that of slavery."[90]

This sort of moral equivocating could easily descend to moral obtuseness.

For his part, Thomas, borrowing from his friend Andrews's hailed sanctity of individual sovereignty, objected to the North's attempted coercion of the South.[91] While there is condescension to African Americans in Thomas's pronouncements on the war, the flaw in his reasoning ran deeper than the era's near ubiquitous racism. With their focus on visions of universal transformation, the Nichols, like Fourier, Brisbane, and others, thought chattel slavery a secondary issue that would be resolved when more fundamental reform got under way. Focused like so many other antebellum reformers—including their friends the Fowlers—on individual self-improvement, they continued to hope, long after the casualty count mounted, that if only people ate well and had meaningful sexual relations the problems besetting country and world would take care of themselves.

6

Thoreau's Nullification

In 1851 Stephen Pearl Andrews published *The True Constitution of Government in the Sovereignty of the Individual as the Final Development of Protestantism, Democracy and Socialism*, the first in a proposed series of tracts, *The Science of Society*. In it, he offered his justification for the philosophical underpinnings of the utopian experiment that he and Josiah Warren were undertaking at Modern Times, on Long Island, whose inhabitants included Mary Gove Nichols and her husband, Thomas. Specifically, Andrews argued that the "Sovereignty of the Individual" underlay all three of the great social developments identified in the book's title and, moreover, was the only basis on which mankind could ever realize a just society.[1]

The relationship of the individual to the rise of Protestantism and democracy was evident. Protestantism freed the individual from the religious hierarchy, and democracy gave every citizen a voice. But it was not as clear why Andrews linked individuality as well to socialism. He had in mind the theories of Charles Fourier so much then in vogue, and, in particular, the French social theorist's celebrated equation, "destinies are proportionate to attractions." Andrews understood this to mean that reformers had to reorganize society so that every individual was empowered "to choose and vary his own destiny or condition and pursuits in life, untrammeled by social restrictions."[2] Viewed in this way, Andrews believed, Fourier's elaborate and sometimes extravagant social engineering—socialism—proved secondary to its chief premises, the uniqueness of each individual and society's obligation to respect his or her material, social, and psychological needs. What socialism demanded, Andrews explained, was nothing less than the emancipation of the individual from social bondage "by whatsoever means will effect that design," just as Protestantism had demanded the emancipation of the individual from ecclesiastical bondage, and democracy from political.[3] Every man, Andrews prophesied, would be a law unto himself.[4]

Andrews also understood that many people misconceived how "Individuality" could be "the great remedy for the prevalent ills of the social state." Individuality did not imply isolation, he explained, or "the severance of all personal relations with one's fellow-men," for he understood that men and women were social beings. But, there was more to it than a vague pull toward community. Here the "final development" of Andrews' title asserted itself. He understood that mankind could attain "harmonic cooperation and universal brotherhood" only through "the Individualization of interests." The chief misconception was to suppose that because "individuality" as it was then understood had not resulted in harmony, somehow it was itself at fault.[5] Not so. Before a better society could emerge, mankind had to restructure social arrangements to accommodate a yet greater degree of personal liberty and autonomy, no matter what an individual's needs. This personal liberty would not descend into rank selfishness and chaos, but instead produce the harmonies of a universal brotherhood, which was in his time awaiting realization.

Andrews's contemporary Henry Thoreau was another highly vocal proponent of such individual self-sufficiency. As much as he would have agreed with Andrews on many points, though, he fashioned a different and in some ways still more extreme individualism. In particular, like his one-time mentor Emerson, he doubted that men acting in concert could ever ameliorate social conditions without first reforming themselves. As was true for so many of his contemporary reformers, he believed that the problem was within, not without. Just after graduating from college, Thoreau began to elaborate this premise, which he then put to a practical test in the mid-1840s in the two years he lived alone at Walden Pond.

In his view, the specific causes his countrymen took up to reform American society—temperance, for example, or women's rights, or abolition—allowed them to sidestep more incisive, radical action. It never brought them to what he thought was the heart of the matter: the need for self-purification and a life lived so close to the bone that one came to know the higher laws of conscience, a lesson he absorbed from his friend Emerson and other Transcendentalists who lived in and around Thoreau's hometown of Concord, Massachusetts. Eventually, such knowledge informed Thoreau's position on the greatest moral issue of his day, slavery, and was vividly exemplified in his brave defense of Captain John Brown after his raid on the United States arsenal at Harpers Ferry.

Thoreau in 1837

David Henry Thoreau (as he first was called) graduated from Harvard in 1837 at the age of twenty. He distinguished himself enough to gain a part in the commencement festivities, but unlike many of his classmates, who came from wealthier families—his father John Thoreau was a mere "mechanic" (in his case, a pencil maker) and his mother took in boarders—he did not gravitate toward the law, ministry, or medicine. The Panic of 1837, casting a decadelong shadow over the national economy, also complicated his search for work, for Concord, one of the commercial centers of Middlesex County, deeply felt the depression's repercussions.

Initially, Thoreau obtained a good position teaching in the Central Grammar School in the Concord public schools, but he did not hold it long. Two weeks into the term a school board member visited his class and reprimanded Thoreau for not enforcing stricter discipline. Miffed, for he did not believe in corporal punishment, the young teacher selected several students at random, caned them, and promptly resigned, an example of the kind of headstrong behavior that soon became one of Thoreau's hallmarks.[6]

As he cast about for other, comparable work, he befriended his Concord neighbor Emerson, who a year earlier had published his important Transcendentalist manifesto, *Nature*. Emerson then was emerging as one of the region's prominent intellectuals. As part of Harvard's commencement activities in 1837, for example, he had delivered the Phi Beta Kappa address, "The American Scholar" (it is unclear if Thoreau heard it), and he was at the center of what became known as the "Transcendental Club," which met to discuss timely issues in religion and philosophy, among other topics. During this period, Thoreau continued to inquire after teaching jobs in Massachusetts, New York, Virginia, and Maine, and even considered going to the Ohio Valley. Not having any luck in this search, in 1838 he opened a small academy of his own and began teaching a handful of students. His brother John, two years older, soon joined him.

By 1840 Thoreau began to travel among Transcendentalists, at first by attending meetings of the informal discussion club organized by Emerson, George Ripley, and a few others. He also took an interest in the group's new periodical, the *Dial*, to which Emerson urged him to contribute and in which appeared his first published work, on Roman satirical poets. During this period, too, Thoreau fell in love for what appears the only time in his life, with Ellen Sewall of Scituate, Massachusetts. He pursued her; but so did his brother. Thoreau was crushed when later her parents asked her to cut off relations with both young men—John had actually proposed—whose family they regarded as too "advanced"—that is, radical—in their politics, particularly because of their abolitionist leanings. This emotional imbroglio only grew more tangled in 1840 when, after cutting himself shaving, John was stricken with tetanus and died within days. Henry was so affected by the death of his beloved sibling and, for a time, rival, that for several days he came down with psychosomatic symptoms that made his family fear that he, too, would die.

Throughout this period, at Emerson's urging, Thoreau wrote voluminously in a journal, recording his thoughts on nature, society, and self. He knew that he wanted to become a writer, and Emerson provided him with a model and mentor. Thoreau also knew that he wanted to live a meaningful life, not one in which he prostituted himself—as so many of his countrymen did—to debilitating and dehumanizing work. He did not become a major player per se among the Transcendentalists but learned from their various examples that others, too, questioned the premises on which the nation based its purported progress and uniqueness. Thoreau's writings would center more specifically on how a life lived close to nature allowed personal fulfillment of a sort that was all too rare among his contemporaries, for whom economic success seemed all.

Because Thoreau's private school was not lucrative enough for him to justify continuing it, in April 1840 he moved into the Emerson household on the Lexington Road, his chief task to look after household affairs for Emerson's wife and children while the master of the house was off on increasingly frequent and lengthy lecture tours. It was a heady time for the young Thoreau, who was not treated as a hired man but an intimate of the family. This placed him as close to the epicenter of Transcendentalism as one could be. At this time, for example, when in addition to the emergence of the Transcendentalists' *Dial* as a new voice in American letters, Emerson's cousin Ripley was soliciting support for his utopian experiment, Brook Farm. It was in this crucible that Thoreau wrestled with just how to forge his own path as thinker, writer, and social critic. After two years with the Emersons, he began that work in earnest.

Thoreau and the New York Associationists

In the spring of 1843, Thoreau traveled to Staten Island, New York, to tutor the children of William Emerson, his friend Waldo Emerson's brother. After two years as general factotum to the Emerson family, at Waldo's urging he undertook this trip not only for the employment but also to further his budding literary career. Thanks again to Emerson, who with Margaret Fuller was editing the *Dial*, Thoreau had seen some of his work published. As young and green an author as he was, however, he realized that the center of the literary world was shifting from Boston to New York. Hence, he wished to make overtures there.

Through his friendship with Emerson and others in his circle, in New York City Thoreau quickly met a pride of literary and intellectual lions. Not surprisingly, given the ferment that spilled over from Ripley's Brook Farm experiment, many had connections to Fourier and the Associationist movement. Among others, Thoreau was introduced to William Henry Channing, the renowned Boston Unitarian clergyman William Ellery Channing's nephew, who already had spent much time at Brook Farm. When Thoreau met him, Channing was well along in planning for a periodical devoted to reform, *The Present*, but Thoreau found him sadly wanting in self-confidence. He seemed "a concave man," Thoreau wrote, for one saw "by his attitude, and the lines of his face that he is retreating from himself and from yourself, with sad doubts."[7] Not through such an individual, Thoreau implied, would the necessary changes come upon the world!

Another fellow traveler in the socialist movement was Henry James Sr., good friend of Emerson, and soon to be a major proselytizer for Swedeborgianism as well as an advocate for women's rights in marriage. In contrast to how he felt about Channing, Thoreau liked James very much. After a three-hour visit, he observed that his new acquaintance was "a refreshing and forward-moving man" who "naturalized and humanized New York" for him. "I never was more kindly and faithfully catechized," Thoreau continued. Indeed, he had never met anyone "so patient and determined to have the good" of one.[8]

Then there was Albert Brisbane, Fourier's foremost American exponent and proponent, who already had issued his major work on Association, *Social Destiny of Man* (1840). Thoreau (like others) found him prickly and self-centered, and, as Emerson had noted, completely in thrall to the Frenchman, "always reciting paragraphs out of his master's book." As a warning to Thoreau for what he might expect, Emerson had written his young friend that when he had last seen Brisbane, he had just given Emerson "a faithful hour & a half of what he calls his principles." It was all he could do to keep from laughing "incredulous[ly]" as Brisbane recited descriptions of "the self[-] augmenting potency of the solar system which is destined to contain 132 bodies . . . and his urgent inculcation of our *stellar duties*."[9] Thoreau concurred with Emerson's assessment, finding Brisbane's obsession with Fourier so pervasive that it seemed to affect the reformer's health. He "looks like a man," Thoreau reported wryly, "who has lived in a cellar, far gone in consumption."[10] The implication was clear: no hope of fundamental reform, of the self or of society, promised to stem from Brisbane's efforts.

Emerson's young friends Giles Waldo and William Tappan, Thoreau's de facto guides to the city, also introduced him to Horace Greeley, editor of the *New-York Tribune*.[11] Thoreau quickly warmed to this "hearty New Hampshire boy," whom he found "cheerfully earnest" and utterly devoted to his work.[12] Although only thirty-three, Greeley knew virtually everyone in the city's world of print culture, and he soon proved most helpful to Thoreau's literary ambition. Long after Thoreau left the city—he found it "a thousand times meaner" than he could have imagined, with the pigs in the street seeming "the most respectable portion of the population"— Greeley continued to act as his new friend's literary agent as well as to remind him of the value of the Associationist project.[13]

In his attempt to forward his literary prospects, Thoreau made the rounds of several editorial offices of literary journals, including those of the *New Mirror, Brother Jonathan,* and the *New World,* but found that "all were overwhelmed with contributions which cost nothing, and are worth no more." He glumly wrote his mother back in Concord that even a better journal, the prominent Whig periodical the *Knickerbocker,* was too "poor" to offer anything for his work, leaving only the prospect of the middlebrow, domestic *Ladies' Companion,* which could pay, but was hardly the sort of venue in which Thoreau imagined publishing his poetry or essays. "My bait will not tempt the rats," he added sharply, "they are too well fed."[14] Despondent, he was reduced to canvassing for subscriptions to the *American Agriculturalist,* a periodical for farmers, traveling north through Manhattanville as far as the recently completed Croton Reservoir; but even in this work he met with little success.[15]

Thoreau had in hand two completed works, "A Winter Walk," a lyrical essay that provided an account of precisely what the title indicates; and a lengthy book review called "Paradise (to be) Regained," in which he evaluated the second edition of the utopian J[ohn] A[dolphus] Etzler's *The Paradise Within the Reach of All Men, Without Labor, by Powers of Nature and Machinery* (1842). He had written this piece for Emerson, who thought it might fit the *Dial,* but instead the young author carried it to the New York editors to show them of what he was capable. Eventually, he brought it to the Democratic Party stalwart John L. O'Sullivan at the *United States Magazine, and Democratic Review,* who coined the deathless term "Manifest Destiny."[16]

Thoreau had met O'Sullivan the previous January at the Boston
Athenaeum and subsequently took tea with him and Nathaniel
Hawthorne, another Concord neighbor and, like O' Sullivan, a
Democrat. Thoreau remembered the editor as a "rather puny looking
man," not at all striking. But he soon warmed to him, for he was
"one of the not—bad," that is, who "does not by any means take
you—by storm—no—nor by calm," which was, Thoreau concluded,
"the best way." The two got along well enough for O'Sullivan to
solicit Thoreau to write for his journal, which he said he would be
glad to do.[17]

A few months later he took up O'Sullivan's offer. Serendipitously,
the editor had heard of Etzler's work and thought it warranted notice, but he had not seen a copy. At first, he rejected Thoreau's essay
but clearly remained interested, for he asked if the young writer
might drop off Etzler's book to peruse. Thoreau could not oblige,
for he had read and returned Emerson's copy, sent to him from
England by another Concord neighbor and Transcendentalist,
Bronson Alcott. Soon enough, though, O'Sullivan changed his
mind and told Thoreau that he would indeed like to publish the
young writer's piece, if Thoreau would revise it to suit what he reported as the editor's "peculiar notion on the subject."[18]

In a letter to Emerson, Thoreau bluntly explained O'Sullivan's
objection: in his essay Thoreau displayed an evident "want of sympathy with the Communities."[19] The allusion was to the Associationist communal experiments that were springing up all over the
northeastern states (including in West Roxbury, Massachusetts, the
site of Brook Farm, and at Harvard, Massachusetts, where that
spring Alcott was beginning his own experiment) and those of the
"Northwest Territory," and in whose fortunes O'Sullivan's readership, disappointed as many of them were with the nation's course
after the Panic of 1837, had much interest.

Thoreau's review of Etzler's idiosyncratic work was his first extended engagement with the world of socialist reform and formed

the backdrop to his future domestic adventure at Walden Pond. Two years earlier he had rejected out of hand Ripley's appeal that he join his band of communitarians, many of whom were linked to the Transcendentalist movement. "As for these communities [like Brook Farm]," he wrote in his journal, "I think I had rather keep bachelor's hall in hell than go to board in heaven," a sentiment remarkably similar to Emerson's demurrer when he too refused to join Ripley's experiment.[20] But Etzler's was a radically different approach to bringing heaven to earth, far more the dream of an engineer than a former clergyman. Reflecting an era of rampant mechanization that already was irrevocably altering the natural world, Etzler spun a vision of vast energies channeled to realize a very tangible paradise. What did Thoreau make of this? How would he treat a subject so close to his heart? O'Sullivan's readers found out in the fall of 1843, for Thoreau did indeed revise the review to the editor's satisfaction.

John Adolphus Etzler

It is perfectly fitting that Alcott, the consummate Transcendentalist dreamer, had sent Emerson Etzler's *Paradise within the Reach of All Men* when he came across the London reprint while traveling in England.[21] He had been visiting at the invitation of a group of men who, at a school called "Alcott House," were experimenting with the same pedagogy that its namesake had used in the mid-1830s at his Temple School in Boston. Now, however, Alcott's mind was on other matters, particularly utopian communities; upon his return to the United States he would start Fruitlands. Known more as a dreamer than a doer, and constitutionally incapable of finding a lucrative profession, it is little wonder that Alcott was interested in such labor-saving projects as Etzler proposed.

In *Paradise within the Reach of All Men*, Etzler promised his readers "the means of creating a paradise within ten years, where every thing desirable for human life may be had for every man in superabundance, without labor, without pay." By paradise, Etzler promised more than just material abundance, but for those willing to follow him, "a life of continual happiness, of enjoyments yet unknown."[22] He would accomplish this by rendering "the whole face of nature" into "the most beautiful form of which it is capable," even as men "accomplish[ed], without his labor, in one year more than hitherto could be done in thousands of years." He went on rapturously, man would "level mountains, sink valleys, create lakes, drain lakes and swamps, intersect everywhere the land with beautiful canals." And he would "provide himself with means unheard of yet, for increasing his knowledge of the world, and so his intelligence."[23] How could such a prospect not seduce Alcott or, indeed, any American reformer?

Such were the dreams of Etzler, a mechanic and visionary born in 1791 in the central German state of Thüringen.[24] Trained in engineering at his town's gymnasium—one of his classmates and friends was John Augustus Roebling, future designer of the Brooklyn Bridge—in his twenties Etzler was swept up in the region's radical politics. Bristling under the stern eyes of an entrenched aristocracy that strictly ruled the German states, in 1822 he and his friend Roebling left for the United States, where Etzler spent the next seven years, most of them in Pennsylvania.

He liked what he saw and returned home to try to convince others to join him in casting their lot across the Atlantic. This brought him afoul of the state's reactionary authorities, who jailed him for preaching what they regarded as incendiary criticism of their regime. Released from prison after a year, Etzler organized an emigration society with Roebling, and, in 1831, with a few hundred acolytes, they recrossed the Atlantic.

Soon after the group's arrival in Philadelphia, however, they split, some casting their lots with Roebling, who had lured them with talk of a projected utopian farming village that Etzler thought ill founded. Instead, Etzler persuaded his group to consider a more industrial vision. He dreamed of applying what he knew of engineering to remake the social world with unlimited and yet untapped sources of power derived from nature.

Etzler and his group traveled west to Cincinnati, home to a sizable German émigré settlement and where he wrote what became *Paradise within the Reach of All Men.* He moved back east to Pittsburgh, the site of another large German community, and found work as editor of a German-American newspaper. There in 1833 he published his utopian tract in the hope that, given the country's growing interest in communitarian schemes meant in part to forge a healthier relationship between capital and labor, his book would find a large and sympathetic readership. He promised a sequel in which he would address more concretely the kinds of machinery needed for his ventures. Eight years later he was good to his word, issuing *The New World.*[25]

Etzler believed that, with proper engineering and machinery, there could be a burgeoning economy, as well as attendant social benefits, that could continue to grow indefinitely without depleting the world's natural resources in the ways industry currently demanded. He understood that the key to unlimited economic development, and so a more just and equitable society, lay not in raw materials like wood or coal, but in sources of perpetually renewable energy. Earlier than most economic theorists, he saw that the industrial economy's reliance on finite energy sources, then steam engines run on coal and wood, would prove untenable.

Etzler also understood an important side effect of this reliance. Those who controlled the extraction of these limited resources controlled as well the greatest amount of wealth and lived in most comfort. To create a more equitable distribution of wealth as well as to preserve the order of the natural world, man had to harness different sources of power. If they could be used "continually and uniformly," they would power mechanisms whose moving parts were replaceable, turning them into "perpetual motion machines."[26]

The visionary Etzler thus proposed an economy—indeed, an entire civilization—based on inexhaustible sources of energy that could not be monopolized for profit. "There are powers in nature," he explained, "a million times greater than all men on earth could effect, with their united exertions, by their nerves and sinews." But what were they? Quite simply, they were the wind; the waves and the tide, "or the rise and fall of the ocean caused by the gravity between the moon and the ocean"; and the sun, whose heat could transform water into steam. Properly harnessed by machinery of Etzler's design, energy from these free, renewable sources would enable and sustain a new kind of society, one of unlimited bounty and free of class struggle.[27]

When such energy was universally harnessed—Etzler envisioned, for example, huge mirrors to capture the power of the sun, and elaborate raftlike structures that caught and transformed wave movement—the way man lived would change. Where now much of humanity lived in hovels, there would be huge palacelike structures a thousand feet long, comprising "seven thousand private rooms," all with views of gardens and forests that no longer need be decimated for energy needs. The surrounding landscape would be rearranged to appear "in the most beautiful order, with walks, colonnades, aqueducts, canals, ponds, plains, amphitheaters, terraces, fountains, sculptural works, pavilions, gondolas, [and] places for public amusement" everywhere available to all. At night, cities would be illuminated by gaslights, which, amidst "the mazes of many-colored crystal-like colonnade and vaultings," would reflect brilliance like that of gems.[28]

Inside the living quarters, remarkable comforts would abound. Anyone could procure "all the common articles of his daily wants, by a short turn of some crank," without leaving his apartment. In the privacy of one's rooms, one would bathe in hot or cold water, or in steam, "or in some artificially prepared liquor for invigorating health." The air in these living quarters would be controlled "to the temperature that suits [one's] feeling best." And one could admit "agreeable" scents of various kinds to perfume the rooms. All this was now possible without any undue exertion of physical labor, for in this new world, machines performed all such, and for humanity there was "nothing but enjoyment and delight."[29]

Etzler's baroque vision of physical and architectural space bespeaks indebtedness to none other than Fourier, one of whose phalansteries Etzler could have been describing.[30] Indeed, the frontispiece to Fourier's American disciple Albert Brisbane's *Social Destiny of Man*—a foldout engraving of a palatial phalanstery and its environs—provides a visual counterpart to Etzler's elaborate verbal description.[31]

Moreover, like Fourier, Etzler knew that before any government would adopt his ideas wholesale, he had to show their feasibility and effectiveness. To do this he sought to drum up support for small-scale models, communities of believers who, with Etzler's machinery, would harness nature as he planned. Once again, the most immediate means of fixing the woes of the world was understood to be a shining example of stunning success that others would be compelled to follow. As he put it in terms Fourier would have approved, "the most profitable, shortest and easiest way to put them into operation . . . is to form *associations* . . . so as to enable the rich and poor to participate fully in all the possible benefits of these discoveries." In more pedestrian terms, he envisioned communities formed on the model of joint-stock corporations.[32]

Etzler's immersion in the nuts and bolts of how one effected such change signaled his confidence in being able to calculate how productivity would perpetually spiral upward. This, too, mirrored Fourier. For all his bizarre cosmological speculations, the French social theorist always had a profoundly practical side. A large part of Etzler's tract similarly described just such seemingly mundane matters. He discussed horsepower, population growth, gears and pulleys, what it took to do various kinds of work for so many people. He believed that such "practicality," on display in *Paradise* but even more so in *The New World*, would go far toward winning converts to his cause.

Thoreau on Etzler and Reformers in General

Thoreau's evaluation of Etzler's scheme shows the evolution of his own ideas about reform. First, he rightly linked the utopian's book to Americans' growing interest in communal associations of all kinds. Thoreau explained that the recent reprinting of Etzler's work was due to the spread of Fourier's doctrines, and this spread was "one of the signs of the times."[33] But Thoreau also linked the book to the current ferment among his New England neighbors, for Etzler recognized that, as Thoreau put it, there was "a transcendentalism in mechanics as well as in ethics."[34]

What did Thoreau mean? The Transcendentalists, he explained, believed that if man reforms himself, "nature and circumstances will be right." But Etzler and others like him argued that only after man "reforms nature and circumstances," would *he* "be right." At first, this seemed to Thoreau to make a certain amount of sense, for "no doubt the simple powers of nature properly directed by man would make it healthy and paradise," just as "the laws of man's own constitution" waited to be obeyed, "to restore him to health and happiness."[35] But as he evaluated Etzler's promises, Thoreau shifted the balance of what at first seemed like a straightforward endorsement.

He was, for example, genuinely approving of Etzler's notion that man could relate to and use nature in more positive, productive ways than he presently did. How "meanly and grossly" man dealt with nature! Thoreau exclaimed. "Can we not do more than cut and trim the forest—, can we not assist in its interior economy, in the circulation of the sap?" Etzler urged his readers that this might be possible, reminding them that there were "innumerable and immeasurable powers already existing in nature, unimproved on a large scale, or for generous and universal ends, amply sufficient" to support a new kind of economy.[36] Thoreau also heartily welcomed the author's understanding of the potential of wind, tides and waves, and sunshine as renewable sources of energy. "Oh ye millwrights, ye engineers, ye operatives and speculators of every class," Thoreau exclaimed, "never again complain of a want of power."[37]

Eventually, however, the Transcendentalist in Thoreau arose and begged Etzler to think even more creatively. The important question that this book raised, Thoreau told readers of the *Democratic Review*, was not "how we shall execute, but what."[38] In other words, what most needed doing? Was it enough to transform the environment, or did mankind need another sort of revolution? Citing Etzler's passage about the gratification of all men's earthly needs by the mere turning of a crank, Thoreau observed, there is "a certain divine energy in every man, sparingly employed as yet, which may be called the crank within,—the crank after all,—the prime mover in all machinery,—quite indispensable to all work." Etzler had neglected to take into account the continuing centrality of the individual to any serious, permanent reform. "We will not be imposed upon by this vast application of forces," Thoreau wrote, for he believed that most things would still be accomplished through each individual's "application called Industry."[39]

"Alas!" Thoreau added plaintively, "the crying sin of the age" is "this want of faith in the prevalence of a man," for nothing could be effected "but by one man." Here then is what O'Sullivan initially objected to in Thoreau's review and that he could not get him fully to purge, a sense that the reform of each individual trumped any effort at widespread social reform through communal association. Thoreau had "little faith in corporations" to reform the world.

"We must first succeed alone," he announced, before we could "enjoy our success together."[40]

Thus, Thoreau warned that Etzler's "castles" would fall to the ground, because they were not built "lofty enough," were not "secured to heaven's roof." The German's chief fault was that he aimed too low and sought "to secure the greatest degree of gross comfort and pleasure merely." Doing so, Etzler advocated merely "a Mahometan's heaven," a garden of sensual rather than spiritual delights. Transcendentalism again asserting itself, Thoreau opined, "If we were to reform this outward life truly and thoroughly, we should find no duty of the inner omitted."[41]

Etzler premised nothing on the inner man. The outward world was all. But a Transcendentalist "conversant with supernal powers" never would worship only "these inferior deities of the wind, the waves, tide, and sunshine." Mankind did not so much need a calculus based on physics and engineering, as on an ethics of "love." Alluding to Etzler's frequent calculations of the physical force necessary to perform certain tasks, Thoreau asked the reader to compare "the moral with the physical, and say how many horsepower the force of love, for instance, blowing on every square foot of man's soul would equal."[42]

Yet even though the wisest men in all ages had labored "to publish this force" and every human heart was "sooner or later, more or less, made to feel it," how infrequently, Thoreau noted, had it been taken into account for "social ends." Love remained the true "motive power" of all "social machinery." But just as mechanical forces had not yet been "generously and largely" applied to make the physical world answer to the ideal, "so the power of love has been put meanly and sparingly applied." It had been used only to create institutions—almshouses, hospitals, Bible societies—that paralleled man's crude industrial machinery, while he awaited a more deep-seated transformation, of the inner self.[43]

Given Thoreau's search for practical solutions to nineteenth-century challenges, his praise of Etzler's plan to use nature's powers in a more economical way is understandable. But more important was his announcement, for the first time in print, that the pressing question was not how to reform society, but how to reform *individuals* so that the society they created was more just and equitable. To Thoreau, this occurred not in communal settings but only when people participated in a higher economy in which charity was the coin of the realm.

In a letter to his sister, a month or so before publication of his review of Etzler, Thoreau had expressed just such misgivings about what he saw as many of the Associationists' evident self-centeredness, a predictable by-product of their stress on the material rather than the spiritual. His objection to William Henry Channing, he wrote Helen Thoreau, "and all that fraternity"—that is, the other communitarians—was, that they "need and deserve sympathy themselves, rather than are able to render it to others." They mistook "their private ail for an infected atmosphere" generally. But let any one of them "right his particular grievance"—that is, overcome what troubled him specifically—and he ceased to be devoted to large-scale societal reform.[44]

In a draft of an almost-completed essay or lecture from this period, "Reform and Reformers" (1844), Thoreau elaborated on this notion. He depicted a dichotomy likely derived from Emerson's lecture, "The Conservative" (1841), in which his mentor had divided people into the party of "Conservatism" and that of "Innovation."[45] Thoreau likewise identified people as "Conservatives" or "Reformers." The former often had the annoying and self-righteous proclivity to say, "*We* and *Our*, as if they had never been assured of an individual existence," he complained. They were "public men, fashionable men, ambitious men," those of "property, standing and respectability, for the most part, and in all cases created by society," and unaware or dismissive of all the "social disorder and imperfection" around them. They understood their chief duty to "preserve the law and order and institution" already in place.[46]

Reformers, on the other hand, personified such disorder and imperfection, and sought to "heal and reform" society. How? By discovering "the divine order and conform[ing] to it," earnestly asking "the cooperation of all men" to do so.[47] But, as in his review of Etzler, Thoreau faulted this group for not being radical enough because most of them only "meddl[ed] with the exposed roots of innocent institutions" rather than exploring their own deep structure. Effective reform, Thoreau believed, had to be approached as "a private and individual enterprise" because most likely "the evil" was "private also."[48] Any reformer who recommended to his fellow men a new institution or system, Thoreau wrote, could not rely merely on the strength of his own logic or argument (as, say, Fourier or Etzler had done) but had to "see that he represents one pretty perfect institution in himself, the centre and circumference of all others, an erect man."[49]

Thoreau asked of all who urged on others such causes as "Temperance—Justice—Charity—Peace, the Family, Community or Associative life" not to preach "their theory and wisdom only" but to offer an example of the fruits of such reform, "a small specimen of [their] own manufactures." Each man, he advised, should take care "to emit his own fragrance." Thoreau did not want to know about someone's devotion to a cause but of its effect on that individual, to see "the flower and fruit of the man—some fragrance at least as of fresh spring life."[50] From the temperance man Thoreau wanted to savor the result of his temperance, to see "if it be good." He wanted to enjoy "the blessings of liberty" from the "Just man" and to taste "the sweets of Community life" from the "Community man"—to experience the divine order evidenced by individuals acting in clear conformity with such order.[51]

Too often, however, when Thoreau asked "the schemer" to show him "the material of which his structure is to be built," all he got

were "fair looking words, resolute and solid words for the underpinning, convenient and homely words for the body of the edifice,
poems and flights of the imagination for the cupola," but no strong
foundation for the project in the reformer's own life.[52] He reminded
his audience that what prophets had said often was forgotten, and
that the wisdom of the oracles usually decayed. History, though,
remembered what "heroes and saints" had done.[53] Deeds always
mattered more than words.

By stressing the significance of such "fragrance" that emanated
from a man whose works flowed from his deepest self, Thoreau
emphasized each person's essential and inviolable individuality,
that which often was lost in the organizational complexities of
communal life. He did not object "to action in societies or communities" per se, as long as an individual used "the society as his instrument, rather than the society using the individual," as frequently
was the case in communities like Fourier's and, presumably, would
be in Etzler's.[54]

Criticizing his countrymen's penchant for starting out for des-
tinations far from their homes (and using words he reworked only
slightly for the conclusion of *Walden* [1854]), Thoreau counseled
inward exploration. "Those who dwell in Oregon and the far west,"
he observed, were not so solitary "as the enterprising and independent thinker, applying his discoveries to his own life."[55] Too many
people, he complained, seemed always "outward bound, they live
out and out, are going and coming, looking before and behind, all
out of doors and in the air." Rather, for the greatest reward they
should be "inward bound." Already in his twenties, Thoreau knew
that there was nothing "which can delight or astonish the eyes,"
but one could discover it on "the private sea, the Atlantic and Pacific of one's being alone," even as, for example, one rowed on a neighborhood pond.[56]

Thoreau at Walden Pond

In the late fall of 1843 Thoreau returned from New York City and moved in with his parents. He helped his father in his pencil-making business and also continued writing, although the demise of the *Dial* early in 1844 closed off the venue where most of his work had appeared. A new friend, Isaac Hecker, who had circulated through Brook Farm and Fruitlands looking to anchor himself in one of those communities but was disappointed by both, asked Thoreau to join him on a walking trip through Europe.

Hecker had boarded for a few months in the Thoreau family home and was fond of Thoreau, as Thoreau was of him. But Thoreau demurred, explaining that, although the proposal strongly tempted him and made him experience "a decided schism between [his] outward and inward tendencies," wandering through Europe did not seem as rewarding as "exploring the *Farther Indies,* which are to be reached you know by other routs [*sic*] and other methods of travel."[57] Back from his short stay in New York, Thoreau was beginning to understand that his own "higher latitudes" offered an opportunity for more and different adventures, ones that were possible even as he still boarded in his beloved Concord.

His decision proved epochal, for in the spring of 1845, on land near Walden Pond that Emerson recently had purchased, Thoreau began to build a one-room cabin that he completed in the fall. He cut and squared timbers from pine trees on the acreage, and with friends raised the frame. He purchased an Irishman's shanty for the clapboards and hardware, boarded and roofed his new home, and move into it on the Fourth of July, Independence Day. It had cost him a little more than twenty-eight dollars, about the same amount, he noted wryly, that a student paid annually for a room at Harvard College. For two years, two months, and two days, this was the site of Thoreau's radical experiment in "Individual Sovereignty" very different from that which Ripley would advocate at

Brook Farms, Andrews champion on Long Island, or Etzler would eventually, disastrously, attempt in South America.[58]

Later, when Thoreau reported his adventure in *Walden* (1854), he explained his motivation through a psychological observation. Going against the American grain, he questioned why, given the nation's belief that constant progress guaranteed the greatest happiness of the greatest number, so many of his neighbors seemed deeply unhappy. "The mass of men," he wrote memorably, lead "lives of quiet desperation," for what was "called resignation is confirmed desperation." He had not extrapolated this observation from a mere handful of examples or from secondhand reports. He had traveled a "good deal in Concord," he reminded his readers, "and everywhere, in shops, and offices, and fields," its citizens seemed beaten down and "doing penance in a thousand remarkable ways."[59]

Sadly, whether or not they acknowledged it, his townspeople—indeed, all Americans—led "sneaking lives." They were always "promising to pay, to-morrow, and dying to-day, insolvent." They sought to "curry favor" with their neighbors, and so lied to and flattered them, "contracting [themselves] into a nutshell of civility" so that they might persuade someone to let them "make his shoes, or his hat, or his coat, or his carriage, or import his groceries for him," making themselves sick, that they might "lay up something against a sick day."[60]

His neighbors' "desperation" was endemic to the economic system in which they were inextricably tangled, and thus they stood as prime exhibits of the fruits of American capitalism. Rather than bringing them bounty and contentment, the economic system had dehumanized them, made them into mere "machines" and "the tools of their tools."[61] In the years after the Panic of 1837, this must have seemed especially clear, as men and women were revealed to be pawns in a game they could not control, part of a system that played by its own inhuman rules. Moving to Walden Pond, Thoreau rejected this system. He wanted to live a different, simpler life even than those who had taken part in quasi-socialist experiments like Brook Farm. He wanted to discover whether one could attain true happiness through work that flowed from one's conscience, even if it led to what the majority of his townspeople considered an "unproductive" life. "My purpose in going to Walden Pond," Thoreau wrote, "was not to live cheaply nor to live dearly there, but to transact some private business with the fewest obstacles."[62] He returned to the metaphor he had already tested in one of his lectures. The "business" was daring and personal, to explore his own "higher latitudes," the "private sea, the Atlantic and Pacific Ocean of one's being alone."[63]

Thoreau knew enough of Brook Farm to realize that he could not accomplish this there. Noble as their goals seemed, its members, and those of other such communities, had not fully removed themselves from the competitive capitalist system. Ripley's utopia, for example, was chartered as a joint-stock company, and both Fourier and Etzler counseled similar arrangements. Thoreau wanted to "get" a living differently, honestly, without speculation, and with freedom left for his own pursuits, without sullying himself with the "curse of trade."[64] As liberating as life at Brook Farm seemed to many of his friends, for him it failed the crucial test of allowing one to live without seeking advantage over one's fellow men and women. The cost of something, he explained, "is the amount of what I will call life which is required to be exchanged for it, immediately or in the long run."[65] He was not going into debt for something of little or no value, or that he found psychologically debilitating, or that guaranteed success only at his neighbor's expense.

"Simplify, simplify," Thoreau counseled himself, and he stayed true to his command.[66] His house at Walden stood in stark contrast to Etzler's (and Fourier's) envisioned domiciles, so like grand palaces, each with its hundreds of rooms, constructed and furnished to provide everyone with hitherto unrealized comfort and pleasure.

Thoreau's was a one-room cabin, with two windows and a door, heated by a fireplace, and containing a minimum of furnishings—a table, a desk, a bed, three chairs. The Spartan accommodations had their purpose. Before we adorn our houses with beautiful objects, he explained, "the walls must be stripped, and our lives must be stripped, and beautiful housekeeping and beautiful living be laid for a foundation."[67] Then a habitation was ready for occupancy.

It also was important that Thoreau had built his own dwelling, literally from the ground up, with skills that once were commonplace but had become rare. As mechanization proliferated, people no longer "worked"; instead, one had a particular "job." Someone was a tailor, a merchant, a shoemaker, or a tinsmith, for example, whereas fifteen years earlier he might have done all such things as part of his way of "making a living." Instead of the kind of infinite parsing of work into "attractive" specialties that Fourier imagined, or its virtual elimination through machinery, as did Etzler, Thoreau urged competence at a variety of tasks. Where would "this division of labor" end? Who had "advanced" more at the end of a month, he asked rhetorically, a boy who made his own jackknife from ore which he had dug and smelted after he read how to do it, or one who had attended "lectures on metallurgy at the Institute in the mean while," and who had been given a penknife by his father?[68]

Thoreau's countrymen had been brainwashed to believe that industrialization and its attendant division of labor "improved" life. But, given the culture's emphasis on competition, Thoreau showed it to be a sleight-of-hand trick. He lit on a telling metaphor to illustrate this. Men have "an indistinct notion," he observed, that if they kept up "this activity of joint stocks and spades long enough," all would at length "ride somewhere, in next to no time, and for nothing." But though a crowd rushed to the depot and the conductor shouted "All Aboard!" when the smoke blew away and the vapor condensed, "it will be perceived that a few are riding, but the rest are run over,—and it will be called, and will be, 'A melancholy accident.'"[69] Indeed. Thoreau had seen enough of the factories around Concord to know that Etzler's and others' optimistic faith in the machine to ameliorate everyday life was wrongheaded. Urging constant economic growth rather than individual fulfillment, such reformers misunderstood the true grounds of human happiness.

Etzler had promised a new paradise within decades. Thoreau, however, realized what he sought in a much shorter span—a few months. He had found, for example, that "by working about six weeks in a year," cultivating his bean field and picking up spare work at surveying or carpentry, he might cover all his annual expenses and have the remaining time for his own pursuits, his nature study and writing.[70] At Walden Pond he learned what no member of the intentional communities had yet realized, that to maintain one's self on this earth was "not a hardship but a pastime," if one lived "simply and wisely," according to the "higher laws" that were revealed when one lived the simple life.[71]

To his credit, unlike many self-righteous reformers who saw their ways as the only ways, Thoreau did not believe that others should simply replicate how he lived at Walden Pond. Yes, the nation was in dire straits because everyone bought into the same dream of perpetual economic growth. But the solution was not to go to Walden Pond or to join a community in the belief that such association would effect one's transformation. Rather, each person should be "very careful to find out and pursue his own way, and not his father's or his mother's or his neighbor's instead." Thoreau knew that the cooperation found in the utopian experiments was always "exceedingly partial and superficial" unless the community found a way to respect and preserve each person's individuality within its particular social arrangements. "If a man has faith he will cooperate with equal faith every where," Thoreau counseled. If he did not believe in himself, he simply continued to "live like the rest of the world, whatever company he is joined to," on Concord's Mill Dam or at Brook Farm.[72] The discovery and turning of the "crank within" was the hard work that, once done, promised meaningful change.

In a chapter of *Walden* called "Solitude," Thoreau explained his penchant for the solitary life over that lived within the complex social arrangements of the communities. Society, he complained, was "commonly too cheap." Further, even though people met each other frequently in the new, frenetic economy, this was frequently only at "very short intervals" and thus did not allow "any time to acquire any new value for each other." They encountered each other only at times established by custom—at three meals a day, say, or at the post office, and at the fireside at night, where they were "sociable." In these ways, "We live thick and are in each other's way, and stumble over one another," but usually without any true meeting of minds and hearts.[73]

Why was this so? Why this fear of true communication between independent beings? Try as one might to mitigate or deny the fact, Thoreau believed, each person was profoundly and permanently singular. This is what it meant to be a prisoner in one's self-consciousness. Sounding like a twenty-first-century practitioner of mindfulness meditation, Thoreau explained that, however intense any experience he had, "I always was conscious of the presence and criticism of a part of me, which, as it were, is not a part of me, but a spectator, sharing no experience, but taking note of it; and that is no more I than it is you." When "the play of life" is over, he continued, "the spectator goes his way." The experience is simply "a kind of fiction" that occurs in consciousness.[74]

A life of solitude, with attendant integrity and self-sufficiency, allowed one to understand such things, the true ground of existence, and thus to discover those "higher laws" by which man lives a truly moral life. "The nation itself," Thoreau explained, "with all its so-called internal improvements" (that in fact were merely "external and superficial") had become "an unwieldy and overgrown establishment," ruined "by luxury and needless expense." The only cure was for each person to adopt a "rigid economy," "a stern and more than Spartan simplicity of life and elevation of purpose" that led him to what was truly valuable in life.[75] New Englanders, he explained, continued to live the "mean life" they did because they did not look beyond "the surface of things." "We think that *is*," he observed, "which *appears* to be." Thoreau's countrymen had to know how to be satisfied with what they had, and thus to stop always wanting something newer and greater. "God himself culminates in the present moment," he declared, "and will never be more divine in the lapse of all the ages."[76]

Here was the divine backstop to Thoreau's musings on individual reform born of self-reflection but capable of promising wider reform: the indwelling universal laws accessible to all who earnestly sought them. When one understands God's presence in each moment, morality becomes self-evident. If one lives with true integrity, as Thoreau urged, one will "pass an invisible boundary." "New, universal, and more liberal laws" begin "to establish themselves around and within him, or the old laws" expand and are interpreted "in his favor in a more liberal sense." This person now lives "with the license of a higher order of beings." If that meant that one contradicted or trespassed the laws of society, so be it, for man should not be mindlessly in their thrall. Instead, he should "maintain himself in whatever attitude he find[s] himself through obedience to the laws of his being, which will never be one of opposition to a just government," if, Thoreau added sarcastically, "he should chance to meet with such."[77]

After he left Walden Pond, Thoreau's problem was precisely this—how to behave toward a society (and its representative government) that everywhere trampled what should be the inviolable rights of the individual vouched for by higher laws than man's. He left his cabin, he told his readers, because he had "several more lives to live" and could not "spare any more time for that one."[78] He had learned what he needed from his sojourn, and now he had to use that knowledge to structure a meaningful life among his townspeople. Knowing his aloneness, he wanted to reenter the social world as a sovereign individual and to offer his example, or in Thoreau's own terms, share his "fragrance," with others. He did so in part by continuing to explore how and to what extent someone who knew "higher laws" should position himself in relation to a morally (and financially) bankrupt society.

"Resistance to Civil Government"

Thoreau did not have long to wait before something tested his newfound resolve to live from within. Like many New Englanders, he regarded the government's declaration of war against Mexico in 1846 as a blatant ploy by Southern states to gain territory south of the Mason-Dixon Line into which slavery could eventually be extended. Unlike many, however, he took concrete action. To show his disgust at and disapproval of the federal government's actions, he refused to pay his local poll tax for several years and eventually was briefly jailed until a relative paid off what he owed.

He recorded his experience in "Resistance to Civil Government," an essay that he published in 1849 in the sole issue of Transcendentalist Elizabeth Peabody's *Aesthetic Papers*. Renamed "Civil Disobedience" when it was reissued after his death, it indicts a political system that disregards the rights of the minority. It also was a clarion call to citizens to throw their weight against the state if any of its actions ran counter to "higher laws" discerned by conscience.

At the heart of Thoreau's plea was the self-sufficiency and sanctity of the individual, for a government in which the majority ruled "in all cases" was not one "based on justice." Instead, one needed a government in which "majorities do not virtually decide right or wrong, but conscience." Why should man have such a faculty, he

asked, if he has to "resign" it to the whims of legislators for whom
expediency was the highest law? Instead, he wanted to awaken
readers to cultivate not so much "a respect for the law, so much as
for the right."[79] Although there were thousands who were "*in
opinion*" opposed to certain societal injustices, he knew that they
did nothing "*in effect*" to end them because they feared contradicting
the majority, whose position was to be supported because they were
just that, the majority. His countrymen "hesitate[d], and regret[ted],
and sometimes they petition[ed]," but they did "nothing in earnest
and with effect" to halt social injustice. As a result, he asked rhetorically, what was "the price-current of an honest man and patriot
today?"[80]

Even the much-vaunted right to vote was a sham, Thoreau explained, because, while it made the individual think that in casting
a ballot he had done right, he simply had participated in a system
that empowered the will of the majority. Voting thus was nothing
but "a sort of gaming, like chequers or backgammon, with a slight
moral tinge to it, a playing with right and wrong, with moral questions." Again, even if a man cast his vote and thought that he had
done his duty in the matter, he was not "vitally concerned" that
right should then prevail, because he was willing to leave the decision to the majority. So, to vote "*for the right*," Thoreau explained,
in fact was "*doing* nothing for it."[81] White male citizens simply
soothed their consciences by voting.

After his experience at Walden Pond, Thoreau could no longer
accept such majority rule. When it was evident that unjust laws
existed, he asked, should the good man "be content to obey them,"
or "attempt to amend them, and obey them" until they were
changed, or "transgress them at once?" To a man of conscience,
the answer was clear. If the evil was such that it required one "to
be an agent of injustice to another," one had to break the law. "Let
your life," Thoreau counseled, "be a counter friction to stop the machine," for it mattered "not how small the beginning might seem"

but, rather, that the man of conscience made the gesture and understood that what is "once well done is done forever."[82] There will never be "a really free and enlightened State," Thoreau concluded, until it recognized the individual "as a higher and independent power" from which all its power and authority were derived.[83]

Outraged by the Mexican War, in his journal Thoreau further explored his dismissal of oppressive government. The chief outward obstacles that always stood in his way as he sought to live morally, he complained, "were not living men—but dead institutions." The only "highwayman"—that is, robber—he had ever met was the "State" itself, for when he refused to pay the tax that it demanded to prosecute what he viewed as an illegal war, it pretended to offer him protection but instead took away his right to act according to higher law. More insidiously, when he asserted something as basic as "the freedom it [had] declared [for all men]," the state imprisoned him. "Not thieves & highwaymen but Constables & judges" were at the root of the nation's problems—"not sinners but priests—not the ignorant but pedants & pedagogues—not foreign foes but standing armies—not pirates but men of war." And "not free malevolence—but organized benevolence"—these threatened the sacred freedom of each individual.[84]

The passage of the Fugitive Slave Law in 1850 similarly incensed Thoreau, prompting a lecture, "Slavery in Massachusetts," in which he extended his thoughts about the sovereignty of the individual in matters of moral concern. He reminded his readers that they had been men first, and Americans "only at a late and convenient hour." Laws were fine and good, to protect one's property, say. But no matter how valuable, they were worthless if they "did not keep you and humanity together."[85]

Clearly the laws as currently written were blatantly divisive. Judges, lawyers, and the like, for example, did not care whether the Fugitive Slave Law was "right" but whether it was "constitutional." But, Thoreau asked, "is virtue constitutional, or vice?" Is "equity constitutional, or iniquity?" The question was not whether seventy years ago one's grandfather entered into an agreement "to serve the devil," as the Founders had when they legalized slavery, but "whether you will not now, for once and at last, serve God."[86] The nation did not need men of "policy, but of probity," those who recognized "a higher law than the Constitution, or the decision of the majority."[87] Such men and women were the only truly "sovereign individuals," and they had to stand against a government that returned fugitive slaves to their masters.

"Life without Principle"

The Mexican War had provided a blatant example of the country's pursuit of economic expansion despite the objection of a minority. Within two years, another such folly, the "California Gold Rush," provided Thoreau with more ammunition with which to attack the American way to wealth.

In "Life without Principle," a lecture he delivered several times in the 1850s and which he prepared for publication shortly before his death, he recurred to overt criticism of the nation's economic system, based as it was on a capitalism that tolerated slavery. He asked his readers to consider the ways in which most of them spent their lives, immersed, he suggested, most likely "in a world of business." It was nothing "but work, work, work," he complained, as his compatriots labored to accumulate wealth and prestige, at someone else's expense.[88] And if like Thoreau, however, one questioned the reason behind and final value of such labor, and sought to "walk in the woods for love of them half of each day," one's neighbors could not fathom such a waste of time. Any man who acted in this way was in danger of being regarded a mere "loafer."[89]

Thoreau's contemporaries' problem was compounded because, virtually "without exception," economic success led "downward"; that is, it buried man's higher nature.[90] Given such a melancholy state of affairs, Thoreau found it "remarkable" that there had been "little or nothing written on the subject of getting a living," and specifically, about how work might be "not merely honest and honorable, but altogether inviting and glorious."[91] Instead, most people tried to avoid it, the rush to the California goldfields but the latest example. The forty-niners' goal was not to reap the reward of their industry but to quickly become rich and never again have to labor.

But the gold fever was emblematic of an even deeper malaise, an utter disregard for how one made money. "As for the means of living," Thoreau noted, "it is wonderful how indifferent men of all classes are about it, even reformers, so called,—whether they inherit, or earn, or steal it."[92] So what did this mean for how one should actually seek to live? His contemporaries obviously misunderstood "wisdom," for how could one be "wise" if this meant simply that one was "only more cunning and intellectually subtle" than his neighbor? The latest example of such selfishness was indeed "the rush to California," and the approval of it, "not merely of merchants, but of philosophers and prophets, so called, in relation to it," which reflected "the greatest disgrace on mankind." That so many people were ready "to live by luck, and so get the means of commanding the labor of those less lucky, without contributing anything of value to society" seemed sheer madness as well as stupidity.[93]

Thoreau could conceive of no more startling development of "the immorality of trade" than this mad dash for western riches. Panning for gold made God, he bitterly observed, into nothing more than "a moneyed gentleman who scatters a handful of pennies in order to see mankind scramble for them." The gold digger was no hard-working, industrious soul potentially rewarded for his productive work but the enemy of honest laborers, no better than a gambler in San Francisco's saloons, shaking "dirt" instead of "dice."[94] Better, Thoreau knew, "to sink a shaft down to the gold within . . . and work that mine," where true riches lay.[95]

California, however, was merely a mirror of New England, for the gold diggers were "bred at her own school and church" where profit always came first.[96] And likewise New England was a synecdoche for the nation itself, for, even if one granted that Americans had freed themselves from "a political tyrant," in their insatiable desire for more wealth they showed themselves nothing but slaves to "an economical and moral" one. "We tax ourselves unjustly," he wrote, invoking his countrymen's enshrinement of the days of 1776, for there is "a part of us which is not represented." Yes, "we quarter troops," but we also "quarter our gross bodies on our poor souls, till the former eat up the latter's substance."[97] Even as many reformers sought to change so many aspects of American life, these idealists did not acknowledge the need for such fundamental self-reform, perhaps because they had not mined themselves as deeply as Thoreau. Or if they had, they had seen that the kinds of changes demanded would take too great a toll on their purses.

The Sovereignty of Individuals, the Freedom of Slaves

Thoreau was convinced that the enshrinement of individual conscience as the highest arbiter pointed the way to the moral life. Concomitantly, as he indicated in "Resistance to Civil Government," he did not encourage participation or even trust in large-scale movements whose proponents sought to eradicate social ills. For him, the answer was individual disengagement from any of the state's immoral policies—hence, his refusal of its right of taxation as long as it sanctioned slavery. "How does it become a man to behave toward this American government today?" he asked. He could not "without disgrace be associated with it" and so had to reject any claim it had over him.[98]

Thoreau resented that the U.S. government had forced him into such choices by having created and justified an institution so immoral that he was forced to act against it. This should not be the government's purpose. Rather, it was meant to be merely "an expedient by which men would fain succeed in letting one another alone" and thus was most successful when the "governed [were] most let alone by it."⁹⁹ This clearly was no longer the case.

Because Thoreau believed in the inalienable right of each individual to conduct whatever private "business" he felt called to transact, because he had "other concerns to engage him," he did not think that it was his job to "devote himself to the eradication of any, even the most enormous wrong," and particularly when the government had created it. But once the injustice was there, as a man of conscience it was his duty "at least to wash his hands of it, and, if he gives it no thought longer, not to give it practically his support."¹⁰⁰ This, Thoreau believed, was required of a man of good conscience, and not that he had to change the course of his life to work to reform the world's manifold evils.

This explains what to many is Thoreau's problematic statement in *Walden*'s first chapter when he wonders how his townspeople could be so "frivolous" as to worry about "the gross but somewhat foreign form of servitude called Negro Slavery," when there were already "so many keen and subtle masters" that enslaved them themselves. "It is hard to have a southern overseer," he admitted, but "worse to have a northern one." Worst of all, however, was "when you are the slave-driver of yourself."¹⁰¹ Thoreau thought that it was fatuous to devote one's time to a problem hundreds of miles away when there was an equally insidious evil right within Concord, one that underlay its very economy.

Rather than joining abolitionist societies and debating endlessly the problem of slavery, those who favored its abolition should, as individuals, immediately disengage themselves from the government, not waiting until they were a majority party but resting assured that it was enough "if they have God on their side." To Thoreau, it sufficed to know that, "any man more right than his neighbors" constituted "a majority of one."¹⁰² "If one thousand," he claimed, "if one hundred, if ten men whom I could name,—if ten *honest* men only, aye, if one HONEST man, in this State of Massachusetts, *ceasing to hold slaves*, were actually to withdraw" his partnership with the state, "and be locked up in the county jail therefor [*sic*], it would be the abolition of slavery in America."[103]

But, would it? Tired of hearing reformers natter on about a problem, Thoreau wanted to see the fruits of their sincerity in immediate, individual gestures. But the U.S. government was perfectly willing to incarcerate whomever broke civil law. What good did it do the millions of the enslaved if such conscientious individuals served their nights in jail? Ever the champion of individual sovereignty, in the early 1850s Thoreau still thought that engaging in civil disobedience and accepting the penalties for it cleansed one of evil so that one was free to live his life as he saw fit. Once a man had negated the government's hold on him, the larger cause—the complete eradication of slavery—was a different concern.

Presumably, one then slept undisturbed by his Southern brothers' and sisters' screams and tears. But what if the sound could not be blocked? What if one's devotion to individual conscience moved him to more extreme civil disobedience, even to physical violence against the government or some of its citizens? Was this what devotion to individual sovereignty implied and allowed? Soon enough, one of Thoreau's acquaintances acted in ways that posed just this question.

7

John Brown and the Bankruptcy of Conscience

After two decades of effort, much of it catalyzed by the Panic of 1837, during which advocates for the nineteenth-century antebellum liberal ethos explored myriad ways to put Americans and America on a better, healthier, more moral track, disaster struck again. Despite hundreds of thousands of Americans—perhaps millions—having literally had their heads examined by phrenologists, despite utopian communities dotting however briefly the landscape from Massachusetts to Ohio, despite the few very public and the uncountable private efforts at individual self-improvement, and even as slavery and sectionalism strained ever more the bonds of nationhood, the economy once again jumped the rails.

In the late summer of 1857, America seemed to be flourishing— as one contemporary remembered, "the country to all appearances was in a high state of prosperity."[1] Then, on August 24, the Ohio Life Insurance and Trust Company, the largest and seemingly most secure bank in Ohio, with important offices in New York City, failed. Its New York director had loaned too freely and then embezzled from the bank's already depleted reserves, and before long the institution had to suspend specie payments. At first, this affected mainly the New York financial sector, but because other of the city's banks worried about their own ability to redeem notes, they began calling in loans from smaller, regional institutions and asked for payment in specie. The Panic of 1857 had begun.

Within two months, more than 260 banks throughout the country were forced to close their doors. Tumbling wages and unemployment followed. Crowds of financially distressed men roamed the streets. One such mob in New York numbered twenty to thirty thousand strong, spilling off of sidewalks and choking the entrances to the banks, demanding specie for notes and checks.[2] Massachusetts Whig politician Robert Winthrop put it succinctly: "The world never seemed to me a less hopeful place than in this month of September, in the Year of our Lord, 1857."[3]

While the failure of the Ohio Life and Trust precipitated the crisis, the same improvident mix of ever-rising land values, fueled this time by the exponential expansion of railroads, particularly in the West, and unrealistic investors and speculators, produced another nationwide panic and collapse.[4] When credit in the East contracted, the rail companies began to tumble, taking the farming and manufacturing sectors down with them. But many saw a more familiar failing as standing behind it all.

"Speculators," the prestigious *North American Review* snarled, "whose only function is to derange prices, unsettle markets, entrap purchasers, defraud sellers, and introduce into transactions intrinsically necessary and honest the hazards and chicanery of the gaming table," were to blame.[5] And what animated these speculators? Selfishness, pure and simple.

Unitarian clergyman and erstwhile Transcendentalist Theodore Parker, who preached to one of the largest congregations in Boston, was unsparing in his indictment of the greed that had brought on the latest financial debacle. Merchants, he inveighed, forsook their legitimate business and dabbled in this or that investment. Then "simple men, seeing these marvels of success," next ventured their hard earnings and went "to gambling likewise." Lawyers followed suit, and then, "that there may be no want of moral sanctity," ministers of the Gospel secretly bought and sold stocks. "Now," Parker concluded, "when the company themselves are gigantic speculators by fraudulent and dishonest means; and when the stock of the company goes up and down the street, carrying in its hand a bowl drugged with gambling, and crowds rush to its intoxication, is it strange that, at length, the head is sick, the whole body faint?"[6] The results of such "intoxication" soon appeared everywhere, and affected high and low alike as the nation revisited the distress that had followed the Panic of 1837.

Just as had occurred two decades earlier, in 1857 fear became contagious, with everyone believing that his business would be next into the abyss. New York diarist George Templeton Strong accurately described the nation's growing trauma: "It is an epidemic of fear and distrust."[7] Numbers of jobless swelled through the fall of 1857, giving rise to widespread anxieties that social unrest soon would follow. In New York, nearly twenty thousand persons were thrown out of employment "in a single fortnight," and, throughout New England, "the distress in large manufacturing towns, for want of work, made the prospect of winter absolutely sickening."[8] In Philadelphia, one concerned citizen noted that "a nightmare broods over society." He added, "Bread riots are dreaded. Winter is coming. God alone foresees the history of the next six months."[9]

A larger problem still lay unattended. Beneath the nation's economic as well as political troubles lay the canker of sectionalism and, of course, slavery. The Panic of 1857 coincided with the protracted and sometimes violent debate over the extension of slavery into new territories—specifically, Kansas and Nebraska—that had followed the notorious Kansas-Nebraska Act of 1854.

By allowing the citizenry of these two new territories to decide for themselves whether slavery should be allowed (what critics called "squatter sovereignty"), the Kansas-Nebraska Act effectively nullified the long-standing Missouri Compromise prohibiting slavery north of the 36° 30' parallel. When the new state of California,

territory won in the Mexican War, excluded slavery, supporters of
the peculiar institution panicked and decided that if they could secure Kansas to their side the tally would be even. Proslavery "Border
Ruffians" flooded the new territories to stuff the ballot boxes, while
antislavery "Jayhawkers," or "Free Staters," many sponsored by
eastern "Emigrant Aid" societies, took advantage of cheap land to
swell the antislavery vote. Inevitable confrontations between the
parties increased, and there followed seven years of political tur-
moil and escalating violence that Horace Greeley dubbed "Bleeding
Kansas." Clearly, the impotent political system that had allowed
the formation of new states to devolve to this level was incapable
of addressing head on the nation's increasing bifurcation over
slavery.

The most notorious episode occurred on 26 May 1856, when fervent abolitionist John Brown and a handful of followers massacred
five proslavery settlers at Pottawatomie Creek as retribution for
the unprovoked killing of five antislavery men over the previous
several months. Brown escaped to fight another day, first at Osawatomie that August, and more infamously at Harpers Ferry, Virginia,
in 1859.

John Brown, Failed Businessman

Brown's peculiar trajectory through American history, which saw
him traverse the lives and interests of many of the reformers tracked
in this book, was set in motion by the Panic of 1837, of which he
was an economic casualty. Thereafter, his never-ending financial
difficulties drove him further and further into radical abolitionism,
until he came to believe that violence was necessary to abolish
slavery. As his son John Brown Jr. put it, "The financial crash came
in 1837, and down came all of father's castles, and buried the reputation he had achieved of possessing at least good common-sense
in respect to business matters."[10] Like so many of his contempo-

raries, failure in the market precipitated an ever more searing self-examination of his faith and conscience.

So, before John Brown was an abolitionist, he was a businessman, but not a very good one, to judge by his experiences between the Panics of 1837 and 1857. As a recent biographer puts it, "Few people in history have failed so miserably in so many different pursuits."[11] He was born in Torrington, Connecticut, in 1800 of poor but respectable parents, orthodox Christians descended from Puritan stock.[12] In his teens Brown had a profound conversion experience and thereafter believed in the divine authority of the Bible and drew from it as well his visceral hatred of the chattel slavery that undergirded the American South and supported the national economy. From his father Brown learned the tanning trade, but over the course of his working life he also was a surveyor, lumber dealer, wool grower, breeder and trainer of racehorses, land speculator, wool factor (wool merchant's agent), wool sorter, and orchardist.[13] Not surprisingly, given his deep religious bent, he also had harbored thoughts of training for the ministry, but recurring eye trouble as well as his family's financial difficulties dashed his wish to attend Amherst College.

Apart from the Bible, he derived most of his wisdom from Benjamin Franklin, absorbing the lessons from Franklin's autobiography and devoting himself with diligence to whatever trade he followed. By 1835, now married and with children—eventually with two wives he fathered twenty—he had found his way to Ohio and established a tannery. He was speculating in real estate as well, hoping to make money from land adjacent to the Pennsylvania and Ohio Canal. The Panic of 1837 dashed any hopes for a profit, and he had to assign all his investments to his creditors. By 1842, to cover other obligations, he also lost his home in Hudson, Ohio, and was briefly imprisoned for bankruptcy.

As he struggled to right his financial situation—through the 1840s he tried to raise himself from his indebtedness by becoming a wool producer and dealer in New England—Brown became a fervent abolitionist. As one historian notes, "It is almost impossible to comprehend Brown's militant crusade against slavery outside the context of his business failures and bankruptcy." He became an "outsider," John Stauffer continues, "rejected the values and beliefs of his material world, and revised his understanding of God and the permanence of sin." He wanted to bring God's law to earth to replace the insufficient and unfair system that men had instituted and continued to defend.[14]

The Cause of Abolition

Brown's increasing devotion to the antislavery effort had other, more immediate sources. For one, Brown, more than almost any other fellow abolitionist, had close relations with black people. In Springfield, Massachusetts, in 1851, for example, he exhorted free blacks to organize into a "League of Gileadites" to resist the recently passed Fugitive Slave Law. But his passion for the movement began earlier, with his family's intense religiosity. And when economic disaster upended his financial prospects, he compensated by directing his heroic energy to another cause, one to which he believed God had called him. His father, Owen Brown, was an admirer of both the great theologian Jonathan Edwards and his son Jonathan Edwards Jr., who in the course of modifying the elder Edwards's theology to the demands of the late eighteenth century also devoted himself to the antislavery cause. Brown's upbringing in this environment was determinative, for there is no denying that one of his distinguishing characteristics was a profound strain of Puritanism that combined a belief in a God-given destiny with that of man's duty to work to bring God's kingdom to earth.

This antinomian strain in Brown's thought, the belief that one has to act from conscience even when its demands abrogate outward, manmade law, surfaced in a variety of ways in the antebellum period. Ralph Waldo Emerson said as much when he observed, "the fertile forms of antinomians among the elder puritans, seemed to have their match in the plenty of the new harvest of reform," in such people, for example, as "the adepts of homeopathy, of hydropathy, of mesmerism, of phrenology" as well as those who "attacked the institution of marriage." He added that "from each of these and other movements," including abolition, there "emerged a good result, an assertion of the sufficiency of the private man."[15]

What distinguished Brown from most other contemporary reformers—and most abolitionists—was his willingness to entertain the prospect of violence to free the slaves. He admired Nat Turner, the slave who had led a bloody uprising in "south side" Virginia in 1831, and as well Cinque, the head of the group of slaves who had revolted aboard the Spanish slaver *Amistad* in 1837. In their fulmination against slavery, other chief antislavery advocates like William Lloyd Garrison and Wendell Phillips, as well as politicians like Henry Clay and Daniel Webster, sought to avoid violence at all costs. Brown knew enough of Southern intransigence to consider a resort to bloodshed likely and perhaps inevitable.

His public resolution to devote his life to ending slavery was the immediate result of the murder by proslavery advocates of antislavery editor Elijah P. Lovejoy in Alton, Illinois. Toward the end of a memorial service for Lovejoy at the fledgling Western Reserve College, Brown dramatically rose, lifted his right hand, and said, "Here, before God, in the presence of these witnesses, from this time, I consecrate my life to the destruction of slavery."[16] Around this same time, he rejected the pacifism that marked so many abolitionists and swore an oath with several of his family members to combat the institution with force of arms if necessary.[17]

Through the 1840s any serious effort in this direction was waylaid by Brown's continuing financial difficulties, but this did not stop him from formulating an elaborate "plan" to liberate Southern slaves, one he had revealed at least as early as November 1847 when he met with escaped slave Frederick Douglass, then on an anti-slavery lecture tour following the recent publication of his autobiography. To a surprised Douglass, Brown broached the idea of invading a Southern state with small bands of men, stationed in the foothills of the Appalachian Mountains. Periodically, Brown explained, these individuals would raid plantations, free the slaves, and send the more timid among them through the Underground Railroad. The others would remain in the mountain camps and thus generate more soldiers for other, similar raids. The point was not to wage outright war, but to frighten Southern slaveholders and encourage more slave rebellions, as well as to generate more anti-slavery activity in the Free States, which in turn would pressure politicians to legislate slavery out of existence.

Douglass demurred, for he still believed that Southerners could be persuaded to end the institution voluntarily and without violence. He worried, too, about retribution to any slaves who were caught in such activities. But he was singularly impressed by Brown's clear and emphatic sympathy for blacks. This openness to other races, including Native Americans, became a hallmark of Brown's activities.[18]

In 1849, after philanthropist and abolitionist Gerrit Smith provided 100,000 acres of land in northern New York near Whiteface Mountain as a place for freed blacks to resettle, Brown moved his own family there to what henceforth became the site of his homestead. His wife and children settled in North Elba, and, in 1851, having failed to make a living in the wool trade or in other employment, he joined them and devoted himself exclusively to raising funds and planning for the elimination of slavery by any means necessary. Pursuing multiple missions, in 1855 he was off to Kansas, where five of his sons sought to homestead on cheap land of the sort that speculators gobbled up and resold, and where he found himself tossed headlong into the border wars.

"Bleeding Kansas"

As Missourians flocked to the Kansas territory so that they could pad the proslavery vote when it came time for statehood, "Free Staters" from all over the East, but particularly New England and New York, met them head on, sometimes in debate, just as often in violent altercations. In 1855 Brown and his sons joined this latter group, their center the town of Lawrence on the Kansas River. By that time the Missourians, who were voting illegally in two states, had made considerable headway in passing draconian proslavery legislation. The Free Staters were committed abolitionists and were not afraid to voice their disgust at how the Missourian Border Ruffians were subverting the political process.

By all objective accounts, the Border Ruffians were very much the instigators, arresting those who proclaimed their abolitionist views and occasionally resorting to outright, unprovoked murder. John Brown arrived in the territory in the midst of what became known as the Wakarusa War. After a posse of Brown's peers freed a prominent abolitionist from arrest, in retaliation the Missourians began to plan an attack on Lawrence, which they rightly viewed as the Free State stronghold.

When Brown and his sons, fully armed and ready for battle, learned of yet more murders of antislavery men, Brown became more convinced that violence against proslavery settlers could not be avoided. At a meeting of antislavery citizens in March 1856, he stood up and declared that "he was an Abolitionist of the old stock—was dyed in the wool and that negroes were his brothers and his equals— that he would rather see this Union dissolved and the country drenched with blood than to pay taxes to the amount of one-hundredth of a mill" to a government that supported slavery.[19]

As violence, including more unprovoked murders, against abolitionists continued through the spring of 1856, Brown readied himself for action. In early May, the Border Ruffians, making good on earlier threats, stormed Lawrence and burned the Free State Hotel, symbolic headquarters of the antislavery citizens. The final accelerant came on May 22, when Preston Brooks, Democratic representative from South Carolina, responding to a perceived slight, severely beat Massachusetts senator Charles Sumner, a staunch abolitionist, on the U.S. Senate floor. When Brown heard of the beating, which had rendered the senator senseless and almost crippled, he was outraged. He became convinced that violence had to be met with violence.

On May 26, Brown decided to avenge the deaths of several of his fellow abolitionists in Kansas, who had died for nothing but their belief in man's equality, by finding and executing prominent proslavery men. At Pottawatomie Creek he found what he was looking for—men active in proslavery politics and who had in one way or another threatened the Brown family for their activities. He and his associates killed five men, hacking them to death with broadswords. Brown justified what amounted to an act of terror by claiming that the antislavery men's penchant for compromise and passivity in the face of Southern outrages simply had to stop. Echoing numerous reformers of more timid inclinations, Brown would show the way by example.

Kansas was in such a state of warfare that, although warrants were issued for Brown and his associates' arrest, they never answered for their crime, which Brown insisted had been justified by his faith. Following their heinous actions, Brown and his men became a feared guerrilla force throughout the territory, and he continued to speak out against slavery. In all other parts of his life he had lived as a humble, moral Christian. But when sins against his fellows, black and white, continued, he believed it God's will that he act.

For several more months Brown's ragtag army engaged in several skirmishes with proslavery forces. Most famously, in August at the Battle of Osawatomie, Brown and a much smaller number of fighters used guerrilla warfare to hold their own against a much larger group of Border Ruffians. Eventually, they wisely retreated back into the countryside, only to see their homes and businesses burned in the aftermath. Brown intelligently used this admitted defeat to build his image as a person who could successfully resist a much larger force.

Soon thereafter he returned to the East, where he was lionized for his recent activities in Kansas. He had made the trip to try to gather support for more antislavery activities in Kansas but also wished to stockpile money and weapons for his long-held and most audacious plan, to secure the arsenal at Harpers Ferry, Virginia.

The Road to Martyrdom

By January 1857, even as the consequences of the recent panic roiled the nation, Brown was in the Boston area canvassing for long-term support of his plans. He met with Franklin B. Sanborn, secretary of the Massachusetts State Kansas Committee. In turn, Sanborn introduced him to the Worcester, Massachusetts, minister Thomas Wentworth Higginson, who also had recently been in Kansas working for the antislavery cause. Brown then won the confidence of an even better-known clergyman, Transcendentalist Theodore Parker, active in the city's attempts to shelter or free fugitive slaves. He met with Dr. Samuel Gridley Howe, who worked with the mentally and physically challenged, and who earlier in his career had gone to Europe to aid the freedom fighters in Greece and Poland. George Luther Stearns, a wealthy mill owner active in the attempts to make Kansas a Free State, was also converted to Brown's cause. Finally, he won over philanthropist Gerrit Smith, the man who had given the large tract of land near North Elba as a place for the resettlement of freed slaves and was ready to continue his munificence. This group eventually would be termed "the Secret

Six," those who long knew of and supported Brown's audacious plan to seize Harpers Ferry.

Sanborn, Higginson, and Parker were closely allied with the Transcendentalist circle that gravitated toward Emerson and his Concord friends, among whom Brown now found himself a celebrity. During his visit to the area, for example, he met Emerson, Thoreau, and Bronson Alcott, among others, all of whom attended the lectures that he gave in Concord to explain the need to support his attempts to keep Kansas a Free State. The group, having hitherto refrained from commitment to any overt violence to end slavery, after meeting Brown found themselves more and more swayed by this remarkable man of conscience.

Even though the Concord circle celebrated Brown's bravery and pledged allegiance to his larger end, they were not munificent in their donations. His most generous financial backers remained among the Secret Six, particularly Stearns and Smith, who with Higginson were most adamant that he should undertake his long-contemplated attack on Harpers Ferry sooner rather than later.

In the fall of 1857 Brown returned to Kansas to begin to recruit volunteers for his expedition into Virginia. As he sought to persuade other abolitionists to accompany him, he explained the need to create a genuinely multicultural state, a prospect not all of his putative associates—despite being abolitionists—welcomed. Brown made his seriousness evident, however, in the lengthy "Provisional Constitution and Ordinances of the People of the United States" that he had penned—at the home of the fervent black abolitionist Douglass—and which he wished to substitute for the U.S. Constitution.

He contemplated this brash action because he believed that the United States was de facto a nation whose Constitution not only accepted but also encouraged slavery, something evident as well in recent Supreme Court decisions like the *Dred Scott* case and legislative enactments such as the Fugitive Slave Act and the Kansas-Nebraska Act, all of which denied the equality of blacks. By contrast, his proposed constitution extended equal rights not only to blacks but to women and other minorities, including Native Americans. Importantly, as Brown explained to whomever would listen, he did not seek to overthrow the state and thus dissolve the Union but only to amend that by which it was constituted.

But first slavery had to be abolished and blacks freed. To that end, Brown had a simple plan, a variant of what he had been talking about for years: "with a small body of picked men, [to] inaugurate and maintain a Negro insurrection in the mountains of Virginia, which would produce so much annoyance to the United States Government, and create such a feeling of dread and insecurity in the minds of slaveholders, that slavery would ultimately be abolished."[20] In search of more potential recruits, he ventured to Canada, where thousands of American blacks had escaped and where at Chatham in Ontario he held an antislavery convention. On this trip he met both Harriet Tubman, an escaped slave who had assisted in freeing hundreds of other blacks from the American South, and Martin Delany, a fiery advocate of black emigration to the Caribbean or Africa, where American blacks could establish a nation free of white racism. After Delany heard Brown's plan, he supported it, maintaining, however, that the U.S. government should be overthrown.

At the Chatham convention, attended by about fifty blacks and whites, Brown explained his grand strategy: invade one of the Southern states to free slaves. News of this action would, he predicted, encourage those on other plantations to rise up and join Brown's contingent in the mountains. From there they would continue and enlarge such raids. Terrified slave owners, he believed, would realize that the end of their time had come. Antislavery whites would push for political reform that would permanently abolish slavery, and the Union would be preserved.

In June 1858 Brown headed back to Kansas to gather his supporters, whom he had left to study the forms of guerrilla warfare that he had originated at Osawatomie and that he wished to carry into the Virginia countryside. Adding to his already considerable legend for bravery, in retaliation for the murder of five Free Staters a few months earlier, he carried out a surprise raid in which he rescued eleven Missouri slaves. This bold action—he guided them all the way to Detroit so that they could cross to Canada—only whetted his appetite to move on Harpers Ferry.

He was stymied, however, by a lack of necessary financial support. Early in 1859 he returned to New England and continued to appeal to the Secret Six and their friends, the Transcendentalists. Even the ethereal Bronson Alcott lined up behind him. Brown was, Alcott wrote, "superior to legal traditions, and a disciple of the Right in ideality and affairs of state." The abolitionist was "equal to anything he dares," he explained, and was "the man to do the deed, if it must be done, and with the martyr's temper and purpose," lines that turned out to be prophetic.[21]

The Arsenal at Harpers Ferry

In July, Brown, now fifty-nine years old, began to move his men and equipment outside of Harpers Ferry, where they rented a rural farmhouse from which they reconnoitered. He had picked this town because it was home not only to Hall's Rifle Works, which produced around ten thousand arms each year; but also a U.S. arsenal. Twenty-one recruits, black and white, were with him, less than half the number he sought, but he had cast the die. October 16 would be the day.

At first, all proceeded well. In the early morning hours, facing little resistance, Brown secured the armory, the arsenal, and the rifle manufactory. Now he had to get word to local slaves of what was occurring so that they could revolt, armed with the weapons

he would supply them with. Six of his men went to nearby plantations and took both freed slaves and hostages back to the arsenal.
But now things went awry, for Brown lingered, not retreating with
the freedmen and his arms to the hinterlands as planned. He had
expected and awaited rebellion to jump like wildfire from plantation
to plantation, but the freed slaves reacted with caution, fear, and
reluctance. He had in mind the example of Nat Turner's Rebellion,
but nothing comparable was occurring on the plantations around
Harpers Ferry.

Instead of retreating to the hills, Brown waited at the armory
through the night, allowing time for word of what was occurring
to spread. But blood had been shed during the raids, when Brown's
men killed several civilians, and townspeople, awakened to what
was happening, began to organize a response. They started to take
back the buildings. They blocked Brown's only escape routes, across
the bridges to the island on which Harpers Ferry stood. After
another few hours, local militias, eventually swelling to twelve in
number, marched to the area, and federal troops were called in as
well. Before long, Brown and his men were trapped. After attempts
to negotiate his escape, using his thirty hostages as bargaining
chips, failed, only further fighting remained.

With only his small group of soldiery and some of the freed
blacks guarding the hostages, Brown managed somehow to hold his
own against what had swelled to hundreds of soldiers from all over
the region. The episode at Harpers Ferry ended when a detachment
of U.S. Marines, led by Lieutenant Colonel Robert E. Lee, overran
his redoubt. Bleeding profusely from a saber wound, Brown was
taken prisoner. Ten of his men, including two of his sons, were
killed; seven (including Brown) were captured; and four others escaped but were later apprehended. On the other side, two marines
and six civilians died during the initial raid or ensuing siege.

Over the next six weeks, during Brown's imprisonment and trial,
public opinion swayed, some declaring him a deluded madman,

others presenting him as a blessed martyr for the antislavery cause. For his part, all Brown wanted the public, and the jurors, to know was that he had attacked the arsenal solely to liberate slaves, which he took as both a patriotic and a God-directed imperative. He had not intended any murder nor had he mistreated any of his hostages. When the situation in Harpers Ferry devolved, he explained, there had been unforeseen and unsought casualties. But the larger goal had been nothing short of the beginning of full emancipation.

His own words to the court make this clear. He reminded the assembled of the honesty of his intentions, and that he had performed a similar action in Missouri the previous year, when he had rescued a group of slaves and delivered them to freedom without any violence. All he designed at Harpers Ferry was "to have done the same thing on a larger scale." He never intended "murder, or treason, or the destruction of property, or to incite slaves to rebellion, or to make insurrection."

He also sharply reminded the jurors that they claimed to acknowledge, as he did, "the validity of the law of God." From his seat in the court he had watched "a book kissed," he said, "which I suppose to be the Bible, or at least the New Testament." The same holy text acknowledged by the court was that which had taught him "whatsoever I would that men should do to me, I should do even to them." He endeavored to act on that principle. "I believe that to have interfered as I have done—as I have always freely admitted I have done—in behalf of His despised poor," Brown declared to court, country, and posterity, "was not wrong, but right."[22] He had only followed the divine law as revealed to him.

The jury took only forty-five minutes to return verdicts of guilty on charges of treason (against the state of Virginia), murder, and inciting slave revolt. Later, when his sentence was handed down, death by hanging, by all accounts Brown took it calmly. He passed his last days in prison with the same calm, issuing letters and statements that circulated widely in the national press. Once one of

God's warriors in Kansas, he now prepared to sacrifice his life for a noble cause, taking the suffering Christ as a role model. Years earlier, when O. S. Fowler had taken Brown's measure by the shape of his skull, he had rightly noted Brown's fortitude and forthrightness. All he missed was his client's eventual martyrdom.

Authorities allowed Brown's wife to visit, which she did on December 1. The next day, while she waited in her hotel, John Brown was hanged, his body remanded to her for burial at their homestead in North Elba, where black and white people lived together harmoniously, a dream that he had harbored for all America.

Thoreau's Defense of Brown

By 1859 Henry Thoreau was debilitated from battling consumption, a disease that had ravaged other members of his family. But when he learned of Brown's raid, he was electrified. He received the news of Harpers Ferry on October 19 while he and Bronson Alcott were visiting Emerson. Returning to his journal, Thoreau immediately framed Brown's action in light of what he had written a decade earlier in "Resistance to Civil Government." "When a government puts forth its strength, on the side of injustice," he wrote, "as ours (especially to-day) to maintain slavery and kill the liberators of the slave, what a merely brute, or worse than brute, force it is seen to be! A demonical force!"[23]

Over the next few days, particularly as he read in the national press that damned Brown as demented, he continued to write indignantly in his journal. Many of these passages would later find their way into his public celebration of Brown's actions. In their first iteration, they dripped disgust. "The Republican editors, obliged to get their sentences ready for the morning edition,—and their dinner ready before afternoon—," spoke of Brown and his men as "'deluded fanatics,' 'mistaken men,' 'insane,' or 'crazed.' Did

it ever occur to you what a *sane* set of editors we are blessed
with!—not 'mistaken men'; who know very well on which side their
bread is buttered!" He continued vehemently, "What has Massachusetts and the North sent a few *sane* senators to Congress for of
late years?" "All their speeches put together and boiled down," Thoreau continued, "do not match for simple and manly directness,
force and effectiveness the few casual remarks of insane John Brown
on the floor of the Harper's Ferry engine-house."[24]

To those who wondered what Brown thought he would gain by
his actions, Thoreau had a simple answer. "I don't suppose he could
get four-and-six-pence a day for being hung," he wrote to his penny-
pinching townspeople, but "he stands a chance to save a considerable part of his soul—and such a soul—!" His neighbors, Thoreau
implied, were blinded to truth and goodness by their fatuous worship of profit and gain. The self-evident righteousness of Brown's
cause eclipsed such mundane concerns and such petty individuals.
Thoreau's Northern neighbors believed that they could "get more
in [their] market for a quart of milk than a quart of blood, but that
is not the market that heroes carry their blood to."[25]

Soon enough, Thoreau decided to make his thoughts public, pro-
posing a speech on October 30 in Concord's town hall in support
of Brown. His plan met resistance from many, including the community's antislavery committee, who thought such a course rash
and likely only to inflame an already heated debate. To critics who
counseled caution he had a brief but sharp retort: "I did not send
to you for your advice, but to announce that I am to speak."[26] The
message was clear. Thoreau, in a manner echoing Brown's own actions, would act according to higher principles. Resistance to Thoreau's appearance continued to the very day of his lecture, when
recalcitrant officials refused to ring the meetinghouse bell to
summon townspeople to the lecture. Unfazed, Thoreau pulled the
bell rope himself.

Those at the lecture, "A Plea for Captain John Brown," heard the most powerful defense of Brown that had yet been issued. Incensed by Brown's treatment in the national press, Thoreau wanted to make sure his neighbors realized the true nobility of what Brown had undertaken. Brown was the nation's exemplar of individual sovereignty, of a morality centered on private conscience, not on mindless adherence to outward law.

Thoreau began by claiming that Brown's patriotism—one of the charges against him was treason—was never in doubt. "I should say," he told his auditors, "that he was an old-fashioned man in his respect for the Constitution, and his faith in the permanence of the Union," and he deemed slavery "wholly opposed to these, and he was its determined foe."[27] Invoking places linked in his townspeople's minds to the American Revolution, Thoreau reminded them that Brown was "like the best of those who stood at Concord Bridge once, on Lexington Common, and on Bunker Hill, only he was firmer and higher principled," for while they bravely faced their country's foes, Brown "had the courage to face his country itself, when she was in the wrong." Dismissing any sense that Brown's actions in Kansas had made him an outlaw and murderer, Thoreau explained that in fact Brown there "finally commenced the public practice of Humanity."[28]

Thoreau saw something of himself in this rebel, for he praised Brown's "Spartan habits" and "scrupulous" diet, which mirrored his own. And like him, Brown was "a man of rare common sense and directness of speech," and "a transcendentalist above all, a man of ideas and principles—that was what distinguished him." Commenting on how dispassionately Brown spoke of the atrocities his family endured, Thoreau resorted to a striking image: Brown was like "a volcano with an ordinary chimney flu," someone whose fortitude was never in doubt. When Thoreau had asked him how he dared to live in Kansas when he had a price on his head, Brown calmly replied, "It is perfectly well understood that I will not be taken."[29]

Paired to a certainty born of adherence to higher principles was a faith in the greater good, even greater efficacy of reform by example. Brown's critics did not realize that, "like the seed is the fruit," and that, "in the moral world, when good seed is planted, good fruit is inevitable." So, too, with men, for "when you plant, or bury, a hero in his field, a crop of heroes is sure to spring up." For years Brown had been challenging "the legions of Slavery, in obedience to a higher command," and Harpers Ferry was just another example of his commitment to what he believed was right.[30] His detractors, particularly editors and politicians, simply did not know what type of man he really was. "They have got to conceive of a man of faith and of religious principle," Thoreau explained, someone who did not recognize "unjust human laws, but resisted them as he was bid." With Brown's example, Thoreau proclaimed, "for once we are lifted out of the trivialness and dust of politics into the region of truth and manhood."[31]

Brown's nobility consisted in the fact that "no man in America" had ever "stood up so persistently and effectively for the dignity of human nature, knowing himself for a man, and the equal of any and all governments." In that sense, Thoreau continued, Brown "was the most American of us all," someone who "could not have been tried by a jury of his peers, because his peers did not exist."[32] In contrast, Thoreau's fellow citizens chattered of a "*representative* government," but what they had instead was monstrous: a government in which "the noblest faculties of the mind, and the *whole* heart, are not *represented*." Thoreau's support of Brown's violent actions was unequivocal. "I agree with him," Thoreau proclaimed, and "I shall not be forward to think him mistaken in his method who quickest succeeds to liberate the slave."[33]

"Is it not possible," Thoreau asked, "that an individual may be right and a government wrong?" Were laws to be enforced merely because they were made? "What right," he continued sharply, "have you to enter into a compact with yourself that you will do thus or so, against the light within you?"[34] He was unafraid to follow his logic out to its obvious consequences. The only government that Thoreau recognized was one that "establishes justice in the land, never that which establishes injustice." What could one think of a government, he continued, "to which all brave and just men in the land are enemies, standing between it and those whom it oppresses?"[35]

Toward the end of his address Thoreau made his most remarkable assertion, that he regarded Brown as a saint. He was speaking, he explained, not to plead for Brown's life, "but for his character—his immortal life," for "some eighteen hundred years ago Christ was crucified," and "this morning, perchance, Captain Brown was hung." "These are two ends of a chain," Thoreau explained, "which is not without its links," for he was "not Old Brown any longer" but "an Angel of Light."[36]

Soon after he delivered this ringing lecture, Thoreau repeated it in Worcester, Massachusetts, and again on November 1 at the Tremont Temple in Boston, where he substituted for none other than Frederick Douglass. Two days later, friends in Worcester asked him to return to repeat his words. Newspapers up and down the East Coast reported Thoreau's "Plea for Captain John Brown," and soon thereafter Thoreau sent it to James Redpath for his anthology of the John Brown affair, *Echoes of Harper's Ferry* (1860), where it was first published and led off a section that included contributions by Emerson, Parker, Henry Ward Beecher, and Wendell Phillips, among others.

Clearly Thoreau's effort impressed those who eventually came to regard Brown similarly, for Thoreau also was asked to speak at the memorial celebration of Brown's life in North Elba on July 4, 1860. For this event, he prepared "The Last Days of John Brown," but he did not travel to the Brown homestead. Instead, one of the organizers, R. J. Hinton, read his words. Hinton prefaced his delivery by rightly reminding the assembled, that "Mr. Thoreau's voice was the first which broke the disgraceful silence or hushed the senseless babble with which the grandest deed of our time was met."[37]

Thoreau was equally effusive in this piece. "John Brown's career," he said, "for the last six weeks of his life was meteor-like, flashing through the darkness in which we live." He continued, "I know of nothing so miraculous in our history," for since his death Brown had awakened a new sensibility, that is, aroused the "moral sense" among many in the North who before were hesitant to strike at slavery. "The North," Thoreau said, "I mean the *living* North, was suddenly all transcendental," for as it came together behind Brown, "it went behind the human law, it went behind the apparent failure, and recognized eternal justice and glory."[38]

Recurring to the same image, he imagined Brown's body in a railroad car, passing north from Virginia through Philadelphia and New York, "like a meteor" shooting "through the Union from the southern regions to the north!" When Thoreau heard that Brown finally had been hanged, he did not even believe that the rebel was dead, for "on the day of his translation," Thoreau continued, it seemed that "of all the men who were said to be my contemporaries," he "was the only one who *had not died*." "I meet him at every turn," Thoreau concluded, for "he is more alive than he ever was." Quite simply, "he has earned immortality."[39]

Coda

John Brown found a fitting eulogist in Thoreau. Arguably, no American better understood what had inspired Brown's choices or was better able to explain the reasoning that led Brown to his death for his chosen cause. To be sure, Brown's principles were based in a Calvinism far removed from the Transcendentalism that inspired

Thoreau's spiritual life, but the result was the same: a deep-seated belief in the sanctity of individual conscience, itself derived from divine inspiration, either from the miracle of God's grace or one's connection to what Emerson termed the Oversoul. Thoreau's celebration—indeed, his canonization—of Brown was the high-water mark of a certain attitude that underlay much antebellum reform. Particularly following the Panic of 1837, American reformers sought to replace a failing democratic experiment. When they looked out upon the disruption, devastation, and corruption that the panic laid bare and wished for a more equitable society respectful of individual rights, they imagined solutions, and ultimately a nation, based on higher laws than those men devised. Men and women like George Ripley, Horace Greeley, William B. Greene, Orson Squire Fowler, Mary Gove Nichols, Henry Thoreau, and John Brown all believed themselves prophets of a new moral and social order to be achieved when everyone accessed the internal, God-given power to align one's self with God's will. When individuals were so armed, no social ill—from economic inequality to the gross moral stain of slavery—was beyond repair. Indeed, an Ezlter and his followers and a Fourier and his followers foresaw paradise. It is worth briefly trying to view the world through such lenses: unimpeachable answers, demonstrable in sovereign individuals' divinely directed decisions and behavior, awaited discovery. Once demonstrated, these answers and solutions would be beacons to neighbors, citizens, the world, for only the foolish or the irredeemable would ignore a well-lit path to perfection.

But John Brown's actions indicate the inherent danger of this belief, for his frustration at his fellow citizens' callous disregard of the slave's plight—his realization that slaveholders were not going to change their mind's voluntarily—forced him into acts of violence that were difficult for most people to condone. Brown's unshakable faith in his right to act as he had acted, and to ask his fellow Americans to excuse, accept, and even emulate his actions, rested ultimately on his belief that his actions had transcendent sanction.

The Civil War has claimed Brown's historical place in our memory, casting him as a harbinger of the bloodshed to come. It is less often that we view him solely within the 1830s, 1840s, and 1850s, an America caught between two financial panics, its politicians beggared of solutions to the country's multiplying problems. The world-changing events to come, and the changed world they ushered in, can blind us to Brown's true contemporaries. Many of them believed that they, too, had a mission to reform the world. The great Mormon leader Joseph Smith comes to mind, and his acquaintance Robert Matthews, also known as the Prophet Matthias, who like Smith prophesied a new world and recruited many New Yorkers to await its arrival in a settlement he called the Kingdom.[40] So, too, the reformers discussed in previous chapters had varied plans for righting the nation's course. But as Brown's actions in Kansas and Virginia showed, such a belief in an internal directive that empowers one to demand of one's fellow citizens radical social change sets one on a slippery slope. In Brown's case, a devotion to higher principle led to murder in Kansas and Virginia.

The Civil War's horror and magnitude would finally exhaust the idealism that had inspired so much antebellum reform. After Appomattox, prophetic, self-righteous voices like Brown's and others discussed herein faded, their once-inspiring rhetoric falling increasingly on deaf ears. The decades of Reconstruction to follow and the federal and local efforts to reknit the nation were not laboratories for sovereign individualism. The war taught Americans, North and South, that their social problems were of such a scale that they could not be addressed by the example of a few divinely inspired reformers.

The nation's Reconstruction had to be addressed through ever more complicated efforts in social engineering. For example, the Bureau of Refugees, Freedmen, and Abandoned Lands, or popularly, the Freedmen's Bureau, was the antithesis of a Brook Farm or any Phalanx imaginable by Fourier. Agents spread across the Southern states dispensed medical care and food, oversaw education, resolved disputes, reunited families, and by everyone's measure then and since did all of it imperfectly. But perfection, at least, had never been the aspiration. By the 1870s, the increasingly operative word was pragmatism, and the ideal on everyone's lips, compromise. There was no longer any use for a Romantic belief in the unlimited, transformative power of the self, once so prominent.

The work of social transformation had not taken place, as Fowler, Nichols, Thoreau, and others had counseled, inside the individual, but rather outside, in a world where self-reliance no longer had God-given sanction. No longer did the reformer claim that by personal example he or she could make the world perfect and restore some lost paradise. Instead, the goal was to make the world better, through slow, incremental action that demanded redefinition of one's methods and end. No longer was there a supernal calculus against which progress was measured; rather, the specific needs of the world itself served as the measure.

The individuals discussed herein found their various missions because they were under great pressure—initially economic, then psychological—as they struggled to understand such national traumas as the Panics of 1837 and 1857, a political system that failed to address key structural needs, and the horrors of slavery. As they sought to redirect their lives from what Thoreau so aptly termed their "quiet desperation," they looked within for their deficiencies. When they located them—in diet, hygiene, or imbalance of "passions," for example—they then set about convincing their fellow citizens that the same cankers ate at these citizens and that everyone had to combat these cankers similarly, following the reformers' examples. What was more, this effort promised far-reaching solutions to the problems afflicting country and world. Antebellum reformers had retreated into themselves, where they found what they regarded as unimpeachable certainties about how to behave, which if only adhered to would redeem the world unraveling around them. Much good came of such soul-searching, but when the reformers' efforts to guide others into similar enlightenment were stymied or failed outright, these idealists could be moved to despair or desperate action.

John Brown was a manifestation of the nineteenth-century bankruptcy of a noble ideal, the ideal that in a democratic society properly conceived all men and women, regardless of class, gender, race, or ethnicity, should be treated fairly and with dignity because they were irreducibly equal in spirit. By heeding this ideal, John Brown believed, people could bring about a better world. But as a Calvinist, he should have been more aware of the inherent danger—palpably visible in how poorly men and women treated each other, and explicable through the doctrine of original sin, selfishness—of extrapolating his own experience of God to that of all others. Inspirational as the ideal was, it foundered on the rock of self-righteousness and shattered under the weight of the war's hundreds of thousands dead.

When people emerged from the Civil War's maelstrom, they found a strange new world where truth was not some divine gift to all mankind but what best fit with the rest of their and their fellow citizens' experience. In the face of such pragmatism, what William James felicitously called truth's "cash-value," the antebellum reformers' dreams of perfect harmony crumbled and silently disappeared.[41] They had great if finally misguided faith in human nature.

NOTES

ACKNOWLEDGMENTS

INDEX

Notes

Introduction

1. Daniel Webster, *Writings and Speeches of Daniel Webster*, 18 vols. (Boston: Little, Brown, 1903), 2:233–34. This was on May 18, 1837.

2. Ralph Waldo Emerson, 21 May 1837, *Journals and Miscellaneous Notebooks*, ed. William H. Gilman, et al. 16 vols. (Cambridge, MA: Belknap Press, 1960–1982), 5:331–2. See Scott A. Sandage, *Born Losers: A History of Failure in America* (Cambridge, MA: Harvard University Press, 2005), 6–7, for examples of suicide brought on by the panic. A writer for the then new literary periodical *Arcturus* agreed. It was the "age of suicides and mysterious disappearances," as those in debt sought to escape their problems one way or another. Everywhere people gathered into "noisy and tumultuous masses—shouting for change, reform, and progress" (*Arcturus* 1 [1841]: 133). Recently, Jessica M. Lepler, in *The Many Panics of 1837: People, Politics, and the Creation of a Transatlantic Financial Crisis* (New York: Cambridge University Press, 2013), has investigated the varieties of responses, including transatlantic, to the panic.

3. Emerson, *Journals and Miscellaneous Notebooks*, 8:295.

4. Joseph G. Baldwin, *The Flush Times of Alabama and Mississippi* (1853; New York: Sagamore Press, 1957), esp. 59–63. Also see Philip Hone, *The Diary of Philip Hone, 1821–1851* (New York: Dodd, Mead and Company, 1927), 1:261. On the notion of "flush times," see Joshua Rothman, *Flush Times and Fever*

Dreams: A Story of Capitalism and Slavery in the Age of Jackson (Athens: University of Georgia Press, 2012). Also see Sandage, *Born Losers*, 22–27, for examples of the kinds of phrases that people used to describe the flush, and then the hard, times. In general on the panic and its effect, see Alasdair Robert, *America's First Great Depression: Economic Crisis and Political Disorder after the Panic of 1837* (Ithaca, NY: Cornell University Press, 2012); Scott Reynolds Nelson, *A Nation of Deadbeats: An Uncommon History of America's Financial Disasters* (New York: Knopf, 2012), chap. 6; and Reginald McGrane, *The Panic of 1837: Some Financial Problems of the Jacksonian Era* (New York: Russell and Russell, 1965). The whole question of the "market revolution" and its impact on the Panic of 1837 is nicely summarized in John Lauritz Larson, *The Market Revolution in America: Liberty, Ambition, and the Eclipse of the Common Good* (Cambridge: Cambridge University Press, 2009). The best economic history of Jackson's era is still Peter Temin, *The Jacksonian Economy* (New York: W. W. Norton, 1969).

5. Angela Lakwete, *Inventing the Cotton Gin: Machine and Myth in Antebellum America* (Baltimore: Johns Hopkins University Press, 2003), 102–3, 100.

6. Ibid., 104; and Sven Beckert, *Empire of Cotton: A Global History* (New York: Knopf, 2014), esp. chap. 5, "Slavery Takes Command."

7. *A Brief Popular Account of All of the Financial Panics and Commercial Revulsions in the United States from 1690–1857* (New York: J. C. Haney, 1857), 8. One thousand dollars in 1836 is the equivalent of approximately $26,000 today.

8. Ibid., 9, 17.

9. Ibid., 22. Also see Lepler, *Many Panics of 1837*, particularly 67–70.

10. See Samuel Rezneck, "The Social History of an American Depression, 1837–1843," in Rezneck, *Financial Panics: Essays in American Business and Economic History* (New York: Greenwood Press, 1968), 77–78, and passim for a vivid assessment of the social dislocation the financial troubles initiated.

11. William H. Siles, ed., "Quiet Desperation: A Personal View of the Panic of 1837," *New York History* 67 (January 1986): 89–92.

12. James Parton, *Life of Horace Greeley* (1855; Boston: Houghton Mifflin, 1889), 166.

13. Sidney George Fisher, "The Diaries of Sidney George Fisher," *Pennsylvania Magazine of History and Biography* 79, no. 2 (1955): 230.

14. See Rezneck, "Social History," 78.

15. Justin Winsor, *Memorial History of Boston*, 4 vols. (Boston: Osgood, 1883), 4:166.

16. Cited in Rezneck, "Social History," 78.

17. See Lepler, *Many Panics*, 137.

18. Baldwin, *Flush Times*, 61–62.

19. *Knickerbocker* 9 (May 1837): 488.

20. Hone, *Diary*, 1:259.

21. The "better angels of our nature" is from Abraham Lincoln's first inaugural address; also see Heb. 1:4. Dickens had used "our better angels" in his novel *Barnaby Rudge* (1841), chap. 29.

22. Henry David Thoreau, *Walden* (1854; Princeton, NJ: Princeton University Press, 1971), 8.

23. See, for example, Nathan O. Hatch, *The Democratization of American Christianity* (New Haven, CT: Yale University Press, 1989).

24. On Graham, see Steven Nissenbaum, *Sex, Diet, and Debility in Jacksonian America: Sylvester Graham and Health Reform* (Westport, CT: Greenwood Press, 1980).

25. On the water cure, see Susan E. Cayleff, *Wash and Be Healed: The Water-Cure Movement and Women's Health* (Philadelphia: Temple University Press, 1987).

26. John S. Haller Jr., *The History of American Homeopathy: From Rational Medicine to Holistic Health Cure* (New Brunswick, NJ: Rutgers University Press, 2009).

27. Adam W. Sweeting, *Reading Houses and Building Books: Andrew Jackson Downing and the Architecture of Antebellum Literature, 1835–1855* (Hanover, NH: University Press of New England, 1996); Justin Martin, *Genius of Place: The Life of Frederick Law Olmsted* (Cambridge, MA: Da Capo Press, 2011). Darrow's former home is in Kinsman, Ohio.

28. On Wright, see Sean Wilentz, *Chants Democratic: New York City and the Rise of the American Working Class, 1788–1850* (New York: Oxford University Press, 1984), chap. 5; and on Brownson, Patrick W. Carey, *Orestes Brownson: American Religious Weathervane* (Grand Rapids, MI: Wm. B. Eerdmans, 2004).

29. John Davies, *Phrenology, Fad and Science: A 19th Century American Crusade* (New Haven, CT: Yale University Press, 1955).

30. On physiognomy, see Christopher J. Lukasik, *Discerning Characters: The Culture of Appearance in Early America* (Philadelphia: University of Pennsylvania Press, 2011); for its influence on racialism, see William Ragan Stanton, *The Leopard's Spots: Scientific Attitudes toward Race in America, 1815–59* (Chicago: University of Chicago Press, 1960).

31. Robert C. Fuller, *Mesmerism and the American Cure of Souls* (Philadelphia: University of Pennsylvania Press, 1982); and Howard Kerr, *Mediums, and Spirit-Rappers, and Roaring Radicals: Spiritualism in American Literature, 1850–1900* (Urbana: University of Illinois Press, 1972).

32. John S. Haller Jr., *Swedenborg, Mesmer, and the Mind/Body Connection: The Roots of Complementary Medicine* (West Chester, PA: Swedenborg Foundation, 2010). Marguerite Beck Block, *The New Church in the New World: A Study of Swedenborgianism in America* (New York: H. Holt and Company, 1932).

33. Gail Thain Parker, *Mind Cure in New England: From the Civil War to World War I* (Hanover, NH: University Press of New England, 1973); and Ann Braude, *Radical Spirits: Spiritualism and Women's Rights in Nineteenth Century America* (Bloomington: Indiana University Press, 2001).

34. Ralph Waldo Emerson, "The Chardon Street Convention," in *Lectures and Biographical Sketches, Works of Ralph Waldo Emerson*, 14 vols. (Boston: Houghton, Mifflin, 1883), 10:352–53. "Dunkers" were members of the Church of the Brethren, a German pietist group with American branches. "Muggletonians" were followers of Lodowicke Muggleton, who during the English Civil War proclaimed that his followers were the prophets foretold in the Book of Revelation. "Come-Outers" were those who in the antebellum period left the established churches because the institutions refused to condemn slavery.

35. Entry for 17 February 1850 in Bronson Alcott's "Journal for 1850," quoted in Joel Myerson, *The New England Transcendentalists and The Dial: A History of the Magazine and Its Contributors* (Rutherford, NJ: Fairleigh Dickinson University Press, 1980), 6. "Groton" refers to a convention held in Groton, Massachusetts, in 1840 and attended by Alcott, George Ripley, and others interested in reform. "Non-resistants" are followers of abolitionist William Lloyd Garrison who eschewed the use of any overt force to end slavery. "Symposeum" was another name for the meetings of the Transcendental Club, between 1836–1840. The *Dial* (1840–1844) was the Transcendentalists' chief

periodical. "Fruitlands" and "Brook Farm" were two utopian ventures started by, respectively, Alcott and Ripley. "Parkerism" refers to the version of liberal religion and reform activities overseen by Transcendentalist minister Theodore Parker. "Conversations" refer to meetings of a discussion group, primarily of women, led by Transcendentalist and feminist Margaret Fuller.

36. *Memoirs of John Quincy Adams,* ed. Charles Francis Adams, 5 vols. (Philadelphia: Lippincott, 1974–1977), 3:345. "Marat democrats" refers to followers of Jean-Paul Marat, a radical political theorist during the French Revolution, a strong advocate of democratic principles.

1. George Ripley, Transcendentalist Dreamer

1. George Ripley, *The Temptations of the Times* (Boston: Hilliard, Gray, and Co., 1837), 12.

2. Ibid., 9.

3. For Ripley's biography, see Charles R. Crowe, *George Ripley, Transcendentalist and Utopian Socialist* (Athens: University of Georgia Press, 1967); and Octavius Brooks Frothingham, *George Ripley* (Boston: Houghton, Mifflin, 1882).

4. On Andover, see Jerry Wayne Brown, *The Rise of Biblical Criticism in America, 1800–1870: The New England Scholars* (Middletown, CT: Wesleyan University Press, 1969); and Jon H. Giltner, *Moses Stuart: The Father of Biblical Science in America* (Atlanta: Scholar Press, 1988).

5. On the rise of American Unitarianism, see Daniel Walker Howe, *The Unitarian Conscience: Harvard Moral Philosophy, 1805–1861* (Cambridge, MA: Harvard University Press, 1970).

6. George Ripley to John Sullivan Dwight, 7 July 1840, cited in Sterling Delano, *Brook Farm: The Dark Side of Utopia* (Cambridge, MA: Belknap Press, 2004), 331, n. 3.

7. On German Idealism among Ripley and his cohort, see Philip F. Gura, *American Transcendentalism: A History* (New York: Hill & Wang, 2007), esp. 46–68.

8. Ripley quoted in Frothingham, *George Ripley,* 84–85.

9. The best modern biography of Brownson is Patrick W. Carey, *Orestes Brownson: American Religious Weathervane* (Grand Rapids, MI: Wm. B. Eerdmans, 2004). On the Working Men's Party, see Sean Wilentz, *Chants*

Democratic: New York City and the Rise of the American Working Class, 1788–1850 (New York: Oxford University Press, 1984), chap. 5.

10. On Tuckerman's work, see Howe, *Unitarian Conscience,* 246–55.

11. On Transcendentalism's emergence, see Gura, *American Transcendentalism,* 69–97.

12. Ralph Waldo Emerson, "Lecture on the Times," in *Essays and Lectures,* ed. Joel Porte (New York: Library of America, 1983), 163.

13. See James Murdock, *Sketches of Modern Philosophy, Especially among the Germans* (1842; New York: M. W. Dodd, 1844), 181, chap. 15.

14. Margaret Fuller to William Henry Channing, 1840, in Robert N. Hudspeth, ed., *The Letters of Margaret Fuller,* 6 vols. (Ithaca, NY: Cornell University Press, 1983–1994), 2:108.

15. Elizabeth Palmer Peabody, *Reminiscences of the Rev. William Ellery Channing, D. D.* (Boston: Roberts Brothers, 1880), 373.

16. *New-York Daily Tribune,* 19 March 1842, 3.

17. Henry James, *Moralism and Christianity; or, Man's Experience and Destiny* (New York: J. S. Redfield, 1850), 84.

18. See Gura, *American Transcendentalism,* 76–79.

19. George Ripley, review of Friedrich Lücke, "Recollections of Schleiermacher," *Christian Examiner* 20 (March 1836): 3–4.

20. Samuel K. Lothrop, "Existing Commercial Establishments," *Christian Examiner* 22 (July 1837): 398.

21. Brownson published "The Laboring Classes" and its defense in his *Boston Quarterly Review* (July, October 1840); both are found in its entirety in Patrick W. Carey, ed., *The Early Works of Orestes A. Brownson,* 5 vols. to date (Milwaukee: Marquette University Press, 2000–), 5:298–401; quotation on 308.

22. Ibid., 310–12.

23. Ibid., 321–23.

24. Cited in Delano, *Brook Farm,* 10.

25. Ralph Waldo Emerson to Margaret Fuller, 27 (?) or 29 (?) May 1840, in *Letters of Ralph Waldo Emerson,* eds. Ralph L. Rusk and Eleanor M. Tilton, 10 vols. (New York: Columbia University Press, 1939–1995), 2:299.

26. [George Ripley], *A Letter to the Congregational Church in Purchase Street by Its Pastor* (Boston: Printed, Not Published, by Request, for the Purchase Street Church, 1840), 5. Also in Frothingham, *Ripley,* 63–91.

27. [Ripley,] *Letter*, 14.

28. George Ripley, *A Farewell Discourse, Delivered to the Congregational Church in Purchase Street, March 28, 1841* (Boston: Freeman and Bolles, 1841), 18–19.

29. Elizabeth Palmer Peabody to John Sullivan Dwight, 20 September 1840, in Bruce A. Ronda, ed., *Letters of Elizabeth Palmer Peabody: American Renaissance Woman* (Middletown, CT: Wesleyan University Press, 1984), 245–47.

30. On Alcott and Fruitlands, see Richard Francis, *The Alcott Family and Their Search for Utopia* (New Haven, CT: Yale University Press, 2010).

31. See Margaret Fuller to William Henry Channing, 29 March 1841, in Hudspeth, *Letters of Fuller,* 2:205.

32. Margaret Fuller to William Henry Channing, [ca. 31 October 1840], ibid., 2:179–80.

33. In Frothingham, *Ripley,* 307–8.

34. Ralph Waldo Emerson to George Ripley, 15 December 1840, in Rusk, *Letters of Ralph Waldo Emerson,* 2:368–71; and Emerson, *Journals and Miscellaneous Notebooks,* ed. William H. Gilman et al., 16 vols. (Cambridge, MA: Belknap Press, 1960–1982), 7:407–8.

35. Delano fully presents Brook Farm's story in his *Brook Farm,* the best modern study. In what follows, I draw on his narrative.

36. Sophia Ripley, "Letter," *Dial* 2 (July 1841): 122–29.

37. See Adin Ballou, *History of the Hopedale Community* (Lowell, MA: Thompson and Hill, 1897); and Edward K. Spann, *Hopedale: From Commune to Company Town, 1840–1920* (Columbus: Ohio State University Press, 1992). This meeting between Ballou and Ripley is described by Butler Wilmarth in William H. Fish, *Memoir of Butler Wilmarth, M. D.* (Boston: Crosby, Nichols, 1854), 88–89.

38. Cited in *Monthly Miscellany of Religion and Letters* (May 1841), 293.

39. See Delano, *Brook Farm,* for the best account of this period. See also the relevant section in Richard Francis, *Transcendentalist Utopias: Individual and Community at Brook Farm, Fruitlands, and Walden* (Ithaca, NY: Cornell University Press, 1997).

40. Peabody's descriptions are "The Community at West Roxbury," in the *Monthly Miscellany of Religion and Letters* 5 (August 1841): 113–18; "A Glimpse

of Christ's Idea of Society," *Dial* 2 (October 1841): 214–28; and "Plan of the West Roxbury Community," *Dial* 2 (January 1842): 361–72.

41. Quoted in Delano, *Brook Farm*, 64–65.

42. See Peabody, "Plan of the West Roxbury Community," passim.

43. Elizabeth Palmer Peabody to John Sullivan Dwight, 26 August [1841], in Ronda, *Letters of Peabody*, 249.

44. Peabody, "Plan of the West Roxbury Community," passim.

45. Ibid.

46. Nathaniel Hawthorne, *The Blithedale Romance* (1852), in *Novels* (New York: Library of America, 1983), 649.

47. John Thomas Codman, *Brook Farm: Historic and Personal Memoirs* (Boston: Arena Publishing Company, 1894), 79–81.

48. John Van Der Zee Sears, *My Friends at Brook Farm* (New York: Desmond Fitzgerald, 1912), 141–42.

49. See Codman, *Brook Farm*, passim; and Lindsay Swift, *Brook Farm: Its Members, Scholars, Visitors* (1900; New York: Corinth Books, 1961).

50. Hawthorne, *Blithedale Romance*, 686.

51. Georgiana Bruce Kirby, *Years of Experience, An Autobiographical Narrative* (New York: G. P. Putnam's Sons, 1887), 102.

52. Brisbane, *Social Destiny*, 311.

53. Codman, *Brook Farm*, 77.

54. Charles Lane, "Brook Farm," *Dial* 4 (January 1844): 351; also see Franklin B. Sanborn, *A. Bronson Alcott: His Life and Philosophy*, 2 vols. (Boston: Roberts Brothers, 1893), 2:382–83.

55. George William Curtis to John Sullivan Dwight, 3 March 1844, in George Willis Cooke, ed., *Early Letters of George Wm. Curtis to John S. Dwight* (New York: Harper & Brothers, 1898), 157.

56. Codman, *Brook Farm*, 26.

57. On the Northampton Association, see Christopher Clark, *The Communitarian Moment: The Radical Challenge of the Northampton Association* (Ithaca, NY: Cornell University Press, 1995).

58. Codman, *Brook Farm*, 55.

59. Samuel Osgood to John Sullivan Dwight, 21 November 1840, in Zoltán Haraszti, *The Idyll of Brook Farm, As Revealed in Unpublished Letters in the Boston Public Library* (Boston: Trustees of the Public Library, 1937), 14. Al-

bert Brisbane's book was *Social Destiny of Man* (1840), which I discuss more fully in the subsequent chapter.

60. Octavius B. Frothingham, *Memoir of William Henry Channing* (Boston: Houghton, Mifflin and Company, 1886), 218.

61. Emerson, *Journals and Miscellaneous Notebooks*, [1843] 8:392–93. "*Sansculottes*" refers to lower class people in France in the late eighteenth century, many of whom became radicalized and thus strong supporters of the French Revolution. The term *sans-culotte* literally means "without knee breeches," by extension, those who did not wear the fashionable clothing of the wealthier classes.

62. Ralph Waldo Emerson, "Historic Notes of Life and Letters in New England," in *Complete Works of Ralph Waldo Emerson*, ed. Edward W. Emerson, 12 vols. (Boston: Houghton Mifflin Company, 1904), 10:364.

63. Henry James, "Democracy and Its Issues," in *Lectures and Miscellanies* (New York: Redfield, 1852), 9.

64. Hawthorne, *Blithedale Romance*, 640.

65. George P. Bradford, "Philosophic Thought in Boston," in Justin Winsor, *Memorial History of Boston*, 4 vols. (James R. Osgood, 1882–1886), 4:311–12.

2. Horace Greeley and the French Connection

1. John Van der Zee Sears, *My Friends at Brook Farm* (New York: Desmond Fitzgerald, 1912), 154; and Walt Whitman, "New York Dissected," in *New York Dissected,* ed. Emory Holloway and Ralph Adimari (New York: R. R. Wilson, 1936), 129. See, too, Arthur E. Bestor Jr., "Albert Brisbane—Propagandist for Socialism in the 1840s," *New York History* 28 (April 1947): 131–49.

2. Albert Brisbane quoted in the *Phalanx* 1 (20 April 1844): 116.

3. Thomas Wentworth Higginson, *Margaret Fuller Ossoli* (Boston: Houghton, Mifflin and Co., 1884), 205.

4. Greeley later hired Ripley as his chief book reviewer for the *Tribune.*

5. Biographical details taken from Robert Chadwell Williams, *Horace Greeley: Champion of American Freedom* (New York: NYU Press, 2006); Horace Greeley, *Recollections of a Busy Life* (1868; New York: E. B. Treat, 1872); James Parton, *The Life of Horace Greeley* (1855; New York: Arno, 1970); and Adam-Max Tuchinsky, *Horace Greeley's* New-York Tribune*: Civil War–Era Socialism and the Crisis of Free Labor* (Ithaca, NY: Cornell University Press, 2009).

6. Greeley, *Recollections*, 41.

7. Ibid., 38–40.

8. Ibid., 41.

9. Ibid., 50.

10. Ibid., 55.

11. See ibid., chap. 8.

12. Ibid., 65

13. Ibid., chap. 9.

14. Ibid., 84.

15. Ibid, 87.

16. On boardinghouse life, see Thomas Augst, *The Clerk's Tale: Young Men and Moral Life in Nineteenth-Century America* (Chicago: University of Chicago Press, 2003) and Wendy Gamber, *The Boardinghouse in Nineteenth-Century-America* (Baltimore: Johns Hopkins University Press, 2007); and on Sylvester Graham and diet, see Stephen Nissenbaum, *Sex, Diet, and Debility in Nineteenth-Century America: Sylvester Graham and Health Reform* (Westport, CT: Greenwood Press, 1980).

17. Logan Uriah Reavis, *A Representative Life of Horace Greeley* (New York: G. W. Carleton, 1872), 182–83.

18. Williams, *Horace Greeley*, 39–40.

19. Greeley, *Recollections*, 96.

20. Ibid., 122–24.

21. See Williams, *Horace Greeley*, 41–43.

22. Greeley, *Recollections*, 137.

23. Ibid., 144.

24. Ibid., 145.

25. Ibid., 145–46.

26. Ibid., 146.

27. Ibid., 146.

28. Ibid., 146–47.

29. Ibid., 147.

30. Horace Greeley, *Hints toward Reforms, in Lectures, Addresses, and Other Writings* (New York: Harper & Brothers, 1850), 8.

31. Greeley, *Recollections*, 503.

32. Ibid., 147–48.

33. Ibid., 149.

34. Greeley, *Hints toward Reforms*, 8.

35. Greeley, *Recollections*, 145.

36. Daniel Walker Howe, *The Political Culture of the America Whigs* (Chicago: University of Chicago Press, 1979), passim.

37. Greeley, *Recollections*, 147.

38. See Jonathan Beecher, *Charles Fourier: The Visionary and His World* (Los Angeles: University of California Press, 1986), chap. 17.

39. See Carl J. Guarneri, *The Utopian Alternative: Fourierism in Nineteenth-Century America* (Ithaca, NY: Cornell University Press, 1991), 17–18; and Jonathan Beecher and Richard Bienvenu, eds., *The Utopian Vision of Charles Fourier: Selected Texts on Work, Love, and Passionate Attraction* (Boston: Beacon Press, 1971), 399–405.

40. Guarneri, *Utopian Alternative*, 17–18.

41. See Howe, *Political Culture*, 195.

42. Beecher and Bienvenu, *Utopian Vision*, 35–40.

43. Parke Godwin, *Popular View of the Doctrines of Charles Fourier; with the Addition of Democracy, Constructive and Pacific* (New York: J. S. Redfield, 1844), 89.

44. Parke Godwin to Charles A. Dana, 12 August 1846, cited in Tuchinsky, *Greeley's New-York Tribune*, 253 n. 82.

45. Beecher and Bienvenu, *Utopian Vision*, 41–48.

46. Parke Godwin to Charles A. Dana, [undated but probably mid-1840s], in Tuchinsky, *Greeley's New-York Tribune*, 253, n. 82.

47. See ibid., 249, n. 16.

48. Charles A. Dana to Parke Godwin, 8 August 1846, cited in ibid., 47.

49. [Charles Julius Hempel], *The True Organization of the New Church, as Indicated in the Writings of Emanuel Swedenborg and Demonstrated by Charles Fourier* (New York: William Radde, 1848), 339–42; Victor Hennequin, *Love in the Phalanstery*, trans. Henry James (New York: DeWitt and Davenport, 1848).

50. Ralph Waldo Emerson, 12 November 1843, in *Journals and Miscellaneous Notebooks*, ed. William H. Gilman et al., 16 vols. (Cambridge, MA: Belknap Press, 1960–1982), 9:54–55.

51. Albert Brisbane, *Social Destiny of Man; or, Association and Re-Organization of Industry* (Philadelphia: C. F. Stollmeyer, 1840), 19.

52. Ibid., 309–11.

53. Ibid., 311–12.

54. Ibid., 76, 78.

55. Ibid., 90, 96.

56. See Tuchinsky, *Greeley's* New-York Tribune, 27.

57. Greeley, *Recollections*, 152.

58. Ibid., 152; and Horace Greeley to Charles A. Dana, 29 August 1842, quoted in James Harrison Wilson, *The Life of Charles A. Dana* (New York: Harper and Brothers, 1907), 41.

59. Sarah Ripley to Ralph Waldo Emerson, 9 July 1843, in Sterling Delano, *Brook Farm: The Dark Side of Utopia* (Cambridge, MA: Belknap Press, 2004), 122.

60. John Thomas Codman, *Brook Farm: Historic and Personal Memoirs* (Boston: Arena Publishing Company, 1894), 73. The pamphlet was Albert Brisbane, *Association; or, A Concise Exposition of the Practical Part of Fourier's Social Science* (New York: J. S. Redfield, 1843).

61. Godwin, too, remained important to Greeley's goals but was not as close to him as Brisbane.

62. Codman, *Brook Farm*, 74.

63. Ibid., 74.

64. Ibid., 62.

65. Ibid., 273.

66. Ibid., 277.

67. Ibid., 282.

68. Ibid., 284–85.

69. George Ripley, *Harbinger* 1, no. 1 (June 14, 1845): 8–9.

70. Convers Francis to Theodore Parker, 22 June 1844, cited in Guarneri, *Utopian Alternative*, 432, n. 6.

71. Ralph Waldo Emerson, Introduction to Albert Brisbane, "Fourier and the Socialists," *Dial* 3 (July 1842): 86–88. Amelia E. Russell, *Home Life of the Brook Farm Association* (Boston: Little Brown, 1900), 64.

72. Greeley, *Recollections*, 153.

73. See Howe, *Political Culture*, 187–95.

74. Horace Greeley, "The Social Architects: Fourier," in *Hints toward Reforms*, 285–86.

75. Francis Brown, *Raymond of the Times* (New York: W. W. Norton, 1951), 24.

76. See Tuchinsky, *Greeley's* New-York Tribune, 42–57, for an account of this debate.

77. Greeley, "Fourier," in *Hints toward Reforms*, 290.

78. Ibid., 290–91.

79. Ibid., 294.

80. Ibid., 297–98.

81. Brisbane, *Social Destiny*, 97.

82. Horatio Greenough to Samuel F. B. Morse, 3 June 1832, in *Letters of Horatio Greenough*, ed. Nathalia Wright (Madison: University of Wisconsin Press, 1972), 131.

83. Brisbane, *Social Destiny*, 97–98, 103.

84. Greeley, *Recollections*, 503.

85. Brisbane, *Social Destiny*, 114.

86. Parke Godwin, *Democracy, Constructive and Pacific* (New York: J. Winchester, 1844), 24.

87. Greeley, *Recollections*, 158.

3. William B. Greene and the Allure of Mutualism

1. Ralph Waldo Emerson, "Historic Notes of Life and Letters in New England," in *Lectures and Biographical Sketches* (1883), in *Complete Works of Ralph Waldo Emerson*, ed. Edward Waldo Emerson (Boston: Houghton, Mifflin, 1903–1904), 10:329.

2. Margaret Fuller to Ralph Waldo Emerson, 9 November 1841, cited in *Letters of Ralph Waldo Emerson*, ed. Ralph L. Rusk and Eleanor M. Tilton, 10 vols. (New York: Columba University Press, 1939–1995), 2:462 n.

3. Annie T. Fields, *Whittier: Notes of His Life and of His Friendships* (New York: Harper, 1893), 23.

4. For a good history of this region when Greene was there, see Christopher Clark, *The Heart of the Commonwealth: Society and Political Culture in Worcester County, Massachusetts, 1713–1861* (New York: Cambridge University Press, 1989).

5. Obituary in the *Boston Evening Transcript*, June 1878, reprinted in Kenneth Walter Cameron, "Emerson and William Batchelder Greene's Creativity and Questioning," *American Renaissance Literary Report X* (Hartford, CT: Transcendental Books, 1996), 82.

6. The main biographical sources for Greene are George Willis Cooke, *An Historical and Biographical Introduction to Accompany the Dial*, 2 vols. (Cleveland, OH: Rowfant Club, 1902), 2:117–28; Joel Myerson, *New England Transcendentalists and the Dial: A History of the Magazine and Its Contributors* (Rutherford, NJ: Fairleigh Dickinson University Press, 1980), 155–56; and Cameron, "Greene's Creativity," passim. Also see Philip F. Gura, "Beyond Transcendentalism: The Radical Individualism of William B. Greene," in *The Transient and Permanent in American Transcendentalism*, ed. Conrad Wright and Charles Capper (Boston: Northeastern University Press, 2000), 471–496.

7. Elizabeth Palmer Peabody, *Reminiscences of Rev. William Ellery Channing, D. D.* (Boston: Roberts Brothers, 1880), 435 ff.

8. Two other contemporary Trinitarian clergymen influenced by the New Thought were James Marsh and Caleb Sprague Henry. Marsh was a Burlington, Vermont, clergyman whose "Preliminary Essay" to his reprinting (1829) of Coleridge's *Aids to Reflection* circulated widely among Transcendentalists in their formative period. See Peter C. Carafiol, *Transcendent Reason: James Marsh and the Forms of Romantic Thought* (Tallahassee: University Presses of Florida, 1982). On Henry, see Ronald V. Wells, *Three Christian Transcendentalists: James Marsh, Caleb Sprague Henry, and Frederic Henry Hedge* (New York: Columbia University Press, 1943).

9. Peabody, *Channing*, 435; Cameron, "Greene's Creativity," 22.

10. William B. Greene, *The Incarnation: A Letter to the Rev. John Fiske, D. D.* (West Brookfield, MA: Merriam and Chapin, 1848), 20.

11. Thomas Wentworth Higginson, *Cheerful Yesterdays* (Boston: Houghton, Mifflin and Company, 1898), 106.

12. William B. Greene, "First Principles," *Dial* 2, no. 3 (January 1841): 273–85; and *The Doctrine of Life with Some of Its Theological Applications* (Boston: B. H. Greene, 1843).

13. See Greene, *The Incarnation: The Doctrine of the Trinity Briefly and Impartially Examined in the Light of History and Philosophy* (West Brookfield, MA: Merriam and Chapin, 1847); *Remarks in Refutation of the Treatise of*

Jonathan Edwards in the Freedom of the Will (West Brookfield, MA: Merriam and Chapin, 1848); *Transcendentalism* (West Brookfield, MA: Oliver S. Cooke and Company, 1849); and *Remarks on the Science of History; Followed by an A Priori Autobiography* (Boston: Crosby and Nichols, 1849).

14. On Buchez, see D. G. Charlton, *Secular Religions in France, 1815–1870* (London: Oxford University Press for the University of Hull, 1963), 182–84; Robert Flint, *The Philosophy of History in Europe*, 2 vols. (Edinburgh: Blackwood, 1884), 1:242–52; Edward Berenson, *Populist Religion and Left-Wing Politics in France, 1830–1852* (Princeton, NJ: Princeton University Press, 1984); Shirley M. Gruner, *Economic Materialism and Social Moralism: A Study of the History of Ideas in France from the Latter Part of the 18th Century to the Middle of the 19th* (The Hague: Mouton, 1977), chap. 20; and Francis-André Isambert, *Politique, religion et science de l'homme chez Philippe Buchez* (Paris: Cujas, 1967).

15. On Leroux, see Flint, *Philosophy of History in Europe*, 1:252–58; David Owen Evans, *Social Romanticism in France, 1830–1848* (Oxford: Clarendon Press, 1951); Charlton, *Secular Religions in France*, 82–87; and Jake Bakunin, *Pierre Leroux and the Birth of Democratic Socialism* (New York: Revisionist Press, 1976).

16. Peabody, *Channing*, 439–40. Also see Greene, *Incarnation*, 28–29.

17. Higginson, *Cheerful Yesterdays*, 106–7; Peabody, *Channing*, 364.

18. Ednah Dow Cheney, "Reminiscences of Mr. Alcott's Conversations, Part I," *Open Court* 2 (9 August 1888): 1131–33; reprinted in Kenneth Walter Cameron, *American Renaissance Literary Report VI* (Hartford, CT: Transcendental Books, 1992), 95.

19. Peabody, *Channing*, 435.

20. Greene, *Transcendentalism*, 1.

21. Ralph Waldo Emerson, *Nature* (1836), in *Essays and Lectures* (New York: Library of America, 1983), 48.

22. Greene, *Transcendentalism*, 18, 41.

23. Peabody, *Channing*, 373.

24. Greene, *Incarnation*, 27.

25. Ibid., 41–43.

26. See Pierre Leroux, *De l'Humanité, de son Principe, et de son Venir* (Paris: Perrotin, 1840), 189.

27. Greene, *Incarnation*, 25–27.

28. Edward Kellogg, *Usury, The Evil and the Remedy* [New York: Burgess and Stringer, 1843]; Godek Gardwell, *Currency: The Evil and the Remedy* (New York: Burgess and Stringer, 1844); *Labor and Other Capital* (New York: By the Author, 1849). Also see *A New Monetary System* (Philadelphia: Baird, 1861), edited by Kellogg's daughter, Mary Kellogg Putnam.

29. Philip F. Gura, "The Reverend Parsons Cooke and Ware Factory Village: A New Missionary Field," in *The Crossroads of American History and Literature* (University Park: Pennsylvania State University Press, 1996), 140–56.

30. William B. Greene, *Equality* (West Brookfield, MA: O. S. Cooke and Company, 1849), 3.

31. Ibid., 32. Proudhon made his statement in *Qu'est-ce que la Propriété? ou Recherche sur le principe du Droit et du Gouvernement (1840)* (Paris: Garnier Frères, 1849), xii.

32. Greene, *Equality*, 62–64.

33. Ibid., 65–69.

34. Ibid., 70.

35. Ibid., 72–74.

36. See Carl J. Guarneri, *The Utopian Alternative: Fourierism in Nineteenth-Century America* (Ithaca, NY: Cornell University Press, 1991), 287–88, 341. Dana had heard Proudhon speak on the topic in Paris in 1848 and reported that some French Fourierists were adopting his views.

37. William B. Greene, *Mutual Banking* (West Brookfield, MA: O. S. Cooke and Company, 1850), 11–12.

38. Ibid., 18–23. He referred as well to the works of John Stuart Mill, Antoine Destutt de Tracy, and other theorists of social organization.

39. Beck quoted in ibid., "Appendix" (xi–xiii) and 75.

40. Ibid., 75–76.

41. Ibid., 15.

42. Ibid., 23–24, and, on Proudhon's work *Organisation du Crédit et de la Circulation*, 16–24 passim.

43. Ibid., 15, 24–25.

44. Ibid., 24.

45. Ibid., 24–25.

46. Ibid., 49.

47. Ibid., 25–26.

48. Ibid., 30.

49. Ibid., 38.

50. Ibid., 42–43.

51. Ibid., 52.

52. Ibid., 56–58.

53. Ibid., 63–65, 67.

54. Ibid., 77.

55. Ibid., 84.

56. Ibid., 27–28; and William B. Greene, The *Radical Deficiency of the Existing Circulating Medium* (Boston: B. H. Greene, 1857), 7–19.

57. Greene, *Radical Deficiency*, 19.

58. "Reformatory: Speech of William B. Greene, of Brookfield," *The Liberator* 23.33 (19 August 1853), p. 132.

59. Ibid.

60. See Timothy Mason Roberts, *Distant Revolutions: 1848 and the Challenge to American Exceptionalism* (Charlottesville: University of Virginia Press, 2009), 146–67.

61. "The Brookfield Letter" and "Remarks of Rev. William B. Greene," in Lajos Kossuth et al., *Kossuth in New England: A Full Account of the Hungarian Governor's Visit to Massachusetts* (Boston: John P. Jewett, 1852), 41–45.

62. Alfred Seelye Roe, "A Sketch of the First Massachusetts Heavy Artillery," *The Melvin Memorial* (Cambridge, MA: privately printed by The Riverside Press, 1910): 141–44.

63. Greene to Butler, Jamaica Plain, MA, 16 March 1864, http://libertarian -labyrinth.blogspot.com/2006/11/william-b-greene-to-gen-b-f-butler .html, accessed 16 November 2014.

64. William B. Greene, *The Blazing Star: With an Appendix Treating of the Jewish Kabbala* (Boston: Rand, Avery, and Frye, 1872), 80. Poe made this claim in his mystical *Eureka: A Prose Poem* (1848); see Edgar Allan Poe, *Poetry and Tales* (New York: Library of America, 1984), 1342.

65. William B. Greene, *Socialistic, Communistic, Mutualistic, and Financial Fragments* (Boston: Lee and Shepard, 1875).

66. Greene, *Radical Deficiency*, 15, 35.

67. See, for example, James J. Martin, *Men against the State: The Exposition of Individualist Anarchism in America, 1827–1908* (Colorado Springs, CO:

Ralph Myles, 1970), 34–35; William O. Reichert, *Partisans of Freedom: A Study in American Anarchism* (Bowling Green, KY: Bowling Green State University Press, 1976), chap. 3; and Rudolph Rocker, *Pioneers of American Freedom: Origin of Liberal and Radical Thought in America* (Los Angeles: Rocker Publications Committee, 1949), 97–112.

68. Orestes Brownson, *Works of Orestes A. Brownson,* ed. Henry F. Brownson, 20 vols. (Detroit: T. Nourse, 1882–1887), 1:222–23.

69. Peabody, *Channing,* 435.

4. Orson Squire Fowler: Reading the National Character, for a Price

1. Stephen Nissenbaum, *Sex, Diet, and Debility in Jacksonian America: Sylvester Graham and Health Reform* (Westport, CT: Greenwood Press, 1980).

2. Cited in ibid., 3.

3. David Meredith Reese, *Hum-Bugs of New York; Being a Remonstrance against Popular Delusion, Whether in Science, Philosophy, or Religion* (New York: Taylor, 1838), 64; John D. Davies, *Phrenology, Fad and Science: A 19th-Century American Crusade* (New Haven, CT: Yale University Press, 1955), 3–5.

4. "Horace Greeley," *American Phrenological Journal* 11 (December 1847): 361–68, repr. in Madeleine B. Stern, ed., *Phrenological Dictionary of Nineteenth-Century Americans* (Westport, CT: Greenwood Press, 1982), 20–26.

5. The best biographical source on Fowler is Madeleine B. Stern, *Heads & Headlines: The Phrenological Fowlers* (Norman: University of Oklahoma Press, 1971).

6. On Beecher, see Debby Applegate, *The Most Famous Man in America: The Biography of Henry Ward Beecher* (New York: Doubleday, 2006).

7. Nelson Sizer, *Forty Years in Phrenology, Embracing Recollections of History, Anecdote and Experience* (1882; New York: Fowler and Wells, 1891), 13–14.

8. Orson Squire Fowler, *Human Science or Phrenology* (n.p., n.d.), 213 ff.

9. Orson Squire Fowler, *Self-Culture and Perfection of Character, Including the Management of Youth* (New York: Fowlers and Wells, 1847), 85; Jessie Allen Fowler, "The American Institute of Phrenology," *American Phrenological Journal* 122, no. 11 (November 1909): 366.

10. Stern, *Heads & Headlines,* 16–17.

11. Orson Squire and Lorenzo Niles Fowler, *Phrenology Proved, Illustrated, and Applied* (New York: For the Authors, 1836).

12. See Stern, *Heads & Headlines,* passim.

13. On physiognomy, see Christopher J. Lukasik, *Discerning Characters: The Culture of Appearance in Early America* (Philadelphia: University of Pennsylvania Press, 2011).

14. See Frederic Henry Hedge, "Pretensions of Phrenology Examined," *Christian Examiner* 17 (November 1834): 249–69.

15. Davies, *Phrenology,* 16.

16. George Combe, *Notes on the United States of North America during a Phrenological Visit in 1838—1839—1840,* 2 vols. (Edinburgh: Maclachlan, Stewart, 1841).

17. Ibid., 1:126.

18. Roger Cooter, *The Cultural Meaning of Phrenology and the Organization of Consent in Nineteenth-Century Britain* (Cambridge: Cambridge University Press, 1984), 120.

19. George Combe, *The Constitution of Man Considered in Relation to External Objects* (Boston: Marsh, Capen & Lyon, 1835), viii, iv.

20. Ralph Waldo Emerson, *Journals and Miscellaneous Notebooks,* ed. William H. Gilman et al., 16 vols. (Cambridge, MA: Belknap Press, 1960–1982), 8: 134. Also see Emerson to William and Edward Emerson, 4 January 1830, in *The Letters of Ralph Waldo Emerson,* eds. Ralph L. Rusk and Eleanor M. Tilton, 10 vols. (New York: Columbia University Press, 1939–1995), 1:291.

21. Ralph Waldo Emerson, Introduction to Albert Brisbane, "Fourierism and the Socialists," *Dial* 3 (July 1842): 87.

22. James John Garth Wilkinson, *Emanuel Swedenborg: A Biography* (Boston: O. Clapp, 1849), 86. Swedenborg's description of his ecstatic conversion is at p. 75

23. Sampson Reed, *Observations on the Growth of the Mind* (Boston: Hilliard and Metcalf, 1826), 24.

24. George Bush, *Mesmer and Swedenborg; or, The Relation of the Developments of Mesmerism to the Doctrines and Disclosures of Swedenborg* (New York: John Allen, 1847).

25. Ibid., 17, 168.

26. John S. Haller Jr., *Swedenborg, Mesmer, and The Mind/Body Connection: The Roots of Complementary Medicine* (West Chester, PA: Swedenborg Foundation, 2010), 17–27.

27. [Charles Julius Hempel], *The True Organization of the New Church, as Indicated in the Writings of Emanuel Swedenborg and Demonstrated by Charles Fourier* (New York: William Radde, 1848), 339–44; Victor Hennequin, trans. Henry James, *Love in the Phalanstery* (New York: DeWitt and Davenport, 1848).

28. Ralph Waldo Emerson, "Swedenborg; or, The Mystic," in *Representative Men, Works of Ralph Waldo Emerson,* 14 vols. (Boston: Houghton, Mifflin, 1883), 4:117.

29. Lydia Maria Child, *Letters from New York, Second Series* (New York: Francis & Company, 1847), 64.

30. *American Phrenological Journal* 6 (1844): 23.

31. Ibid., 12 (1849): 12.

32. In Andrew Combe, *Principles of Physiology Applied to the Preservation of Health* (New York: Harper and Brothers, 1840), x.

33. Stern, *Heads & Headlines,* 59.

34. O. S. Fowler, *Phrenology, Proved, Illustrated, and Applied* (New York: Wells, 1837).

35. Reprinted in Stern, *Phrenological Dictionary,* 30–36.

36. Oliver Wendell Holmes, "The Professor at the Breakfast Table," *Atlantic Monthly* 4, no. 22 (August 1859): 232–43.

37. Reese, *Hum-Bugs,* 74.

38. Sizer, *Forty Years,* 3.

39. Sizer, cited in Stern, *Heads & Headlines,* 134.

40. Ibid., 128.

41. Reese, *Hum-Bugs,* 21–22. Maria Monk was a Canadian woman who claimed to have been abused in a convent and whose book *Awful Disclosures of Maria Monk, or, The Hidden Secrets of a Nun's Life in a Convent Exposed* (1836) was a print-culture sensation, greatly exacerbating tensions between Protestants and Catholics.

42. William A. Alcott recounts his remarkable career in *Forty Years in the Wilderness of Pills and Powders; or, The Cogitations and Confessions of an Aged Physician* (Boston: John P. Jewett, 1859).

43. Stern, *Heads & Headlines*, 49.

44. See Susan E. Cayleff, *Wash and Be Healed: The Water-Cure Movement and Women's Health* (Philadelphia: Temple University Press, 1987), passim, for the history of this health movement.

45. Hedge, "Pretensions of Phrenology Examined," 268.

46. O. S. Fowler, *New Illustrated Self-Instructor in Phrenology and Physiology* (1859; New York: Fowler, 1885), 100–103.

5. Mary Gove Nichols: Individual Health and Sovereignty

1. *New York Morning Herald*, 10 April 1839, 2. Throughout, I refer to Mary Gove Nichols as "Mary," so that there is no confusion with her husband. Similarly, after her marriage to Thomas Low Nichols, I refer to him as "Thomas."

2. Lazarus, M[arx] Edgeworth, *Passional Hygiene and Natural Medicine: Embracing the Harmonies of Man with His Planet* (New York: Fowlers and Wells, 1852).

3. On health reform in general in this period, see James C. Whorton, *Crusaders for Fitness: The History of American Health Reformers* (Princeton, NJ: Princeton University Press, 1982). On the radicalism of Nichols's views on sexuality, see Joanne E. Passett, *Sex Radicals and the Quest for Women's Equality* (Urbana: University of Illinois Press, 2003), esp. 27–34; and as well John C. Spurlock, *Free Love: Marriage and Middle-Class Radicalism in America, 1825–1860* (New York: New York University Press, 1988), 182–201.

4. Jean L. Silver-Isenstadt, *Shameless: The Visionary Life of Mary Gove Nichols* (Baltimore: Johns Hopkins University Press, 2002) is the best modern biography, which I draw from throughout this chapter unless otherwise noted. Patricia Cline Cohen now is preparing another, and I am indebted to her for her close reading of this chapter and the many clarifications she provided. See her "The 'Anti-Marriage Theory' of Thomas and Mary Gove Nichols: A Radical Critique of Monogamy in the 1850s," *Journal of the Early Republic* 34, no. 1 (Spring 2014): 1–20. Also see Passett, *Sex Radicals*, 19–38; and John B. Blake, "Mary Gove Nichols, Prophetess of Health," *Proceedings of the American Philosophical Society* 106 (June 1962): 219–34.

5. Mary Gove Nichols, *Mary Lyndon, or, Revelations of a Life: An Autobiography* (New York: Stringer and Townsend, 1855), 36–38. Also see Joel

Myerson, "Mary Gove Nichols' *Mary Lyndon:* A Forgotten Reform Novel," *American Literature* 58, no. 4 (December 1986): 523–39.

6. Nichols, *Mary Lyndon,* 77–79.

7. Ibid., 116–23.

8. Ibid., 120–21.

9. Ibid., 121.

10. See Nichols's *A Woman's Work in Water Cure and Sanitary Education* (London: Nichols & Company, 1874), 11.

11. Mary Gove Nichols and Thomas Low Nichols, *Marriage in All Ages and Nations: As It Has Been, As It Might Be. Its History, Physiology, Morals and Laws* (London: W. Foulsham and Co., 1886), 194; and Silver-Eisenstadt, *Shameless,* 28.

12. Harriot K. Hunt, *Glances and Glimpses; or, Fifty Years' Social, Including Twenty Years' Professional Life* (Boston: J. P. Jewett and Company, 1856), 139. "Ultras" refers to reformers who hold extreme views.

13. Quoted in Silver-Eisenstadt, *Shameless,* 39.

14. *Morning Herald,* 10 April 1839, 2. Cohen, "Mary Gove Nichols," n. 7.

15. George Combe, *Notes on the United States of North America during a Phrenological Visit in 1838–39–40,* 2 vols. (Philadelphia: Carey & Hart, 1841), 2:32, 216.

16. Lucretia Mott to Nathaniel Barney, 6 March 1841, in *Selected Letters of Lucretia Coffin Mott,* ed. Beverley Wilson Palmer (Urbana: University of Illinois Press, 2002), 88–89.

17. *Baltimore Sun,* 10 June 1841.

18. Nichols, *Mary Lyndon,* 156–57.

19. Ibid., 179–85.

20. Ibid., 196.

21. Ibid., 200.

22. Ibid., 225.

23. Ibid., 240.

24. Ibid., 257–64.

25. Susan E. Cayleff, *Wash and Be Healed: The Water-Cure Movement and Women's Health* (Philadelphia: Temple University Press, 1987), 20–21. This study offers the best modern account of the water cure in the United States.

Also see Harry B. Weiss and Howard R. Kemble, *The Great American Water-Cure Craze: A History of Hydropathy in the United States* (Trenton, NJ: Past Times Press, 1967).

26. Cayleff, *Wash and Be Healed*, 23.

27. R. T. Trall, *Hydropathic Encyclopedia*, 2 vols. (New York: Fowler and Wells, 1850) 1:4.

28. Catharine E. Beecher, *Letters to the People on Health and Happiness* (New York: Harper and Brothers, 1855), 117–18. A series of articles in the *Vermont Phoenix* in the summer of 1847 by a patient-*cum*-journalist provide a vivid first-hand account of the rigor of what she likely experienced; see particularly 9 July and 19 August 1847.

29. Joan D. Hedrick, *Harriet Beecher Stowe: A Life* (New York: Oxford University Press, 1995), chap. 16.

30. Mary Gove Nichols, *Woman's Work*, 23.

31. Carl Guarneri, *The Utopian Alternative: Fourierism in Nineteenth-Century America* (Ithaca, NY: Cornell University Press, 1991), 356–57; and Cohen, "'Anti-Marriage Theory,'" 14.

32. Anne C. Rose, in *Transcendentalism As a Social Movement, 1830–1850* (New Haven, CT: Yale University Press, 1981), 137, 128, n. 73, citing the Brook Farm records for 24 September 1843, suggests that the Brook Farmers may have wanted to distance themselves from her increasingly radical views. Also see Guarneri, *Utopian Alternative*, 198.

33. See *Phalanx* 1 (5 February 1844): 64–65. I thank Patricia Cline Cohen for information about the *Social Reformer*, which exists in a unique copy at the Boston Public Library. Brook Farm members John Orvis and Charles Dana also contributed to it.

34. See Cohen, "'Anti-Marriage Theory,'" 14.

35. Lazarus, *Passional Hygiene*, v.

36. Nichols, *Mary Lyndon*, 285.

37. Ibid., 317.

38. Ibid., 285.

39. These novels included *Uncle John; or, "It Is Too Much Trouble"* (1846); *Agnes Morris; or, The Heroine of Domestic Life* (1849); and *The Two Loves; or, Eros and Anteros* (1849). Later, in England, she published *Uncle Angus* (1864) and *Jerry: A Novel of Yankee American Life* (1872).

40. *Mary Lyndon,* 339–41. See Madeleine B. Stern, "The House of Expanding Doors: Anne Lynch's Soirees, 1846," *New York History* 23 (January 1942): 42–51, for Mary's presence at another such gathering.

41. Edgar Allan Poe, "The Literati of New York," in *Essays and Reviews* (New York: Library of America, 1984), 1162.

42. Nichols, *Mary Lyndon,* 338, 340.

43. Ibid., 337–44. See chapter 20 for Mary's recollection of their remarkable letters to each other.

44. On the Flash Press, see Patricia Cline Cohen, Timothy J. Gilfoyle, and Helen Lefkowitz Horowitz, *The Flash Press: Sporting Male Weeklies in 1840s New York* (Chicago: University of Chicago Press, 2008).

45. "The Free Love System: Origin Progress—and Position of Anti-Marriage Movement," *New York Daily Times,* 8 September 1855, 2.

46. *New York Arena,* 27 May 1842.

47. "Animal Magnetism," *Boston Medical and Surgical Journal* (February 1836): 418–19. I thank Patricia Cline Cohen for this reference.

48. Thomas Low Nichols, *Journal in Jail, Kept during a Four Months' Imprisonment for Libel, in the Jail of Erie County* (Buffalo, NY: A. Dinsmore, 1840).

49. Nichols, *Mary Lyndon,* 384.

50. Ibid., 384.

51. See the Marriage column in *New-York Tribune,* 31 July 1848.

52. Poe, "Literati," 1162.

53. Nichols, *Mary Lyndon,* 153.

54. "Woman the Physician," in *Water Cure Journal* 12, no. 4 (October 1851): 74.

55. See Silver-Eisenstadt, *Shameless,* 135–37.

56. Thomas Low Nichols, *Esoteric Anthropology (The Mysteries of Man): A Comprehensive and Confidential Treatise on the Structure, Functions, Passional Attractions, and Perversions, True and False Physical and Social Conditions, and the Most Intimate Relations of Men and Women* (New York: Stringer & Townsend, 1853), 7.

57. Ibid., 140, 212.

58. Ibid., 201.

59. Ibid., 143–44, 209.

60. Ibid., 142, 152–53.

61. Ibid., 147, 100.

62. Ibid., 396–98.

63. Ibid., 402.

64. Ibid., 197–98.

65. Ibid., 142.

66. Silver-Eisenstadt, *Shameless*, 153–55.

67. See Roger Wunderlich, *Low Living and High Thinking at Modern Times, New York* (Syracuse, NY: Syracuse University Press, 1992).

68. John B. Ellis, *Free Love and Its Votaries; or, American Socialism Unmasked* (New York: United States Publishing Company, 1870), 384.

69. See ibid., chap. 23.

70. Josiah Warren, *Practical Details in Equitable Commerce* (New York: Fowlers and Wells, 1852), 115.

71. See Madeleine Stern, *The Pantarch: A Biography of Stephen Pearl Andrews* (Austin: University of Texas Press, 1968), 74.

72. See Taylor Stoehr's *Free Love in America: A Documentary History* (New York: AMS Press, 1979) for a good introduction to the range of contemporary thought on this subject.

73. Ellis, *Free Love*, 386. "Non-resistants" refers to fervent abolitionists like William Lloyd Garrison who called for an end to slavery but abjured any violence to do so.

74. Ibid.

75. *Love, Marriage, and Divorce, and the Sovereignty of the Individual: A Discussion by Henry James, Horace Greeley, and Stephen Pearl Andrews* (1855; Boston: B. R. Tucker, 1889), 11.

76. Ibid., 71–72.

77. Ibid., 17.

78. Thomas Low Nichols and Mary S. Gove Nichols, *Marriage: Its History, Character, and Results; Its Sanctities, and Its Profanities; Its Science and Its Facts* (Cincinnati: V. Nicholson, 1854), 100–101, 114, 178.

79. Ibid., 86–87.

80. Ibid., 119.

81. Ibid., 221, 214.

82. On this phenomenon's appeal, see Ann Braude, *Radical Spirits: Spiritualism and Women's Rights in Nineteenth-Century America* (Bloomington: Indiana University Press, 2001).

83. Nichols and Nichols, *Marriage*, 412–26; and Thomas Nichols, "The Progressive Union," *Nichols' Monthly* (June 1855): 53–59.

84. Silver-Eisenstadt, *Shameless*, 200; and Bertha-Monica Stearns, "Memnonia: The Launching of a Utopia," *New England Quarterly* 15, no. 2 (June 1942), 280–95.

85. Thomas Low Nichols, "The Law of Progression in Harmony," *Nichols' Monthly* 2 (June 1856): 441, in Stoehr, *Free Love in America*, 470.

86. See Philip Gleason, "From Free Love to Catholicism: Dr. and Mrs. Thomas L. Nichols at Yellow Springs," *Ohio Historical Quarterly* 70 (1961): 283–307.

87. See Thomas Low Nichols, *Lectures on Catholicity and Protestantism* (Boston: P. Donahoe, 1859).

88. See Nichols, *Woman's Work in Water Cure*, for Mary's work in England.

89. *Nichols' Journal: A Weekly Newspaper Devoted to Health, Intelligence, Freedom, Individual Sovereignty and Social Harmony* 1, no. 5 (August 1853): 37.

90. Nichols, *Mary Lyndon*, 269.

91. On this topic, also see Thomas Low Nichols, *Forty Years in American Life, 1821–1861* (1864; New York: Stackpole Sons, 1937), chap. 37.

6. Thoreau's Nullification

1. Stephen Pearl Andrews, *The True Constitution of Government in the Sovereignty of the Individual as the Final Development of Protestantism, Democracy and Socialism* (1852; Weston, MA: M & S Rare Books, 1970), 12.

2. Ibid., 10.

3. Ibid., 11.

4. Ibid., 10.

5. Ibid., 39–40.

6. Robert D. Richardson, *Henry Thoreau: A Life of the Mind* (Berkeley: University of California Press, 1986), 5–6. This, along with Walter Harding's *The Days of Henry Thoreau: A Biography* (Princeton, NJ: Princeton University Press, 1992), is the best biographical source.

7. Henry D. Thoreau to Ralph Waldo Emerson, 6 June 1843, in *The Correspondence of Henry D. Thoreau*, vol. 1, *1834–1848*, ed. Robert N. Hudspeth (Princeton, NJ: Princeton University Press, 2014), 180.

8. Ibid., 179.

9. Emerson to Thoreau, February 1843, in ibid., 129–30.

10. Thoreau to Emerson, 8 June 1843, in ibid., 180.

11. These men were young clerks in the Mercantile Agency of William's father, prominent businessman Lewis Tappan.

12. Thoreau to Helen Louisa Thoreau, 21 July 1843, in *Correspondence*, 211.

13. Thoreau to Emerson, 8 June 1843, in ibid., 181.

14. Thoreau to Cynthia Dunbar Thoreau, 1 October 1842, in ibid., 238.

15. Thoreau to Emerson, 14 September 1843, in ibid., 233.

16. See John L. O'Sullivan, "Annexation," *United States Magazine and Democratic Review* 17, no. 1 (July–August 1845), 5–10.

17. Thoreau to Emerson, 24 January 1843, in *Correspondence*, 124.

18. John L. O'Sullivan to Thoreau, 28 July 1843, in ibid., 214.

19. Thoreau to Emerson, 14 September 1843, in ibid., 234.

20. Henry D. Thoreau, 3 March 1841, in *Journal*, ed. John C. Broderick et al., 8 vols. to date (Princeton, NJ: Princeton University Press, 1981–), 1:277. See also Ralph Waldo Emerson, *Journals and Miscellaneous Notebooks*, ed. William H. Gilman et al., 16 vols. (Cambridge, MA: Harvard University Press, 1960–1982), 7:407–8.

21. One of the few modern studies is Stephen Stoll, *The Great Delusion: A Mad Inventor, Death in the Tropics, and the Utopian Origins of Economic Growth* (New York: Hill & Wang, 2008). See also Joel Nydahl's introduction to *Collected Works of John Adolphus Etzler* (Delmar, NY: Scholars' Facsimiles and Reprints, 1977).

22. J. A. Etzler, *Paradise within the Reach of All Men* (Pittsburgh: Stollmeyer, 1833), 1.

23. Ibid., 1–2.

24. For his biography, see Stoll, *Great Delusion*, passim.

25. J. A. Etzler, *The New World, or, Mechanical System: To Perform the Labours of Man and Beast by Inanimate Powers, That Cost Nothing, for Producing and Preparing the Substances of Life* (Philadelphia: Stollmeyer, 1841).

26. Etzler, *Paradise*, 4.

27. Ibid.

28. Ibid., 69–77.

29. Ibid., 78–81.

30. Stoll, *Great Delusion*, 50, 79–80.

31. Etzler's longtime supporter Conrad Stollmeyer published Brisbane's *Social Destiny of Man* in Philadelphia in 1840. And later, in 1842, English Fourierist Hugh Doherty teamed with Stollmeyer, newly returned to England, to try to build one of Etzler's complex labor-saving machines. See Stoll, *Great Delusion*, 100.

32. Etzler, *Paradise*, vi.

33. Thoreau, "Paradise (to be) Regained," in Henry D. Thoreau, *Reform Papers*, ed. Wendell Glick (Princeton, NJ: Princeton University Press, 1973), 19.

34. Ibid., 20.

35. Ibid.

36. Ibid., 22.

37. Ibid., 33.

38. Ibid.

39. Ibid., 40–41.

40. Ibid., 42.

41. Ibid., 44–45.

42. Ibid., 46.

43. Ibid., 47.

44. Thoreau to Helen Thoreau, 18 October 1843, in Thoreau, *Correspondence*, 250.

45. Ralph Waldo Emerson, "The Conservative," in *Essays and Lectures* (New York: Library of America, 1983), 171–90.

46. Henry D. Thoreau, "Reform and Reformers," in Thoreau, *Reform Papers*, 181–82.

47. Ibid., 182.

48. Ibid., 183.

49. Ibid., 184.

50. Ibid., 190.

51. Ibid., 184.

52. Ibid.

53. Ibid., 185.

54. Ibid., 186.

55. Ibid., 193.

56. Ibid., 194.

57. Thoreau to Isaac Thomas Hecker, 14 August 1844, in Thoreau, *Correspondence*, 262.

58. See Stoll, *Great Delusion*, passim.

59. Henry D. Thoreau, *Walden*, ed. J. Lyndon Shanley (1854) (Princeton, NJ: Princeton University Press, 1971), 8, 4.

60. Ibid., 6–7.

61. Ibid., 6, 37.

62. Ibid., 19–20.

63. Ibid., 321.

64. Ibid., 70.

65. Ibid., 31.

66. Ibid., 91.

67. Ibid., 38.

68. Ibid., 89, 51–52.

69. Ibid., 53–54.

70. Ibid., 69.

71. Ibid., 70–71.

72. Ibid., 71.

73. Ibid., 135–36.

74. Ibid., 135.

75. Ibid., 92.

76. Ibid., 96.

77. Ibid., 323–24.

78. Ibid., 323.

79. Henry D. Thoreau, "Resistance to Civil Government," in Thoreau, *Reform Papers*, 64–65.

80. Ibid., 69.

81. Ibid.

82. Ibid., 73–74, 75.

83. Ibid., 89.

84. Thoreau, *Journal,* 2:262–63.

85. Henry D. Thoreau, "Slavery in Massachusetts," in Thoreau, *Reform Papers,* 102.

86. Ibid., 103.

87. Ibid., 104.

88. Henry D. Thoreau, "Life without Principle," in Thoreau, *Reform Papers,* 156.

89. Ibid., 157.

90. Ibid., 158.

91. Ibid., 161.

92. Ibid.

93. Ibid., 162.

94. Ibid., 162–63.

95. Ibid., 164.

96. Ibid., 166.

97. Ibid., 174.

98. Thoreau, "Resistance to Civil Government," in Thoreau, *Reform Papers,* 67.

99. Ibid., 64.

100. Ibid., 71.

101. Thoreau, *Walden,* 7.

102. Thoreau, "Resistance to Civil Government," in Thoreau, *Reform Papers,* 74.

103. Ibid., 75.

7. John Brown and the Bankruptcy of Conscience

1. *A Brief Popular Account of All the Financial Panics and Commercial Revulsions in the United States, from 1690 to 1857: With A More Particular History of the Two Great Revulsions of 1837 and 1857* (New York: J. C. Haney, 1852), 39. Also see Ann Fabian, "Speculation on Distress: The Popular Discourse of the Panics of 1837 and 1857," *Yale Journal of Criticism* 3, no. 1 (Fall 1989): 12–142.

2. *Harper's Weekly,* 24 October 1857, 678.

3. Robert C. Winthrop to John H. Clifford, 21 September 1857, cited in Kenneth M. Stampp, *America in 1857: A Nation on the Brink* (New York: Oxford University Press, 1990), 213.

4. Ibid., 215.

5. *North American Review* 86 (January 1858): 171.

6. Cited in *Brief Popular Account*, 47.

7. *Diary of George Templeton Strong*, ed. Alan Nevins and Milton Halsey Thomas, 4 vols. (New York: Macmillan, 1952), 2:359.

8. *Hunt's Merchants' Magazine* 37 (November 1857): 582.

9. *Life and Letters of Peter and Susan Lesley*, ed. Mary Leslie Ames (New York: G. P. Putnam's Sons, 1909), 1:351.

10. F. B. Sanborn, *Life and Letters of John Brown, Liberator of Kansas, and Martyr of Virginia* (1885; Concord, MA: F. B. Sanborn, 1917), 87–88.

11. David S. Reynolds, *John Brown, Abolitionist: The Man Who Killed Slavery, Sparked the Civil War, and Seeded Civil Rights* (New York: Knopf, 2005), 66.

12. In this section I draw from Stephen B. Oates, *To Purge This Land with Blood: A Biography of John Brown* (New York: Harper & Row, 1970); and Reynolds, *John Brown, Abolitionist*. See also John Stauffer, *The Black Hearts of Men: Radical Abolitionists and the Transformation of Race* (Cambridge, MA: Harvard University Press, 2002).

13. Sanborn, *Life and Letters of John Brown*, 54.

14. Stauffer, *Black Hearts*, 120.

15. Ralph Waldo Emerson, "New England Reformers," in *Essays and Lectures* (New York: Library of America, 1983), 592.

16. Oswald Garrison Villard, *John Brown, 1850–1859: A Biography Fifty Years After* (Boston: Houghton Mifflin, 1910), 46.

17. Reynolds, *John Brown*, 65.

18. Louis Ruchames, ed., *John Brown: The Making of a Revolutionary: The Story of John Brown in His Own Words and in the Words of Those Who Knew Him* (1969; New York: Grossett & Dunlap, 1971), 294.

19. Villard, *John Brown*, 134.

20. Alexander Milton Ross, *Recollections and Experiences of an Abolitionist: From 1855 to 1865* (Toronto: Roswell and Hutchinson, 1875), 50.

21. Sanborn, *Life and Letters*, 504.

22. See *John Brown Speaks: Letters and Statements from Charlestown* (Lanham, MD: Rowman & Littlefield, [2015]), 105, for his statement to the court.

23. Henry David Thoreau, *The Writings of Henry David Thoreau*, ed. Bradford Torrey (Boston: Houghton Mifflin, 1906), 18:400.

24. Ibid., 406–7, 414.

25. Ibid., 414–15.

26. Ralph Waldo Emerson, "Thoreau," in Joel Myerson, ed., *The Transcendentalists: A Reader* (New York: Oxford University Press, 2000), 658.

27. Thoreau, "A Plea for Captain John Brown," in *Reform Papers*, ed. Wendell Glick (Princeton, NJ: Princeton University Press, 1973), 112.

28. Ibid., 113.

29. Ibid., 115–16.

30. Ibid., 119.

31. Ibid., 124–25.

32. Ibid., 125.

33. Ibid., 132–33.

34. Ibid., 136–37.

35. Ibid., 129.

36. Ibid., 137.

37. Thoreau, *Reform Papers*, 363.

38. Thoreau, "Last Days of John Brown," in *Reform Papers*, 146–47.

39. Ibid., 152–53.

40. The scholarship on Smith and Mormonism is legion but Richard Bushman, *Joseph Smith and the Beginnings of Mormonism* (Urbana: University of Illinois Press, 1984) offers a good starting point; on Matthias see Paul E. Johnson and Sean Wilentz, *The Kingdom of Matthias: A Story of Sex and Salvation in 19th-Century America* (New York: Oxford University Press, 2012).

41. William James first used the phrase in 1898 in his address to the Berkeley Philosophical Union, "Philosophical Conceptions and Practical Results," Appendix to James, *Pragmatism*, in *The Works of William James* (Cambridge, MA: Harvard University Press, 1975), 268.

Acknowledgments

First of all, I want to thank my editor, Thomas LeBien. For more than a decade his intelligence and good sense have helped to shape my books. He believed in this project early on and pushed me to see the forest through the trees.

As I was completing this book, the Department of English at the University of North Carolina at Chapel Hill, under the able leadership of Beverly Taylor, and the University Provost's Office, through a Kenan Senior Faculty Research Fund, provided welcome research leaves.

Over all my work loom the examples of Perry Miller, the scholar who memorably insisted that the "mind of man is the basic factor in human history," and of his protégé, Alan Heimert, who observed that "an understanding of any idea, or of a constellation of ideas, requires an awareness of the context of institutions and events out of which thought emerged, and with which it strove to come to terms." "But," he added, "full apprehension depends finally on reading, not between the lines, but, as it were, through and beyond them." For my entire career I have kept these thoughts in mind and strived to write as intelligently and powerfully as they did. Always I am aware of how short I fall.

Over the many years that I have been thinking about this book, I have been fortunate in those students whose doctoral dissertations I directed, for they always pushed their classmates and me in new directions. In chronological order, they are Sam Worley, Wilson Somerville, Richard S. Keating, Glen Blalock, Karen Weyler, Tess Lloyd, Susan M. Ryan, Alan Brew, James Emmett Ryan, Susan Irons, Christopher Smith, Laura Mielke, Michael Everton, David Faflik, Tara Robbins, Bryan Sinche, Christopher Windolph, Timothy Jecmen, Karah Rempe, Maura D'Amore, Zachary Hutchins, Adrian Greene, Kathleen Crosby, and Vera Foley.

Although I had been thinking about this study for decades, I wrote it in two and a half years, from the early summer of 2013 to the late fall of 2015. Most of this period was marked by an unbridled optimism of the sort that fueled the dreams of those I document in this book. But as most of this book's subjects learned, miscalculation, hubris, and lack of judgment and vision can just as quickly bring disappointment and loss.

So, I want particularly to thank my children: Daniel, Katherine, and David, and David's wife, Kate Brannen, for their support and understanding. David and Kate also have recently blessed me with two grandchildren, Maeve and Abel, the dedicatees. Robert Cantwell, Lydia Wegman, Linda Passman, and Steve Finer sustained me with their friendship. At an important time, the first two opened their hearts and summer home on Mount Desert Island. Linda's seemingly inexhaustible sensitivity and wisdom, as well as her common sense, have been a godsend. Steve took much time from his antiquarian bookselling both to listen and to teach me about life as well as books. In the academic world, Patricia Cline Cohen offered generous help, particularly for the section on Mary Gove Nichols, about whom she knows more than anyone.

So, too, I thank my longtime friend Bob Richardson, who helped me to understand how Emerson, who makes several appearances in this work, coped with a dialectic of gain and loss. He who once had counseled the individual "to build therefore [his] own world" finally had to acknowledge that he was at the mercy of the "lords of life," his free will confined by the "threads on the loom of time." So, what to do? How to go on? "To finish the moment," Emerson counseled, "to find the journey's end in every step of the road, to live the greatest number of good hours, is wisdom." This has been Bob's lesson to me; it sustained me as I wrote this book.

Thanks finally to Debra, who wholly unexpectedly taught me what Emerson's friend and neighbor Hawthorne meant when he candidly admitted, "I used to think I could imagine all passions, all feelings, and states of heart and mind." "But," he continued, "how little did I know!" "Indeed," he confessed in a letter to his fiancée, "we are but shadows; we are not endowed with real life, and all that seems most real about us is but the substance of a dream—til the heart be touched." "That touch," he explained, "creates us,—then we begin to be." So it has been.

In the end, one of Emerson's "Lords"—"Succession swift"—life's imperative for movement, for perpetual change—intruded. "Gladly we would anchor," he wrote, "but the anchorage is quicksand." The "onward trick of nature is too strong for us." So it seems to be, even as it helped to shape this book and to redirect a life. It remains to be seen how that which Emerson termed "the inventor of the game / Omnipresent without a name," realigns the "lords of life." In the meantime, with the Concord sage I try to learn to be "thankful for small mercies" and rest content with "the pot-luck of the day."

Index